Studies of the Americas

Series Editor
Maxine Molyneux, Institute of the Americas, University College London, London, UK

The Studies of the Americas Series includes country specific, cross-disciplinary, and comparative research on the United States, Latin America, the Caribbean, and Canada, particularly in the areas of Politics, Economics, History, Sociology, Anthropology, Development, Gender, Social Policy, and the Environment. The series publishes monographs, readers on specific themes and also welcomes proposals for edited collections, that allow exploration of a topic from several different disciplinary angles. The series is published in conjunction with University College London's Institute of the Americas, which is the UK's largest multi-disciplinary unit dedicated to the study of North America, Latin America, and the Caribbean.

Nora Nagels

Gender Equality in Conditional Cash Transfer Designs

A disappearing policy recipe in Latin America and the World Bank?

palgrave
macmillan

Nora Nagels
Montreal, QC, Canada

Studies of the Americas
ISBN 978-3-031-60870-4 ISBN 978-3-031-60871-1 (eBook)
https://doi.org/10.1007/978-3-031-60871-1

This Palgrave Macmillan imprint is published by the registered company Springer Nature Switzerland AG
The registered company address is: Gewerbestrasse 11, 6330 Cham, Switzerland

For Davy, Inès, and Elias
And for Jane, much more than my mentor

Acknowledgments

While writing a book can be a quite solitary and perilously long journey at times, such work would have not been possible without the contributions of many individuals and institutions across three continents. I am profoundly grateful for their care and support, which enriched the quality of the research and made the writing of it possible.

First and foremost, I wish to thank the research participants in Mexico, Brazil, Peru, Bolivia, and the World Bank. They remain anonymous here, but this research could not have existed without the collaboration of all those people who agreed to grant me an interview. Experts, policymakers, strategic (gender equality) entrepreneurs as well as implementers in four countries, and the World Bank have contributed greatly to the work of reconstructing the story of CCT travel in Latin America. I am enduringly grateful to them for opening their homes or offices and sharing that part of their life and work with me, and without compensation.

I want to express my wholehearted gratitude to Jane Jenson, who has been much more than a wonderful mentor these last ten years. She accepted to be the external evaluator of my dissertation, supervised my postdoctoral work as part of her Canada Research Chair in Citizenship and Governance at Université de Montréal and helped me to navigate my first years as a professor at Université du Québec à Montréal. I am extremely lucky to work with her. Her patience, generosity, confidence, care, rigor, sharply critical comments, and honesty have contributed to the quality of my research and of this book and have helped me to be a better (Canadian) and scholarly citizen. Her unparalleled generosity has offered me much more than an academic home in Montreal. She opened her door to her chalet, and her (academic) family and has taught us how to support and care for each other and to build strong ties and maintain solidarity. More than a fantastic mentor, her entire career as a researcher, colleague, friend, and public intellectual inspires me every day.

Her senses of family extended to the *Equipe de Recherche sur la Gouvernance et l'Inclusion en Amérique Latine* (ÉRIGAL), that organized—with her fantastic and inspiring colleague and friend, Françoise Montambeault—an international workshop on my book. I had the immense privilege of getting insights from scholars I regard as brilliant researchers. Special thanks to Juliana Martínez Franzoni, Merike Blofield, Laura Macdonald, Jane Jenson, Mireille Paquet, and Francoise Montambeault for having read the first draft of the manuscript. Your careful, precise, and critical comments have made this book much better.

A large number of colleagues and friends have provided feedback on previous chapter drafts and conference papers and presentations at international Congress or workshops: Maxine Molyneux, Stéphanie Rousseau, Tara Cookson, Silke Staab, Emmanuelle Piccoli, Olivier de Sardan, Armando Barrientos, Blandine Destremau, Bruno Palier, Rianne Mahon, Camila Arza, Bérengère Marques-Pereira, Julián Durazo-Herrmann, Charmain Levy, and Tina Hilgers. They also have shared their wisdom and their work for which I am eternally grateful. Likewise, the anonymous reviewers have provided very rich insights to improve the manuscript. My colleagues and friends at ERIGAL and the Department of Political Science at Université du Québec à Montréal have been extremely supportive. I am grateful to Anne-Marie D'Aoust, Sadio Soukouna, Geneviève Pagé, Carole Clavier, Tania Gosselin, and Allison Harell for our monthly "care lunches" that create and maintain a safe and feminist space among colleagues.

During the fieldwork, I was lucky to count on the support of friends and colleagues to gain access to other interviewees and to discover new political realities. In Peru and Bolivia, special thanks go to Camille Boutron, Robin Cavagnoud, Patricia Ruiz Bravo, Naida Henriquez, Cecilia Blondet, Virginia Vargas, Fernanda Wanderley, Sarah-Lan Mathez, Peter Larsen, and Cecilia Salazar. I am indebted to my assistant researchers, Adriana Pozos and Danielle Coenga-Oliveira, who led the fieldwork in Brazil and Mexico and have become true and marvelous friends. The World Bank doors were easier to open than I thought. I encountered and interviewed generous people there. Thank you.

During the research and the writing of this book, I benefited from the financial, organizational, and logistical support of several organizations and institutions. The whole Ph.D. adventure in optimal conditions was made possible by the National Centre of Competence in Research North-South and the Graduate Institute (Switzerland). The *Fonds de Recherche du Québec – Société et Culture* (FRQSC) and the professor installment fund of my current university funded the research and the fieldwork in Mexico, Brazil, and the World Bank. I am also grateful for the support of the Social Science and Humanities Research Council of Canada (SSHRC), which gave me grants while I was writing the final version of this manuscript.

I would like to thank my editors at Palgrave Macmillan, Esther Sundar and Anca Pusca, who have been extremely present throughout the entire publishing process.

I am thankful to all those persons who participated in the production of the book. Thank you to Kelly Clancy for her writing circles and sessions, which supported the writing process and helped me to think like a writer. I am grateful to Alexia Moyer for the English revision, which has helped me to be a little more comfortable in my third language. A special thanks to my graduated students and research assistants, Maxim Aubrey-Robillard, Martín Bertolotti, Hernán Herbozo, and Naiké Léger who took care of all the tasks I could externalize in order to concentrate on the writing process.

Finally, I offer my greatest thanks to my family and friends. They are the hidden force behind the sometimes-tumultuous travels required of academia. Their emotional and moral support is essential. I am grateful to my friends for life, Caro, Laure and Gaëlle, my transnational and feminist friends, Marième N'Diaye and Maria Martín de Almagro Iniesta, and to have built a chosen family in Montreal, far away from my native Brussels: the extended "Belgian mafia", Lianet, Caro, Carole, Sharmila, Audrey, Noël, Olivier, Marine, Audrey, Elise, and their families. I would like to express my wholehearted gratitude to Mireille Paquet for her support, advice, care, love, and friendship. Thank you for having built a feminist friendship group, with Catherine Xhardez and Sadio Soukouna, to share our everyday (academic) roses and thorns. I am also thankful to my parents, Jacques Nagels and Claudine Cyprès, who participated in who I am, read and commented previous writings leading to this manuscript except this last one since they passed away too early. A special thank you to my sister, Carla, for always believing in me despite the distance and for being a contemporary amazon as well as a great scholar whom I admire. I am also grateful to my godmother, Esther Freifeld, and my mother-in-law, Pilar Gonzalez, for helping us to multitask and conciliate work and family in our long-distance commuter life.

A last and very special thank you goes to Davy Santisteban, my partner and love, who has been ever present and supportive. Words and numbers cannot capture the immense gratitude I feel. I am extremely grateful for his care, and patience, and for sharing in our dreams for all these years, whatever they were. I thank you for traveling with me along this long intellectual and physical journey from Europe to Latin America and Canada. In our little family sailboat, Davy is the mast that allows us to sail across seas and to weather storms. We are accompanied on by two little pirates, Elias, and Inès: You three bring me immense joy and remind me that life is not just about academia.

I do not have any competing interests.

The interviews have been done according to the ethical approval of the Universities where I conducted the research, the Graduate Institute in Geneva for the interviews in Peru and Bolivia and the Université du Québec à Montréal for those in Brazil, Mexico, and the World Bank.

Contents

1 **Introduction** 1
CCT Designs Variations in Relation to Gender Equality Goals 4
Gender Equality in CCT Designs 4
Selection Criteria, Generosity, and Conditions 6
Conditional Cash Transfers, Gender, Diffusion, and the World Bank 9
CCT Development 9
CCT Impact 10
CCT Diffusion 11
Argument in Brief 13
Methodological Insights 16
Structure of the Book 21

2 **Mechanisms and Configuration: Understanding the Travels of a Policy Instrument** 25
Introduction 25
Gender and Gendering 27
Gender Analysis and Historical Institutionalism 30
The How of Change: The Mechanisms of Cooking, Standardization, and Translation 34
Cooking 37
Standardization 39

Translation 41
The Why of Change: The Configuration of Institutions, Actors, and Ideas 42
Social Policies as Institutions and the Products of Institutions 43
Strategic (Gender Equality) Entrepreneurs 45
Knowledge on Gender 49
Conclusion 51

3 **Cooking from a New Recipe: Progresa and Bolsa Família with Gender Equality Goals** 1
Introduction 1
Institutional Legacies of Mexican and Brazilian Welfare Regimes 2
Mexico: Cooking from a New Recipe with Explicit Gender Equality Goals 5
Historical and Institutional Context 7
Strategic Gender Equality Entrepreneurs in an Intimate Instrument Community 8
Institutional Legacies of Feminism and Gender Institutionalization 14
Knowledge on Gender and Poverty 17
Brazil: Cooking Bolsa Família *from Old Subnational Recipes* 24
Subnational CCTs as Strong Institutional Legacies 24
Strategic (Gender Equality) Entrepreneurs Embedded in Institutional Venues 26
Gender Equality as an Implicit Goal and an Informal Institution 32
Conclusion: Institutions Legacies and Venues, Strategic (Gender Equality) Entrepreneurs and Knowledge About Gender 39

4 **Standardization of CCTs Without Gender Equality** 97
Introduction 97
Gendered Institutional Legacies in the World Bank 99
Gender Knowledge Institutionalization in the World Bank in the Post-Washington Consensus 104
Institutional and Organizational Changes to Include Gender Equality Concerns 106
CCTs and Gendered Standardization by the World Bank 110

CCT Certification Without Gender Equality Concerns 111
Gendered Decontextualization and Framing 117
Institutional Legacies of Gender-Discriminatory Norms 117
Knowledge: CCT Mixed Results on Gender Relations 119
Asymmetries Among Policy Entrepreneurs and Their Knowledge 122
Conclusion 130

5 **_Juntos_ and the _Bonos_: Translation with Innovations Rooted in Exclusionary Institutional Legacies** 135
Institutional Legacies of Peruvian and Bolivian Welfare Regimes 136
Standard CCT Model Translation in Peru and Bolivia: Juntos *and the* Bonos 140
Peruvian Translation by Technocratic Entrepreneurs in a Fragmented State Without Gender Equality Concerns 140
Juntos *as a Technocratic Solution to Clientelism* 141
Juntos *as a Technocratic Solution to Social Crisis* 143
Juntos *as a Translation of the World Bank's Standard CCT Recipe with Local Ingredients* 145
Bolivia: Inclusive Top-down CCT Translation Without Gender Equality Concerns 147
Institutional Legacies and Venues 148
The Bono Juancito Pinto*: Strategic Entrepreneurs with Presidential Interferences* 151
Bono Juana Azurduy*: Top-down Design with Resistance to the World Bank* 153
The Bonos*: Translation with Universalism as Its Institutional Innovation* 154
Translation with Innovations Rooted in the Institutional Social Policy Legacy of Maternalism 157
Translation of Essentialist and Instrumental Views of Gender Based on Various Forms of Knowledge 158
Differences in Values Between Men and Women 159
Translation with Innovations Rooted in Exclusionary Institutional Social Policy Legacies of Denigration of Indigenous Women 161
Translation with the Innovation of Extra-official Conditions 161

Translation with the Innovation of Denigration of Indigenous Motherhood 165
Innovation: Using Conditions for Changing Indigenous Maternity Practices 168
Conclusion 170

6 Lessons for Gender Equality and Social Policies 173
Mechanisms: How Changes Occur 174
Context: Why Changes Occur 175
Agency, Mechanisms, Multi-Level Analysis, and Knowledge 176
Implications for the Politics of Social Policies with Gender Equality Concerns 181

References 183

Index 209

List of Figures

Fig. 1.1	Variation in CCT designs (Author's construction)	5
Fig. 2.1	Drawing the argument (Author's construction)	36

CHAPTER 1

Introduction

Few aspects of social policy have been more controversial than the effects of Conditional Cash Transfers (CCTs) on gender relations and policy outcomes on gender relations are linked to policy designs. Development and social policy communities have recognized gender equality as a cornerstone of development and social progress. Nonetheless, designing policy to integrate gender equality goals into social policies is rendered that much more complicated as and when these policies travel. In Mexico in 1997, the first CCT, *Progresa*, looked quite different than CCTs look today. Embedded in the design was Affirmative Action geared toward girls, as was a clearly enunciated concern about the program's effects on female empowerment. For the 2005 Peruvian CCT, Juntos, the story was very different. Its design did not include any gender equality goals and it reproduced long-standing social policy legacies of gendered exclusions. Therefore, this book is about the alteration of Conditional Cash Transfer designs in relation to gender equality goals as they have made their way through Latin America as well as through the World Bank. This book aims to account for "the fading goal of gender equality" (Jenson, 2015) across time as part of this regional trajectory. In short, it tracks the how and the why of this trajectory in relation to gender equality goals.

CCTs are anti-poverty policies that transfer resources—in cash and not in kind—to poor families. They contain conditions linked to health and

N. Nagels, *Gender Equality in Conditional Cash Transfer Designs*, Studies of the Americas,
https://doi.org/10.1007/978-3-031-60871-1_1

education. In the short term, they aim to alleviate poverty in families by increasing their cash resources, while in the long term, their objective is to break the intergenerational cycle of poverty with social investments in the human capital of future generations. With these objectives, they provide subsidies to poor families, channeled through mothers, on condition that they seek medical care during pregnancy, enroll their children in school, and take them for health check-ups. Starting in the mid-1990s and in just over a decade, CCTs spread spectacularly quickly to nearly all countries in Latin America, including the four analyzed in this book—*Progresa*[1] (1997) in Mexico; *Bolsa Família* (2003) in Brazil; *Juntos* (2005) in Peru; and the *Bono Juancito Pinto* (2006) and the *Bono Juana Azurduy* (2009) in Bolivia. CCTs became the flagships of Latin American social policies for more than 25 years from the mid-1990s when states returned to "doing" social policy after the lost decade during neoliberalism. By 2019, such policies reached 21% of the whole Latin American population.

In a social investment logic, CCTs are anti-poverty policies targeting children through the behavior of their mothers. Seeking to shape and even control the actions of women, the CCTs are designed with assumptions and intentions regarding gender relations. They will thus affect gender relations but not always in favor of more equality. This book analyzes CCT design and their commitment, or lack thereof toward gender equality. Are particular CCTs designed with a view to achieving gender equality? A measure of this goal is the following. Those that include gender equality goals aim to empower women and grant them financial autonomy. By contrast, those that give money to women because they are mothers and better spenders on behalf of their children reproduce traditional gender roles.

The fading goal of gender equality constitutes a puzzle because, throughout the period in question, all four countries analyzed in this book had the necessary institutional machinery for advancing gender equality in place within their state apparatuses, while the World Bank, which has promoted CCTs since 2004, has an official mandate to promote gender equality and gender machinery within the institution. Why did the institutional arrangements and policy commitments fail in some cases to ensure

[1] Vincente Fox's administration (2000–2006) changed the name to *Oportunidades* and the Peña Nieto administration (2006–2012) renamed it *Prospera*. López Obrador's administration canceled *Prospera* and transformed it into universal scholarship grants.

that an innovative social policy targeting poor children and their mothers would also empower the latter?

Analyzing this difference reveals a complex story. While some Latin American countries did introduce gender equality goals into their CCT designs, others did not. The CCT pioneers—Mexico's *Progresa* (1997) and Brazil's *Bolsa Família* (2003)—explicitly or implicitly articulated gender equality goals. *Progresa* integrated the goals of gender equality and empowerment of women into its original design and *Bolsa Família* followed a design implicitly sensitive to gender equality. However, *Juntos* (2005) in Peru and the two *Bonos* (2006, 2009) in Bolivia did not pay any attention to gender equality and are coercive instruments that reinforce gender and racial inequalities. The book aims to understand this heterogeneity across countries. The book will also map the World Bank's influence because it is impossible to understand how these policies and their design traveled without taking into account the role played by this international organization. The World Bank was a central actor promoting and diffusing CCTs.

Therefore, this book asks and answers one simple question: Why did attention to gender inequalities and the promotion of gender equality become sidelined and then disappear as CCTs traveled through the region? More specifically, for the four cases, it asks: Why did Mexico design a CCT with an explicit goal of gender equality while Brazil designed one that demonstrated some awareness of the dangers of gender inequalities? How is it that both Peru and Bolivia were seemingly unconcerned about gender equality as they designed and implemented their programs? Additionally, the book scrutinizes the World Bank's influence on these choices compared to the national political configurations.

To respond to these questions and understand the fading goal of gender equality as CCTs made their way through Latin America, the book argues that gendered social policy legacies, strategic (gender equality) entrepreneurs, and knowledge about gender matter. While some CCT designers—embedded in gender-friendly institutions—became true strategic gender equality entrepreneurs and could insert their ideas linking gender inequalities to poverty into CCTs, others were not quite so successful. They could not overthrow social policy legacies that reproduced a long-held unconcern for gender equality. In addition, the World Bank itself a bank of knowledge, championed CCTs without any gender equality goals.

This analysis is essential because while the research has documented most elements about CCTs, including their elaboration, implementation, outcomes, and diffusion, the story about their design in relation to gender equality goals as they traveled through time and space has yet to be told. This book tells this story.

The introduction presents the study, establishes the importance of the puzzle, and sets up the organization of the book. First, I document the CCT designs as they vary in their gender equality goals across the four cases analyzed in the book. Second, I locate the study within the body of research on CCTs, gender, diffusion, and the World Bank. Third, I point to gaps in this research by proposing an innovative multiscale methodology to empirically understand CCT designs and their gender equality goals based on fieldwork in four countries—Mexico, Brazil, Peru, and Bolivia—and in one international development organization—the World Bank. Finally, the chapter briefly explains the case selection process and the data analysis and sets up the structure of the book.

CCT Designs Variations in Relation to Gender Equality Goals

Existing research recognizes that CCT designs vary widely in Latin America (e.g., Borges, 2022; De la O, 2015), ranging from few conditions and extensive coverage offered by the *Bono Juancito Pinto* in Bolivia to the strict conditions and limited coverage of the *Progresa* in Mexico. However, the literature does not offer sustained and systematic analysis of the variations in gender equality goals or how these variations are linked to coverage, conditions, and generosity.

Gender Equality in CCT Designs

As shown in Fig. 1.1, and as are all CCTs in Latin America, the four analyzed in this book are intended to be investments in children by way of families' investment in their education and health. Official and unofficial documents that establish and enforce CCTs such as laws, supreme decrees, operational rules, and so on, stipulate that mothers of these children must receive the cash (CEPAL, 2018).[2] However, only a few CCT designs explicitly include gender equality goals. It is the case of *Progresa*'s operational law that included affirmative action, transferring cash to mothers to promote women's empowerment, with more of that money available to girls than boys as an incentive to educating them (DOF, 1999). *Bolsa Família*'s design (2003) also included gender equality goals in its decision to transfer cash to mothers. While the designers did not make this commitment explicit in any official document, they nonetheless sought to empower mothers by contributing to their financial autonomy and thus altering intra-household relationships (Sugiyama & Hunter, 2020). By contrast, latecomers, *Juntos* (2005) in Peru and the *Bonos* (2006, 2009) in Bolivia, did not pay any attention to gender equality in their CCT designs, leaving plenty of space for long-standing social policy legacies that already contained gender inequalities. Indeed, in Peru and Bolivia the rationale behind cash transfers to mothers was built upon narrow definitions of motherhood and femininity, thus reinforcing traditional gender roles.

	Name	Cash recipients	Gender equality goals	Gender differentialism	Selection criteria	Coverage	Generosity	Conditions	Extra-conditions
Mexico	Progresa (1997)	Mother	Explicit	No	Extreme poor	Low	Low	Strict	No
Brazil	Bolsa Familia (2003)	Mother	Implicit	No	Poor	High	High	Soft	No
Peru	Juntos (2005)	Mother	No	Yes	Extreme poor	Low	High	Strict	Yes
Bolivia	Bono Juancito Pinto (2006); Bono Juana Azurduy (2009)	Mother	No	Yes	Universal	High	Low	Soft	Yes

Fig. 1.1 Variation in CCT designs (Author's construction)

[2] See Non-contributory Social Protection Programmes Database: https://dds.cepal.org/bpsnc/cct, accessed in December 2023, for CCT official national documents in Latin American countries. The only exception to mothers as recipients is when they are absent or cannot receive the payment.

Selection Criteria, Generosity, and Conditions

Social policy design characteristics linked to selection criteria, generosity, and conditions can have consequences for gender equality (Nagels, 2018; Orloff, 1993, 2009; Sainsbury, 2008; Siim, 1994). Therefore, it is important to differentiate CCT designs according to these characteristics. In Mexico, *Progresa* was a narrowly targeted program. Its selection criteria were means-tested on individuals experiencing extreme poverty, first in rural areas and after 2000, with *Oportunidades*, in the urban zone (De la O, 2015: 30). Consequently, the coverage was high in relation to the extreme poverty population but low in relation to the entire population—about 16% in 2001 (Borges, 2022: 87). In the same vein, *Juntos* in Peru targeted only rural and Indigenous persons experiencing extreme poverty based on national census and survey. Its coverage was then low (around 8% in 2019) and excluded a high percentage of persons experiencing poverty (CEPAL, 2018). By contrast, in Brazil and Bolivia, selection criteria were based on the idea of basic income or universalism (Borges, 2022). *Bolsa Família*'s selection criteria were based on self-declaration to minimize errors of exclusion, whereas Mexico and Peru's programs prioritized minimizing errors of inclusion. Therefore, from the outset coverage in the program was high. By 2009, the number of *Bolsa Família* beneficiaries surpassed the number of Brazilian poor people, and in 2019 one in five Brazilians accessed *Bolsa Família* (Borges, 2022: 87). Similarly, in Bolivia, where the selection criteria were based on universalism, all children enrolled in public school under 21 years of age accessed the *Bono Juancito Pinto* (BJP) and all pregnant women or mothers of children under 5 without private health insurance had access to the *Bono Juana Azurduy* (BJA) (CEPAL, 2018). Therefore, coverage of the entire population was high even in the first years of the Bonos (CEPAL, 2018). The *Bono Juancito Pinto* "has the broadest scope of any program in the region—by 2014 it covered essentially all public-school students or about one in five Bolivians—and is, in practice, unconditional" (Borges, 2022: 145). I will demonstrate in the empirical chapters that the Brazilian and Bolivian CCT designers linked the generous selection criteria to the improvement of gender equality by enhancing feelings of belonging to the national community for those women experiencing poverty.

CCT generosity varied in the four cases. A more generous stipend might be expected to better women's financial autonomy. While the Mexican and the Bolivian CCTs transferred small amounts of cash to the recipients in terms of average income for the poor, the Brazilian and Peruvian CCT monthly or bimonthly stipends were high (CEPAL, 2018). *Progresa* transferred “approximately thirty-five U.S. dollars per month, which represents around 25% of the average income for the poor” (De la O, 2015: 29). The Bonos were around 285 US$ per year (around 26 for the BJP and 260 for the BJA) representing around 20% of the average annual income (Marco Navarro, 2012: 9) but the amounts have remained nearly unchanged since the program’s adoption despite declining purchasing power (Borges, 2022: 152). By contrast, the stipend average of *Bolsa Família* and *Juntos* per family in 2008 corresponded to 102% in Brazil and 60% in Peru of the monthly income of poor families (CEPAL, 2018).

The conditions that mothers must fulfill to receive the stipend differ widely from one case to another. While they were strict in Peru and Mexico, conditions were softer in Bolivia and Brazil. *Progresa*’s conditions concerned health check-ups for all household members, 85% school attendance, and participation in workshops and communitarian work. Mothers could lose the cash transfer for a variety of reasons such as the non-respect of conditions or if it was not possible to collect socioeconomic and demographic information for reasons attributable to the family (CEPAL, 2018). Therefore, *Progresa* was the “clearest example of a CCT with a ‘sanctioning’ approach. [...] The design clearly highlights the importance of conditionalities (monitoring and sanctioning) as the main instrument to overcome poverty. Sanctions are carefully established, with stringent rules in cases of noncompliance” (Rossel et al., 2022: 12). *Juntos* used protocols similar to those of *Progresa* (De La O, 2015: 33) sanctioning the household if one of the conditions was not fulfilled (Arroyo, 2010).

In Mexico and Peru, not fulfilling the conditions led to expulsion from the program while in Brazil, this was interpreted as a sign of vulnerability requiring social assistance to intervene, helping a particular household to respect the conditions in health and education. In Bolivia as in Brazil, conditions for the *Bono Juancito Pinto* were soft and not monitored (Borges, 2022: 65). In Bolivia, children must be enrolled in public school, but Morales’s administration did not monitor their mandatory 80% presence in the classroom (CEPAL, 2018). According to Rossel et al. (2022: 6), Bolivia’s *Bono Juancito Pinto* included conditions as a formality in the design. However, in the case of the *Bono Juana Azurduy*, the conditions were stricter. Women were expected to respect health check-ups during pregnancy and during the first five years of their children’s lives to receive the stipend associated with each health check-up (CEPAL, 2018). Strict conditions are seen to worsen gender equality since they impose free domestic and reproductive work on women.

This was especially the case for the extra-official conditions that I encountered in Peru and Bolivia but not in Brazil and Mexico, although I scrutinized carefully the anthropological and political literature on *Bolsa Família* and *Progresa/Oportunidades/Prospera*. Since they are "extra-official", they are not written on any CCT official documents but are enforced in the implementation process. In Peru, *Juntos* local promoters utilized the cash as a means to enforce unofficial requirements including, institutional childbirth; cultivating a garden; owning a cocina mejorada (smokeless stove); attending workshops; using contraceptive methods, joining official parades; displaying the *Juntos* flag on homes; covering local managers' travel costs; compensating teachers for recording school attendance; crafting blankets and vests in *Juntos* colors and wearing the vest to public events (Cookson, 2016; Huber et al., 2009; Jones et al., 2007; Nagels, 2018; Piccoli, 2014; Vargas & Salazar, 2009). In Bolivia, such extra-official conditions were related to the children's weight and height and biomedical and "horizontal" childbirth. Although giving birth in a health center is an official condition of the *Bono Juana Azurduy*, by the legal recognition of Indigenous childbirth practices,[3] women could supposedly access "traditional" birth. However, BJA implementers dismissed this "traditional" childbirth and imposed horizontal and biomedical childbirth. As I will demonstrate in the last analytical chapter, in Peru and Bolivia, these extra-official conditions participated in reproducing gender and racial inequalities.

In this book, I aim to explain why and how these designs vary in these four countries. The answer—developed in the theoretical chapter—builds upon and goes beyond the literature reviewed in the next section.

[3] A chapter in the National Development Plan (2006) was dedicated to the decolonization of health (NDP, 2006: 37–43) and articles 35, 37, and 39 of the Plurinational Constitution of 2009 recognized traditional childbirth principles including vertical birth.

Conditional Cash Transfers, Gender, Diffusion, and the World Bank

The research on CCTs, gender, and CCT diffusion has uncovered what CCTs mean to Latin American social policies, their positive impacts on health, education, and poverty, and their negative or at best mixed impacts on gender as well as the diffusion process. However, the literature does not explain how or why gender equality goals changed as CCTs traveled through Latin America.

CCT Development

The research on CCT development in Latin America has shown how this innovation constitutes a major change in social policy (e.g., Arza et al., 2022; Barrientos, 2009, 2012; Barrientos et al., 2008; Jenson & Nagels, 2022; Molyneux, 2008). During the late 1990s in Latin America, policymakers widely recognized that the neoliberal model failed to generate economic growth and reduce poverty. As a result, the state came back to the social areas with its commitment on behalf of low-income citizens (Carnes & Mares, 2015).[4] After decades of social policy retrenchment between the 1970s and 1990s in Latin America, during the beginning of the twenty-first century, the creation of CCTs was a major component of the expansionary era of social policies, "as governments expanded access to income transfers and social services, incorporating sectors of the population that were previously excluded from such benefits" (Arza et al., 2022: 1). More than temporary measures to mitigate poverty, CCTs acquired firm and stable institutional bases in Ministries of social development (Barrientos & Villa, 2016: 423). With CCTs, the welfare regime began to be more inclusive of historical "outsiders", those without access to social security systems linked to formal labor (Barrientos, 2013; Nagels, 2018). This book contributes to this research by inquiring into how and why this major innovation could in some places integrate gender equality goals and not in others. In addition, by including the World Bank to the analysis, I show that the expansionary era of social policies was also in

[4] The role of the state in this era was different from that of the neoliberal era. While the state was not absent during the latter, it was characterized by systematic interventions aimed at dismantling state interventions in economic planning, labor relations, and social policy (Taylor, 2009: 29–30).

interaction with international organizations and that social policies during this era, were also global.

CCT Impact

According to policy analysts, experts, and scholars, CCTs have proven to be effective in achieving social development objectives, particularly in the areas of education, health, and poverty alleviation. There is a consensus about the positive results of CCTs in education, health, nutrition, and poverty that has been reached over the past 25 years, which is supported by a large amount of evidence. A broad spectrum of international, transnational, and national actors has regarded CCTs as "best practice" in the fight against poverty. This consensus is found in international financial organizations, such as the International Monetary Fund, the World Bank, and the Inter-American Development Bank, in United Nations development agencies, such as the United Nations Development Program, the United Nations Children's Fund, and the Economic Commission for Latin America, in think tanks, such as the International Food Policy Institute, and among academics.[5] This agreement relates to their objectives in terms of education (e.g., Barrientos & Dejong, 2006; Behram et al., 2004; ILO, 2011), health and nutrition (e.g., Adato et al., 2001; Fiszbein & Schady, 2009), poverty and inequality (e.g., Bastagli, 2009; Cecchini & Madariaga, 2011). Based on that evidence, for 25 years, CCTs were the flagship of anti-poverty programs. Latin American governments branded them as innovative and the best instrument to fight poverty and to reach welfare regime outsiders (De la O, 2015: 27).

Nonetheless, research on gender and CCTs has revealed that CCT impact on gender relations are not as positive as in other areas. One of the major CCT innovations was to target households and families, and to transfer the cash to mothers, an initiative that broke partially with the historical social policy legacy centered around the male breadwinner and the female dependent and assumptions about how income is distributed equally within the household (Barrientos et al., 2008: 769). However, this design of targeting only mothers and not fathers also perpetuated a social policy legacy of gender norms that reinforces the dichotomy between male breadwinners and female caregivers. Thus, while CCT

[5] E.g., Villatoro (2004) and Cohen et Franco (2006); and special issues of *Development Policy Review* 2006 and *Global Social Policy* 2009.

policies increased women's access to cash benefits, they "also reinforced gender-biased social norms" (Arza et al., 2022: 42).

Scholars have found that providing income to women through CCT programs has had positive effects on gender relations (e.g., Adato & Roopnaraine, 2010; Adato et al., 2000; Bradshaw, 2008; De Brauw et al., 2014; Escobar Latapí & Gonzalez de la Rocha, 2004; Holmes & Jones, 2013; Hunter & Sugiyama, 2014; Martínez Franzoni & Voorend, 2012; Molyneux, 2008; Nagels, 2011, 2016). Women have been able to achieve some material gains from these transfers, which has increased their financial autonomy from their male partners. CCTs have also led to increased use of contraception, enhanced women's role within the household, and improved education for girls (Bastagli et al., 2016; Holmes & Jones, 2013). For instance, *Progresa/Oportunidades* in Mexico has resulted in a 25.2% increase in the average wage of working girls who received higher levels of education and human capital (Barrientos & Villa, 2016). However, the positive effects of these programs are mostly experienced on an individual and household level. Research indicates that CCTs were still influenced by maternalism (e.g., Gil-García, 2015; Lavinas, 2015; Molyneux, 2007; Nagels, 2016; Tabbush, 2010). Women in CCT programs are primarily viewed as "mothers at the service of the state" instead of as citizens or workers, as noted by Molyneux (2007). These programs have not addressed the structural gender inequalities and gendered division of labor (Cookson, 2018; Molyneux, 2007; Nagels, 2016). They do not consider women's dual roles as caregivers and productive workers, nor do they consider the costs of collecting transfers and respecting conditions, "often at the expense of other income-generating activities" (Holmes & Jones, 2013: 73). If the research explains the mixed impact of CCTs on gender equality by the lack or the weakness of gender equality goals in CCT design (Cookson, 2018; Molyneux, 2007; Nagels, 2016), it did not question why that was the case or even why CCTs targeted women as recipients. The book contributes to this research by addressing this question and part of the answer lies in the role of international organizations—mainly the World Bank—in the promotion and diffusion of CCTs.

CCT Diffusion

CCTs have spread across Latin America. They expanded rapidly throughout the region from the mid-1990s (De la O, 2015; Osorio

Gonnet, 2018) and by 2012, 17 countries had adopted a CCT to reach 27 million of the poorest in the region (De la O, 2015: 3). Individual CCT recipients as part of the total population increased from nearly 4% in 2000 to 20.6% in 2016 with a peak of 22.6% in 2010 (Arza et al., 2022: 7). Scholars have identified this phenomenon of CCT dissemination throughout Latin America and beyond through the lens of the concepts of diffusion or policy transfers (e.g., Borges, 2022; Foli et al., 2018; Howlett et al., 2018; Leisering, 2019; Olivier de Sardan & Piccoli, 2018; Osorio Gonnet, 2017; Peck & Theodore, 2015; Sugiyama, 2011). They have confirmed that the widespread adoption of CCTs throughout Latin America followed from policy diffusion. As Borges writes, "specifically, as the share of countries in the region with CCTs increased, countries without programs became more likely to adopt their own" (Borges, 2022: 119). Diffusion concerns the process through which policies move internationally in time and space and means that "the decisions previously taken by one actor affect others" (Porto De Oliveira, 2020: 135). Scholars have identified social learning as the main process by which CCTs are diffused (e.g., Borges, 2022; Foli et al., 2018; Howlett et al., 2018; Sugiyama, 2011). They emphasize the agency of the adopters, not constrained by international organizations, and the role of networks and "epistemic communities" (Haas, 1992) to explain the spread of CCT as the now widely recognized instrument with which to fight poverty. According to Sugiyama (2011: 262), "cross-national learning likely influenced Latin American emulation decisions". This research has also demonstrated the role played by international organizations, mainly the World Bank (Borges, 2022). In this process, the World Bank was key to producing and promoting knowledge about CCTs as the best instrument to reduce poverty and to create epistemic communities and constituencies around CCTs (Foli et al., 2018; Howlett et al., 2018; Leisering, 2019; Martínez Franzoni & Voorend, 2011). This research reaffirms the role of the World Bank, as a bank of knowledge, as an influential actor in global social policy development, promotion, and diffusion (Deacon, 2007; Mahon, 2021; Martens et al., 2021; Vetterlein, 2007).

The research on diffusion and policy transfer tends to see what is moving as relatively stable leading to policy convergence and homogenization of political institutions. CCT design has not, however, been stable as it has moved through Latin America, as shown for example by De la O (2015) and Borges (2022). They argue that despite the apparent convergence, CCT designs vary, specifically regarding the stringent conditions (Borges, 2022) and "the degree to which operational rules limit politicians' ability to manipulate program resources for political gain" (De la O, 2015: 5). Both stress domestic political dynamics as the main factors influencing CCT design variation. Borges explains that political party ideology—left and right—determined the choice and the model of CCTs. "Whereas the right was attracted to CCTs for their potential to boost human capital, the left was attracted to their potential to reduce poverty and saw them as a step in the direction of providing a universal income floor" (Borges, 2022: 4). De la O (2015) has argued that the process of designing and adopting CCTs was largely influenced by executive-legislative relations. According to her "legislators have become 'blunt veto players' with budgetary powers to cut the appropriations desired by presidents" (De la O, 2015: 11). In a divided government, when the executive faces sharp opposition, legislators of the opposition demand more stringent operational rules for CCTs that suppress political discretion and clientelism.

This book takes a different tack. It draws on this literature but expands upon it, analyzing as it does CCTs design in relation to gender equality goals. My objective is to understand how and why some CCT designs included gender equality goals while others reproduced gender inequalities. Filling the gaps within and between these three sets of literature, my argument shows how the configuration of gendered social policy legacies, strategic (gender equality) entrepreneurs, and knowledge on gender in each country and in the World Bank influenced CCT design in relation to gender equality. Therefore, I reassert the role of international organization in social policies even in the expansionary era.

Argument in Brief

I rely on gender analysis and historical institutionalism to explain why and how gender equality goals changed in CCT design as they traveled through Latin America. In the next chapter, I construct a theoretical framework from a mechanistic approach, and political configuration populated by gendered social policy legacies, strategic (gender equality) entrepreneurs, and knowledge on gender to explain how and why gender equality goals changed in CCT designs. Beyond the search for a direct explanation, the mechanism approach does not look for general macropolitical explanations and grand theory but develops a lower level of analysis to "identify recurrent micro-level processes that contribute to" (Hall, 2003: 388) bigger outcomes. The mechanisms of cooking, standardization, and translation explain the processes through which CCT designs have changed along the way from Mexico and Brazil to their standardization in and by the World Bank and their translation into Peruvian and Bolivian programs. Cooking[6] took place in Mexico and Brazil with the invention of a new, complex, homegrown, and contextualized recipe, with its aim to reduce poverty while reducing gender inequalities. With its "one-size-fits-all approach", standardization—mostly led by the World Bank—transformed the initial recipe into a simpler model excluding contextualized complexity, of which gender equality goals were a part. Translation of the standard recipe by latecomers meant adapting to local institutional social policy legacies that reproduced gender inequalities. In each step, the configuration populated by institutional legacies, strategic gender equality entrepreneurs, and knowledge drove the mechanism's outcomes: CCT designs with or without gender equality goals.

The story opens with the mechanism of cooking and Mexico and Brazil, integrating gender equality goals, the former explicitly and the latter implicitly, into their CCT design. This design was ultimately shaped by institutional constraints, strategic (gender equality) entrepreneurs' strategies, and knowledge on gender. The next phase of CCT travel and development is best be described in terms of a standardization mechanism (Ancelovici & Jenson, 2013; Olivier de Sardan & Piccoli, 2018). It explains how the original and national policy recipes were transformed into an exportable model. With its lack of strategic gender equality entrepreneurs, its reliance on evidence-based policies, and its institutional legacies, the World Bank ultimately erased the gender equality goals during this process of standardization. The last part of this story has to do with the mechanism of translation (Campbell, 2004; Levitt & Merry, 2009). It explains how, within specific ideational, institutional, and agential contexts, Bolivian and Peruvian CCT designers translated and adapted the standard recipe. Not only did the translators not pay any attention to gender equality goals but they also reproduced gender inequalities.

This book focuses only on the design of CCTs and does not analyze their implementation or impacts on other gendered outcomes such as gender-based violence, women's poverty, women's economic autonomy,

[6] I thank Juliana Martínez Franzoni for the idea to name this mechanism "cooking".

maternal mortality, and so on. This is because "institutional design matters" (Kapiszewski et al., 2021: 7). Formal institutional designs encourage and constrain political behavior and policy implementation and impacts. They do not determine policies and programs but affect them. This explains why politicians and bureaucrats could fight over a specific policy design. Moreover, formal designs also provide a baseline for evaluations (Kapiszewski et al., 2021: 7). In the case of CCTs, design affects gender relations. CCT designs did not determine the consequences of CCTs on gender relations, but they had intentions about gender relations. Designs have determined that it is women who should receive the transfers. It could be because, as mothers, they are considered better spenders than fathers as far as their children are concerned or because they can achieve more autonomy in the household thanks to these resources.

To explain how and why CCT designs vary in relation to gender equality goals, my argument stresses the role of the standardization process as CCTs traveled. Standardization, mainly undertaken by the World Bank, led latecomer translators of CCTs, such as Peru and Bolivia, to ignore gender equality goals. Without the specific priorities explored and established by the Mexican and Brazilian iterations, subsequent adopters were enabled to set aside gender equality goals. Mexican and Brazilian designers were freer to invent an original CCT recipe whereas Peruvian and Bolivian CCT designers were at once constrained by a standardized recipe with permission to exclude the optional ingredient of gender equality goals.

Standardization in and of itself is not what has led to the exclusion of gender equality goals. It is rather the specific configuration of CCT entrepreneurs and of social policy institutional legacies and venues and their interactions that have led to this exclusion. I show this by way of the cases of Peru and Bolivia. A mechanistic approach does not rest on a counterfactual understanding of causation in which a cause produces an outcome, "because its absence would result in the absence of the outcome, all other things being held equal" (Beach & Pedersen, 2019: 33). Claiming the existence of one mechanism does not mean that other mechanisms are not also at work since many mechanisms could have different effects on the outcome. The mechanistic approach recognizes that in social science, most outcomes have multiple causes because mechanisms are real processes involving causal power in the real world, "not in logically possible counterfactual worlds" (Beach & Pedersen, 2019: 33).

Methodological Insights

This book traces the process of gender equality goal minimization in CCT designs from the development of the first CCTs in Mexico and Brazil to latecomers Peru and Bolivia, whose iterations first passed through the World Bank. The case selection is therefore based on the role of each state or international organization during the extraordinary tale of CCT travel. I have chosen *Progresa* (1997) in Mexico and *Bolsa Família* (2003) in Brazil (and not Chile *Solidario* for instance created in 2002) because they were historically the first CCTs in the world and because the research highlights their role as the flagship and the model exported throughout Latin America and beyond. A comparison between Mexico and Brazil in the first cooking sequence of CCT travel is justified by the fact that they belong to the same category of dual and conservative welfare regime (Filgueira, 1998; Martínez Franzoni, 2008) but they diverge in relation to the government ideology at work during the design process: the left in Brazil and the right in Mexico.

In the same vein, while other international organizations such as the Inter-American Bank of Development (IADB) or national institutions, such as the Anti-poverty Institute in Brazil financed by the United Nations Development Program, have been active in the promotion and diffusion of CCTs, the research has stressed the key role played by the World Bank in this process (Foli et al., 2018; Howlett et al., 2018; Leisering, 2019; Martínez Franzoni & Voorend, 2011). The World Bank, as a bank of knowledge, has been the principal international organization promoting and disseminating CCTs through the region. In the process of CCT travel, the World Bank has been the major actor in a standardization process that ultimately removed gender equality goals from CCT design. In the subsequent process of translation, latecomer CCT designers Peru and Bolivia were free to exclude gender equality goals in their CCT designs. Therefore, the World Bank is central to the chapter dedicated to standardization.

Finally, I selected the *Juntos* program in Peru and the Bonos in Bolivia because they were both latecomers to CCT adoption. Between 2005 and 2009, Peruvian and Bolivian policymakers translated the standard recipe just built by the World Bank (around 2004). The comparison between Peru and Bolivia makes sense because they pertain to the same category of familialist and informal welfare regimes in Latin America (Filgueira, 1998; Martínez Franzoni, 2008) but they diverge in terms of the government ideology at work during the design process. While Peruvian and Bolivian political contexts were antipodal—still neoliberal in Peru and "revolutionary" and decolonial in Bolivia—they translated the World Bank's CCT standard model without any gender equality goals, thus reproducing long-standing social policy legacies of gender and racial inequalities. In addition, their CCTs are quite dissimilar. While *Juntos* in Peru is often held up as exemplary, the Bonos in Bolivia are more controversial—e.g., for their potential use for clientelism (De la O, 2015) but its steadiness over time.

Therefore, the comparison between the first sequence of CCT cooking innovation in Mexico and Brazil and the last one of translation in Peru and Bolivia speaks to some of the key factors addressed by the literature on comparative social policy, such as policy legacy and left-right cleavages (e.g., Arza et al., 2022; Borges, 2022; Garay, 2016; Huber & Stephen, 2012; Staab, 2017). The similarities between Mexico and Brazil on the one hand and between Bolivia and Peru on the other, despite strong divergences in government ideology are essentially due to the work of strategic (gender equality) entrepreneurs, their shared institutional legacies, and the knowledge they use to link (or not) between gender inequalities and poverty.

To understand the trajectory of fading gender equality goals, the study uses process tracing to document and identify mechanisms to comprehend processes and explain specific outcomes (Beach & Pedersen, 2019; Benett & Chekel, 2015; Falleti, 2010). This method sits well with historical institutionalism that is committed to in-depth case studies. Instead of deductive approaches, historical institutionalism "use[s] narratives to identify mechanisms that shape[-] political contestation over time" (Fioretos et al., 2016: 10). The methodology is based on uncovering the causal mechanisms through the careful study of empirical records. In addition, this methodological approach is coherent with a gender analysis that is also contextual, comparative, and relational (women and femininity are analyzed hand in hand with references to men and masculinity). Therefore, historical institutionalism and gender analysis share an abandonment of "the quest for a general theory, searching instead for the 'complex configurations of factors' that have some causal significance (…). Researchers would aim to 'tell a story'" (Franceschet, 2011: 67, 68). In this book, my aim is to tell a story about the goals of gender equality included or not in CCT design. However, in line with historical institutionalism, the book does more than "tell a story" about CCT design and travel. It also offers a "structured comparison and historical process tracing, it aims to identify the causal mechanisms that lie behind particular empirical processes" (Waylen, 2011: 149).

Like Falleti (2010), my method lies between the macrosocial and the micro-level of the decision-making process. It aims to uncover the micro-foundations of the decision-making process of actors and the more macro social events that influence and constrain actors' agency. Process tracing proceeds "through a combination of induction and deduction" (Bennett & Chekel, 2015: 17). Process tracing uncovers and documents causal mechanisms linking events together in the process under study (Falleti, 2010: 20). It "involves making inferences about processes that link together causes and outcomes" (Beach & Pedersen, 2019: 42) by making explicit the activities in which entities (structures, organizations, institutions, actors) engage that could link together parts of the process (Beach & Pedersen, 2019: 70). It involves identifying how initial conditions led to particular outcomes, "and unpacking this process in a series of steps" (Ancelovici & Jenson, 2012: 298). Events (such as economic crisis and internal war) take place and interact with the spatial and temporal contexts that shape their meaning and their causal effects. A sequence "is a temporally ordered set of events that takes place in a given context" and "process is a particular type of sequence in which the temporally ordered events belong to a single coherent mode of activity" (Falleti & Mahoney, 2015: 213, 214). In the case of this book, the sequence of mechanisms as processes is important: cooking precedes standardization, which precedes translation.[7]

For this book, deduction comes from all that was already known about CCT diffusion and its links to gender relations. However, I have identified the causal mechanisms—cooking, standardization, and translation—by induction, retracing, and analyzing events backward through time from the development of CCTs and their travels in and through Latin America. My data are drawn from the literature, specialized, administrative, and academic on the five cases and from interviews. Fieldwork was conducted in Mexico, Brazil,[8] Washington, Peru, and Bolivia. I have

[7] However, the sub-mechanisms of standardization, described in the next chapter, including decontextualization, framing, and certification, did not occur in sequence. They overlapped (Ancelovici & Jenson, 2012: 297).

[8] Research assistants, Adriana Pozos and Danielle Coenga Oliviera conducted the interviews in Brasilia and in Mexico City, respectively.

analyzed the official documents on CCTs, produced mainly by the four state institutions and the World Bank, the International Food Policy Research Institute, and the Inter-American Development Bank (IADB) in the early 2000s. I have identified those documents about CCTs that promoted them as achieving their social development goals and that were most cited by experts within international organizations and scholars.

Between 2008 and 2009 and between 2016 and 2017, I carried out a total of around 80 interviews with authors of these documents as well as policymakers involved in *Progresa*, *Bolsa Família*, *Juntos*, and the *Bonos* in Mexico, Brasilia, Lima, Ayacucho, La Paz, El Alto, and Washington, DC. Initially, I identified potential interviewees by reviewing academic and secondary research that discussed CCTs in Latin America. Subsequently, I employed the snowball sampling method (Noy, 2008), to identify additional individuals for interviews. I interviewed the majority of designers in each country and the majority of the World Bank staff who have worked with or on CCTs. I asked them similar questions about why transfer the cash to women and got very different answers from enhancing women's empowerment in Mexico and Brazil to stressing the maternal role of women recipients in Peru and Bolivia.

In terms of *Progresa*, *Bolsa Família*, and the World Bank, these interviews took place in 2016 and 2017 at the World Bank, the IADB, and within the Mexican and Brazilian administrations. Of the interviewees, six were individuals who had worked or were currently working at the World Bank, while 16 had actively participated in the development of *Progresa* and *Bolsa Família* and were affiliated with either the World Bank, the IADB, and the Brazilian or Mexican administrations. Additionally, five of the interviewees had served as consultants for *Progresa* during either its formulation or evaluation phase.

From 2008 to 2010, I conducted approximately 50 interviews[9] in Lima, the Peruvian Ayacucho department, La Paz, and El Alto in Bolivia.[10] These interviews involved public officials (civil servants or elected officials) at the central, regional, or local level; experts

[9] A list of these interviews is available in Nagels (2014: 128–132).

[10] The interviews in Peru and Bolivia draw upon fieldwork conducted during my Ph.D. studies (Nagels, 2013) and was supported by the Swiss National Science Foundation through the National Centre of Competence in Research North–South (NCCR N/S). My Ph.D. research also included around 30 interviews with Peruvian and Bolivian CCT's recipients not included in this book.

(e.g., academics or research center members sometimes affiliated with ministries); practitioners (e.g., professors and doctors), and policymakers of *Juntos* and the *Bonos*. While the capitals, Lima, and La Paz, involved discussions with high-ranking public officials, Ayacucho, and El Alto, with more poor people than in the capitals, were the source of discussions with the implementers and practitioners of Peruvian and Bolivian CCTs. Moreover, since *Juntos* is specifically targeted at rural areas, I conducted fieldwork in the Ayacucho department, where the program was initiated in 2006. I conducted interviews in Peru and Bolivia with local implementers and practitioners to get access to information about extra-official conditions since they enforced them and as "extra-official", they were not written. I did not conduct this kind of interviews in Mexico and Brazil since their CCTs did not include extra-official conditions.

I conducted these interviews at different points in time and for various projects[11] from my Ph.D. dissertation. This is a strength and a weakness of the methodology because time is important in the attempt to reconstruct policy design processes. In Peru and Bolivia, I conducted fieldwork on recent programs maximizing the identification of key policymakers and increasing the reliability of their information obtained through in-person interviews (Borges, 2022: 131). In Mexico, Brazil, and the World Bank, the interviews took place long after the design stage of *Progresa* and *Bolsa Família*. Nevertheless, scholars have already tracked and identified the majority of Mexican and Brazilian CCT designers, who became famous in Latin America and within the World Bank. Therefore, I had only to ask them about the gender equality goals of their CCT, a question that other scholars did not focus on.

The quotes included in the book represent the overall content of the interviews conducted and are consistent with other evaluations of CCTs mentioned in the text. Through attention to discourse in these interviews, I gained insights into the narratives surrounding CCT travel, and the alteration of their design linked to gender equality goals. The interview quotes featured in this book capture the main themes derived from the respondents' accounts and experiences. To maintain ethical standards, the quotes have been anonymized, and I take full responsibility for their interpretation.

[11] The Programme *Relève professoral du Fonds de Recherche et Culture du Québec*, Canada, financed part of those.

Structure of the Book

Chapter 2: Mechanisms and Configuration: Understanding the Travels of a Policy Instrument

This chapter outlines the problem and the puzzle that the book addresses. Although the research has demonstrated negative or at best mixed results for gender relations and the role played by the World Bank in promoting and diffusing CCTs, fading gender equality goals in CCTs have yet to be explored and explained. This chapter underscores why the book is therefore a good case for understanding changing gender equality goals when these are institutionalized in the form of social policy and when social policy travels. To understand this trajectory, this theoretical chapter builds on insights from gender analysis and historical institutionalism (e.g., Franceshet, 2011; Jenson, 1997; Orloff, 2017; Staab, 2017) and policy innovation, standardization, and translation (e.g., Ancelovici & Jenson, 2012; Campbell, 2004; Stone, 2012). The book goes beyond the current research by stretching the analysis to include an international actor. The multi-level comparative analysis of three mechanisms—cooking, standardization, and translation—and their configuration of gendered social policy legacies and venues, strategic (gender equality) entrepreneurs, and knowledge about gender explain how and why gender equality goals in CCT design varied as they traveled around Latin America. This configuration allows us to trace the direction of change and to map out the outcomes of CCT designs that included gender equality goals and those that did not.

Chapter 3: Cooking from a New Recipe: Progresa and Bolsa Família with Gender Equality Goals

This chapter presents the first sequence of the CCT trajectory: its creation separately and almost simultaneously in Mexico and Brazil. The parallel analysis of the two cases demonstrates how in the process of cooking from existing and new ingredients, policymakers were able to include gender equality goals in the design of *Progresa* while their Brazilian counterparts were not quite so successful. The chapter begins with a brief contextual and historical account of the social policy legacies in both countries. An analysis of gendered social policy legacies and venues, strategic (gender equality) entrepreneurs, and knowledge on gender in the process of cooking *Progresa* (1997) and *Bolsa Família* (2003) shows that power relations and institutional legacies were more favorable to gender equality in Mexico than they were in Brazil. Nevertheless, *Bolsa Família*'s designers cooked a CCT recipe with attention to gender inequalities and implicit gender equality goals. Therefore, among the outcome for both is the inclusion of gender equality goals in CCT designs.

Chapter 4: Standardization of CCTs Without Gender Equality Goals

I present the analysis of the second sequence of the CCT trajectory in this chapter, involving the standardization of *Bolsa Família* and *Progresa* CCTs mostly by the World Bank as part of a series of anti-poverty actions. After briefly explaining the historical and institutional context of the World Bank in social development and gender, I demonstrate that the World Bank weakened gender equality goals in two significant ways. First, international policy entrepreneurs, with a seemingly unwavering commitment to evidence-based policy choices, omitted gender equality arguments when empirical studies found mixed results concerning the reduction of gender inequalities and the empowerment of women. Second, the chapter argues that, in the framing and decontextualizing processes of CCT standardization, the World Bank privileged quantitative and economic forms of knowledge, while qualitative and contextual knowledge—in this case, in particular, feminist and gender-related research—were marginalized, as were the experts in the institution who carry that knowledge. Therefore, the World Bank's evidence-based approach led to certifying a thin version of CCTs, minus any goals for altering gender relations or outcomes. The chapter highlights the importance of knowledge mobilized by actors constrained by institutional legacies and venues. Retaining only instrumental understanding of gender relations involves the negation of feminist knowledge and actors. Therefore, the outcome of standardization is the exclusion of gender equality goals from CCT design.

Chapter 5: Juntos and the Bonos: Translation with Innovation Rooted in Exclusionary Institutional Legacies

The last analytical chapter focuses on the third sequence of the CCT trajectory in Latin America: translation of the CCT standard model by latecomers Peru and Bolivia. The chapter begins by presenting the historical and institutional context of social policy reforms in Peru and Bolivia.

While the Peruvian political regime, under center-right governments, was still very neoliberal, the Bolivian political regime under the Evo Morales governments promised radical change from the left to dismantle colonialism and neoliberalism. Nevertheless, these two political regimes translated the same instrument as standardized by the World Bank but adapted it to local ingredients. My analysis of the design of *Juntos* (2004) in Peru, and the *Bonos Juancito Pinto* (2006) and the *Bono Juana Azurduy* (2009) in Bolivia demonstrates their understanding of gender relations as limited to motherhood. Without any gender equality goals in the standard CCT recipe promoted by the World Bank, Peruvian and Bolivian policy entrepreneurs translated it and adapted it to local ingredients embedded in strong exclusionary institutional legacies. The outcome of translation is therefore the exclusion of gender equality goals from CCT design and a reinforcement of existing gender inequalities.

Chapter 6: Lessons for Gender Equality and Social Policies

In this chapter, I place the conclusion of the book highlighting the theoretical and policy lessons that can be learned from the empirical cases presented. Then, I explore the differentiated explanations and variations built out of the theoretical framework and compares them to the empirical findings. In doing so, it lays open the implications of the inclusion or not of gender equality goals in social policies, stressing the limits and the potential of each sequence as well as discussing their implications for the study of social policies with a gender lens. After, the chapter discusses the theoretical implications and contributions of the findings for the gender study of social policies, historical institutionalism, and policy transfer. Finally, I unpack the significance of this study for policymakers, politicians, and feminist activists who lead or advocate for such social policies throughout Latin America and beyond.

CHAPTER 2

Mechanisms and Configuration: Understanding the Travels of a Policy Instrument

Introduction

Although the research, reviewed in Chapter 1, has considered gender relations in terms of the development of CCTs and has explained their diffusion, an analysis of *how* or *why* gender equality goals changed in CCT design as these traveled throughout Latin America is missing from the literature. This theoretical chapter develops the concepts that I will use throughout the book to understand the alterations in CCT design through travel. For such an account to be convincing, the conceptual tools must permit an understanding of the processes by which attention to gender inequalities was disappeared. More specifically, as seen in the introduction, for the four cases analyzed in this book, the questions are: Why did Mexico design a CCT with an explicit goal of gender equality while Brazil designed one that demonstrated some awareness of the dangers of gender inequalities? And why is it that Peru and Bolivia were seemingly unconcerned about gender equality in designing their programs? Additionally, what was the World Bank's influence on these choices compared to the national political configurations?

To understand the fading goal of gender equality over this trajectory, this theoretical chapter builds on insights from gender analysis and historical institutionalism, particularly from the literature on policy mechanisms,

N. Nagels, *Gender Equality in Conditional Cash Transfer Designs*, Studies of the Americas,
https://doi.org/10.1007/978-3-031-60871-1_2

and those focused on the configuration of actors, institutions, and ideas—institutional legacies and venues, strategic (gender equality) entrepreneurs acting in instrument communities, and knowledge about gender—influencing the outcomes of such mechanisms. Reliance on these approaches enables me to apply a gender lens to mechanisms of policy development and transfer and to the context in which these mechanisms unfold. While mechanisms help us to understand how change occurs, they do not account for why the change occurs, or for the direction and scope of such change because mechanisms are context-specific (Falleti & Lynch, 2009). Thus, the context must be unpacked to reveal the particular configuration of interconnected gendered institutions, actors, and ideas at each step of CCT travel. Outcomes depend on the context of specific configurations and features of past institutional trajectories, institutions in which changes occur, the strategic entrepreneurs, and the knowledge embedded in institutions. The causal mechanisms at work here are the processes of cooking, standardization, and translation. The gendered configuration explains why CCT design changed and in what way—whether to include gender equality goals, or not.

With this theoretical chapter, I aim to explain a process of varying gender equality goals in CCT design by way of a mechanistic approach, but I do not claim that these mechanisms can be applied to other cases. Since mechanisms unfold in specific cases and are highly sensitive to context, the ability to generalize from "studied cases to other cases is substantially weakened" (Beach & Pedersen, 2019: 41). Such analysis involves deploying a gender lens within historical institutionalism. The next sections of this chapter develop this theoretical framework. The first presents the concepts of gender and gendering in some detail. The second examines the literature that describes gender and historical institutionalism. The third section outlines the causal mechanisms of change at play in the processes of policy development and transfer—cooking, standardization, and translation. The fourth section examines the gendered configuration of change and applies a gender lens to historical institutionalism to extract and track such concepts as institutional legacies and venues, strategic (gender equality) entrepreneurs acting in instrument communities, and knowledge about gender.

Gender and Gendering

Since gender equality goals are central to this book, this first section considers a set of categories and concepts key to the book: gender and gendering.

Gender refers to socially constructed relations, being "the mechanism through which 'woman' and 'man' and 'masculine' and 'feminine" come to be known as legitimate conceptual categories" (Htun & Weldon, 2017: 160). This concept rejects all forms of biological determination of sexual differences and insists on the fundamental fact of the social construction of these differences (Butler, 1990; Dorlin, 2008). As Joan Scott wrote decades ago, we must understand gender as "a constitutive element of social relationships based on perceived differences between the sexes, and gender is a primary way of signifying relationships of power" (Scott, 1986: 1067). Therefore, gender relations are "embodied in the sexual division of labor, compulsory heterosexuality, discourses and ideologies of citizenship, motherhood, masculinity, and femininity" (Orloff, 1996: 51). It is, in other words, essential to appreciate that "gender is not an attribute of individuals but a social relationship, historically varying, and encompassing elements of labor, power, emotion, and language; it crosses individual subjectivities, institutions, cultures, and language" (Orloff, 2009: 318).

The concept has helped reveal that in almost all known societies, men dominate women and monopolize the vast majority of economic, symbolic, material, and political resources (Béreni et al., 2012). Nonetheless, women are not a homogeneous group but are differentiated by class, sexuality, race, ability, and the like (Butler, 2004; Young, 2002). Gender, in other words, intersects with and reinforces other axes of structural domination such as those based on race, age, ability, sexuality, or class (Bilge, 2009; Kergoat, 2012). Therefore, analysis must pay attention to intersectional patterns of social construction, because gender relations produce heterogeneous groups through social and historical processes that are contextual. Therefore, in the analytical chapter, I will show that intentions regarding gender relations as addressed in CCT design are also intentions about other forms of domination, including race.

Gendering first refers to the works of scholars who have been using gender as a concept directed at correcting political science. Across fields, they "gender" the analysis developing research that challenges masculinist assumptions by focusing on organizations, political representation, and public policies that specifically target women. This trend of research is particularly well developed in the analysis of social policies[1] (e.g., Jenson, 1997; Lewis, 1992; Martínez Franzoni, 2008; O'Connor, 1996; Orloff, 1993, 1996; Sainsbury, 2008). These scholars have "gendered" the analysis of welfare regimes by taking into account gender relations as causes and consequences of public policies and institutions. They have shown not only the gendered consequences of social policies but also how these policies are involved in constituting the very definitions of "men" and "women" in a given time and space (Orloff, 1996; Staab, 2017; Waylen, 2014).

Therefore, second, "gendering" adopts a verb form "to capture the active, ongoing, and always incomplete processes that *constitute* (make come into existence) 'women' and 'men' as specific kinds of unequal political subjects" (Bacchi, 2017: 20; stressed in the original). These are co-constructed by other processes of subordination such as racializing, hetero-norming, classing, or third-worldizing processes. In these processes of gendering, public policies "gender" by producing and encouraging behaviors and characteristics defined as masculine or feminine, "making them come to be" (Bacchi, 2017: 20). Policies have key roles in the ongoing social process of construction and negotiation of gender "through what is and is not articulated as a problem to be addressed" (Chanfreau, 2022: 3). It is especially the case for social policies, which "by design or by default, definition or omission (...) shape men's and women's participation and position in the market, the

[1] This is also the case in other sub-fields of political science such as security policies (e.g., Anctill, 2022; D'Aoust, 2022; Enloe, 2004) and policies regulating sexualities (Díez, 2015; Paternotte, 2011). For example, in international relations, feminist scholars have shown the consequence of war for women (Enloe, 2004) but also how international relations, wars, conflicts, and post-conflict scenarios are gendered processes producing certain kinds of "women" and "men" (e.g., Martín de Almagro, 2018; Parashar, 2014; Tickner, 1992). Others, including those using an approach labeled feminist institutionalism, aim to reveal not only who takes institutional decisions but also why some policy outcomes have unexpected gender consequences in social lives (e.g., Chappell, 2000; Debusscher & van der Vleuten, 2017; Guerina et al., 2018; Htun & Weldon, 2017; Jacquot et Mazur, 2019; Kenny, 2007; Mackay et al., 2010; Mazur, 2002, 2009; Norris, 2004; Waylen, 2014). They examine institutions through a gender lens to reveal the relations between men and women in phenomena first seen as gender-neutral. For example, masculinity norms often dominate the most prestigious and influential ministries such as finance or defense even when biological women are responsible for them while women and feminine norms are assigned to institutional instances related to "soft" policy areas, such as education, thereby reducing their influence (Franceschet, 2011: 65).

polity, and the home in conspicuously gendered ways" (Staab, 2017: 22). Social policies mostly reinforce the gendered division of labor by creating dichotomies between "male" productive labor work in the public sphere generating income and reproductive labor in the private sphere, which is seen as both "free" and women's work (Beyeler & Annesley, 2011: 84; Jacquot & Mazur, 2019: 291) contributing to economic inequalities between men and women. For example, policies relating to paid work, family, childcare or anti-poverty, gendered "the worker" and "the parent" through normative assumptions, constructing the main earner as male and the main carer as female in a heteronormative family (Chanfreau, 2022: 2).

I rely on the concept of gender and gendering to follow the various CCT designs as they traveled in Latin America. This literature is essential to understanding what the intentions are beyond the choice to integrate gender equality goals in CCT designs or not. Without analyzing CCT's consequences on gender relations (e.g., the impacts of CCTs on maternal mortality, the violence against women, women's economic autonomy, women's empowerment, the education of girls, etc.), CCT designs including or lacking gender equality goals say something about gender relations and the gendered division of labor. They participate in the fabrication of "men" and "women" as (un)equal subjects by gendering—for example, through normative assumptions—the worker and the carer as men and/or women.

To analyze the processes through which CCT designs have included or sidelined gender equality goals in the different stages of their travels in Latin America, I rely on analytical tools drawn from gender analysis and historical institutionalism.

Gender Analysis and Historical Institutionalism

I rely on historical institutionalism[2] because of its focus on variation across time and space and because of the importance it assigns to power inequalities. Indeed, historical institutionalism and gender analysts, who have a structural and materialist conception of power relations, share an approach that sees institutions shaping power relations with distributional consequences (Waylen, 2014: 216). Scholars using gender analysis, like historical institutionalists, understand institutions as reproducing and reflecting power relations (Kenny, 2007: 96) and human behavior as following rational self-interest but also as dependent upon context and existing rules (Lovenduski, 2011: xi).

While the bulk of the classical literature on historical institutionalism does not apply a gender lens to its objects of analysis, scholars using a range of gender lenses have understood that states, welfare states, and public policies have gendering effects and (re)produce gender relations (e.g., see Shaver, 2018 for a summary of this literature). Even if they have not always explicitly framed their theoretical analysis as historical institutionalism, they have contributed to it through their methodologies and results by documenting, for example, the gender relations embedded in welfare states. One focus has been on early welfare states and the emergence of social policies (Dore & Molyneux, 2000; Ewig, 2010; Jenson, 1989; O'Connor, 1996; Skocpol, 1992).[3]

[2] For historical institutionalism, history, and time matter since institutions are the "legacy of concrete historical processes (...) [and they] emerge from particular historical conflicts and constellations" (Pierson, 2004; Thelen, 1999: 382). Historical institutionalists examine how historical events influence creation and create change in institutions. As Fioretos reminds us, "[u]nderstood as the rules, norms, and practices that organize and constitute social relations, institutions [are] examined for their role in creating constraints and opportunities for political action, in distributing political power, and in shaping political preferences over time" (Fioretos et al., 2016: 8). Institutions are formal and informal rules, mechanisms of enforcement, and systems of meaning that define the context within which individual and collective actors evolve and interact with each other. Therefore, "institutions are the foundation of social life (...) [and] without stable institutions, life becomes chaotic and arduous" (Campbell, 2004: 1). Institutions do more than channel current policy and interests; they also reproduce interests and power conflicts. They reproduce or even increase inequalities of power "deeply embedded in organizations and dominant modes of political action and understanding, as well as in institutional arrangements" (Pierson, 2004: 11; Thelen, 1999: 384).

[3] For example, more than three decades ago, Theda Skocpol (1992) problematized key issues of historical institutionalism showing that the interests of actors depended on how

Beyond historical origins, scholars using a gender lens have made major contributions to understanding post-1945 and contemporary welfare regimes by "incorporating gender into the comparative analysis of welfare states" (O'Connor, 1996: 1). They have analyzed "how gender relations were inscribed in welfare state policies and conversely how policies were a force in patterning gender relations" (Sainsbury, 2008: 100). They have critiqued Esping-Andersen's concept of decommodification. The goal for women is not so much traditional "decommodification" (being protected while out of the labor market due to unemployment, illness, or old age) but "commodification" (the capacity and rights to be employed in the formal labor market, including support for combining maternity and employment), especially in developing countries where the labor market is mostly informal (Razavi & Staab, 2018).[4]

Their research has also critiqued Esping-Andersen's popular typology (1990) of welfare regimes for being gender-blind, ignoring women's unpaid care, reproductive and domestic labor, and their contribution to societal welfare (Orloff, 1996: 65). Some scholars have built typologies

institutions were historically constructed. She argued that exclusionary institutions gave almost all men, including workers and ex-slaves, the right to vote. Women, excluded from the patriarchal, property-holding conception of republican citizenship, developed alternatives around "republican motherhood", using maternalist social policies to fill "the civic space left behind by elite men, who were turning to the individualist-liberal pursuit of market wealth and partisan party power" (Skocpol, 1992: 20). In a similar way, Jane Jenson (1989) followed the different trajectories of French and British social policies during the same period. Analyzing the historical and gendered processes of policymaking, she argued that the different conceptualizations of health and demographic public problems led actor coalitions to different policy positions: in France women's employment was facilitated, while in Britain support went to policies supporting unpaid care work (Jenson, 1986).

[4] Orloff described this as the emancipatory goal for women of gaining the capacity "to form and maintain an autonomous household" (Orloff, 1993: 319) without having to rely on a breadwinner. Lister (1994) further theorized this idea, through the concept of defamiliarization which refers to "the degree to which individual adults can uphold a socially acceptable standard of living, independently of family relationship, either through paid work or social security provision" (Lister, 1994: 37). Building on this literature, Mathieu (2016) proposes the concept of "demotherization" of care work to avoid false ideas of gender neutrality in the notion of defamiliarization. This concept refers "to the degree of independence mothers enjoy from the necessity of performing care work, and most specifically childcare" (Mathieu, 2016: 577). Mothers and not families have historically taken charge of care work and policies that support care inside the family can alter the gendered division of labor (with paternity leave or access to non-parental childcare, for example).

of welfare regimes different from the Esping-Andersen, using the criteria of the degree to which the male-breadwinner model was dominant (e.g., Lewis, 1992; Sainsbury, 1996). Others have focused on the ways social policies reinforce the gendered division of labor by creating dichotomies between "male" productive labor work in the public sphere generating income and reproductive labor in the private sphere which is seen as both "free" and women's work (Beyeler & Annesley, 2011: 84; Jacquot & Mazur, 2019: 291).[5]

In Latin America, feminist scholars also provide in-depth analyses of contemporary social policies and care (e.g., Altamirano Zárate-Tenorio, 2022; Dion, 2006; Ewig, 2010; Gideon, 2014; Holmes & Jones, 2013; Lopez-Estrada, 2017; Molyneux, 2007; Nagels, 2016, 2018, 2022; Pribble, 2006; Staab, 2017). They have similarly shown that social policies are not gender-neutral but rather "reinforce and create ideas about appropriate gender roles" (Ewig, 2010: 12) that accentuate motherhood (Gideon, 2014; Molyneux, 2006). They have made visible women's unpaid domestic and care work, as well as their contribution to overall societal welfare. For example, they have demonstrated that neoliberal reforms to social policies were "male-biased" and constantly rendered invisible the needs of women experiencing poverty (Craske, 2003; Gideon, 1998; Moser, 1993). While post-neoliberal policies, such as CCTs, appear to be gender-conscious (Macdonald & Ruckert, 2009: 10), "women's unpaid care work continues to form the bedrock on which social protection is subsidized, with erosions in state provisioning impacting most strongly on women" (Hassim & Razavi, 2006: 2; Jenson, 2017). Nonetheless, analyzing various social policy reforms in Chile,

[5] One of the major contributions of using a gender lens to analyze welfare states is to include a focus on care (see Daly, 2018; Esquivel, 2018 for a summary in the Global North and South). They have underscored that care work is devalued because it is gendered, having traditionally been performed by women as unpaid work in the private sphere (e.g., Batthyány et al., 2020; Daly, 2022; Jenson & Sineau, 2001; Tronto, 2008). Seeing care as a socially necessary activity that is not often recognized because of its gendered construction, has meant that "providing care is the source of many of women's economic and political disadvantages in wage [...], political and economic life" (Orloff, 2009: 324). Jenson (1997) argued that welfare regimes are not first about work and workers but primarily about care. Unemployment insurance is therefore not the flagship policy of welfare regimes but policies to redistribute care (e.g., early childhood education and care) and the risk of differential needs for care (e.g., health insurance, allowances, and housing benefits), to reduce dependency on others for care (e.g., pensions; maternity and parental leaves), and to guarantee quality care (e.g., public education).

Staab argues that their gendering effects are complex and varied: "While some policies take unpaid care by women for granted, others point to an increasing awareness of inequalities that shape women's and men's differential access to market income and public social benefits" (2012: 299).

Other scholars have undertaken welfare regime analyses. For example, Martínez Franzoni (2008) built a typology of Latin American welfare regimes by analyzing the data about commodification, decommodification, and defamiliarization. She identifies three types of welfare regimes built on the complex relations among labor, markets, families, and states. Following Barrientos (2004), she argues that all Latin American welfare regimes, but to different degrees, are informal—an important part of the workforce is in the informal sector. However, she adds the argument that all Latin American welfare regimes are also familialist—women in the private sphere provide an important part of welfare. Therefore, she constructs three categories of welfare regimes: "state-targeted", "state-stratified", and "informal-familialist". In the first two groups, the state is the main provider of welfare but in the first group social policies are targeted to persons experiencing poverty (Argentina and Chile). By contrast, in the second group, the social risk is funded through social insurance and excludes the informal labor sector (Brazil, Mexico, Costa Rica, Panama, and Uruguay). In the third group, the state is not the main provider of welfare; decommodification is then minimal and the labor force is mainly informal (Peru, Bolivia, Ecuador, Colombia, Paraguay, Venezuela, and the Central American countries). Martínez's typology is a highly useful means of organizing the empirical cases of this book since Mexico and Brazil, the first to develop CCTs, remain in the same category of "state-stratified" welfare regime while Peru and Bolivia, latecomer CCT translators, belong to the third group of "informal-familialist" welfare regimes.

Building upon this literature on gender and historical institutionalism, I construct an analytical framework to make visible the gendered processes of CCTs as these travel throughout Latin America. The combination of historical institutionalism and gender analysis of social policies is possible because they share a contextualized, historical, and relational methodological approach. Both approaches share constructionist and materialist perspectives and are comparative. They propose a middle-range theory of structural constraints but also agency. Both "take a denaturalizing and contingent view of political identities and goals, and both share at least some attachment to egalitarian, or even, emancipatory, politics" (Orloff, 2009: 320). A historical institutionalist with a gender lens approach documents for example "the options not discussed, actors marginalized, or micro-political economies not identified because they are obscured by unexamined assumptions about gender relations" (Lovenduski, 2011: xi).

The literature on historical institutionalism and gender analysis attends to the mechanisms, or the *how* of change. This next section of the chapter follows suit. Cooking, standardization, and translation help us to understand how institutions change, or in this case how CCT designs have changed through travel. But since the mechanisms tell us little about the direction of change—toward including or ignoring gender equality goals—the last section of this chapter seeks to explore the *why* of change. More than institutions and processes, it describes the agents (actors and ideas) that drive the institutions and work the mechanisms.

The How of Change: The Mechanisms of Cooking, Standardization, and Translation

My theoretical framework aims to build middle-range theory by telling a story that identifies factors of change in different contexts and times; causal mechanisms can do this. Historical institutionalism defines mechanisms as a causal pathway between two events or social phenomena. "Mechanisms [are] the workhorses of explanation" (McAdam et al., 2001: 30). They enable an understanding of the details of causal processes by looking at relational patterns and configurations over time. More than a sequence of events telling us who did what, the mechanistic approach tells us "why or how events were linked together in a causal sense" (Beach & Pedersen, 2019: 32). Causal mechanisms are different from a correlation established among variables. Correlations may show that links exist between variables but do not tell us anything about how one variable affects another. Mechanisms, on the other hand, are not variables, because their effects do not derive from their value but from their presence or absence (Ancelovici & Jenson, 2013: 297). Mechanisms are not simply the attributes of the units of analysis but are relational concepts that display the link between causes and outcomes (Beach & Pedersen, 2019: 52). This "suggests, among other things, that the outcomes analyzed result from action (and therefore actors) rather than the "amount" of something, as studies based on the correlation of variables imply" (Ancelovici & Jenson, 2013: 297). According to Falleti and Lynch, "mechanisms tell us how things happen: how actors relate, how individuals come to believe what they do or what they draw from past experiences, how policies and institutions endure or change, how outcomes that are inefficient become hard to reverse, and so on" (Falleti & Lynch, 2009: 1147). Therefore, to understand how and whether the mechanisms operate, "variation in values of causes and outcomes are completely irrelevant" (Beach & Pedersen, 2019: 55).

A mechanistic approach pertains more to an interpretative paradigm than a positivist one. Analyzing causal mechanisms helps in the development of middle-range theory, in which there is attention to agency. Mechanisms are general enough to apply to different situations and settings but not to apply to all because causal mechanisms depend on the context of institutions and actors as these change over time; this is a principle of historical institutionalism (Beach & Pedersen, 2019; Campbell, 2004: 64; Falleti & Lynch, 2009).

As shown in Fig. 2.1, cooking, standardization, and translation are causal mechanisms accounting for how policy transformation—its design, objectives, and intrinsic meanings—takes place at the beginning and the end of the gendered process[6] of CCT travel (Ancelovici & Jenson, 2013; Campbell, 2004; Levitt & Merry, 2009; Stone, 2012). While the cooking mechanism refers to the first sequence of policy processes—their creation and development—the standardization and translation mechanisms belong to the next phases—when the policy travels out of its origins. Concerning the two last sequences, the literature on CCT diffusion (e.g., Leisering, 2019; Olivier de Sardan & Piccoli, 2018; Osorio Gonnet, 2017; Peck & Theodore, 2015; Sugiyama, 2011) has already shown how CCTs have spread through Latin America and beyond. As seen in Chapter 1, these scholars have insisted on the mechanism of social learning to explain how the majority of Latin American policymakers have adopted CCT programs. They have also demonstrated the role played by international organizations, mainly the World Bank, to explain this diffusion.

[6] Processes include mechanisms that are themselves smaller processes. For example, in this case, policy diffusion—that I name traveling—is a process including different mechanisms such as standardization and translation but standardization could also be treated as a process including mechanisms: certification, decontextualization, and framing (Ancelovici & Jenson, 2013: 297).

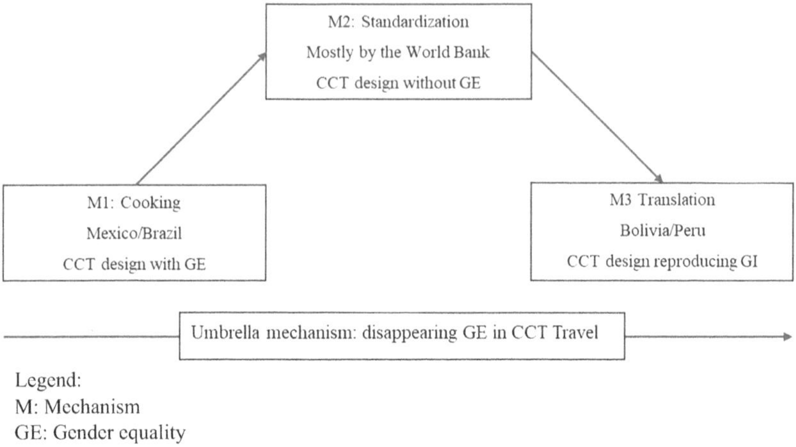

Fig. 2.1 Drawing the argument (Author's construction)

The literature on "diffusion", useful as it is, is too limited. Authors tend to conceive what is moving—policy, instrument, norm, practice, institution, or idea—as relatively stable and fixed. In general, the literature on policy diffusion and transfer argues that diffusion results in the convergence and homogenization of political institutions. They have not questioned the changing content of what is traveling during the process of diffusion. Therefore, I use the term "travel" and not "diffusion". This term underlines that norms and policy are not static or completed but "on-the-way and continuously exposed to influences" (Zwingel, 2012: 124).

In addition, the literature on diffusion generally ignores what happens in the first steps of the process of travel, when local practices, institutions, and ideas are first created and, afterward transformed into a model ready to be diffused (Ancelovici & Jenson, 2013) and overlooks what happens in the last phase of the process when importers adapt the model to be adopted (Campbell, 2004: 78; Levitt & Merry, 2009). As noted by Stone (2012: 487), in the literature on diffusion "'what' is being diffused is sometimes lost in the concern for 'how' diffusion takes place". Therefore, this book is not about diffusion. It does not seek to identify the patterns of CCT diffusion through Latin America; others have already demonstrated this (e.g., Leisering, 2019; Olivier de Sardan & Piccoli,

2018; Osorio Gonnet, 2017; Peck & Theodore, 2015; Sugiyama, 2011). I take for granted that CCTs have been subject to diffusion in Latin America. I am more interested in what was happening to the contents of CCTs—their design related to gender equality goals—when they traveled to new places. What are the causal mechanisms explaining these changes? Therefore, to study the design alterations of CCTs in relation to gender equality goals as they traveled in Latin America, the literature on bricolage (conceptualized as cooking), standardization, and translation is more appropriate. While the mechanistic concept of cooking documents the CCT policy innovation in Mexico and Brazil, the literature on standardization focuses on the first steps of policy travel—valuable here to investigate the role played by the World Bank in standardizing the CCT recipe—the concepts of translation are attached to the final steps of this process, especially helpful to understanding the work of adding local ingredients to the standard CCT recipe in both Peru and Bolivia.

Cooking

The mechanism of cooking is the feminized adaption of the concept of bricolage. Without a direct equivalent in English, this French word refers to the "work done by a bricoleur—very toughly, but not quite, a cross between an odd job man and a handyman" (Milner, 2007: 1). While bricolage is associated with men's work and with masculinity norms, institutions, and outcomes such as a self-built house, cooking is mostly but not exclusively done by women leading to handmade dishes and recipes. Since, this mechanism serves to understand the work of gendered actors—male or female—anchored in gendered institutions and with gendered ideas in the pursuit of the inclusion or not of gender equality in policy CCT designs, I propose the concept of cooking in place of bricolage.

Like bricolage,[7] cooking refers to a mechanism of institutional change resulting from the blending of bits and pieces of different elements that

[7] Levi-Strauss (1966) was one of the first to use this term as a metaphor to explain "primitive" science in comparison to modern science. While modern science uses "concepts" to orient its practice, "primitive" or "concrete" science uses what is available and to dispose to create something new (see Altglas, 2018; Milner, 2007 for a genealogy of the term).

may already be at hand or new ones. Bricolage is then "an innovative recombination of elements that constitutes a new way of configuring organizations, social movements, institutions, and other forms of social activity" (Campbell, 2005: 56). The bricoleur and the cook collect elements—previous ingredients and recipes, species, vegetable, herb, meat, nails, stone, mortar, glass—that have already been used and others new ones—to reassemble them in new combinations and perhaps "granting them new usages for which they were not initially intended" (Alglas, 2018: 1). The bricoleur and the cook work with their hands and use basic skills compared to the expertise and talent of a craftsperson. They are professional "do-it-yourself" men and women. Unlike an engineer or a Chef, who are mostly professional and male, and who chooses her tools and instruments based on a conceptual project, the bricoleur and the cook pick from a set of heterogeneous, existing tools. As Carstensen asserts, "the usefulness of the instruments is not defined by a project but from the practice of making do with whatever is [available]" (Carstensen, 2011: 154). She does not use the new and old elements following an abstract system but rather makes them work together.

Cooking, as bricolage, is a mechanism helpful to understanding evolutionary—and not revolutionary—change[8] and "entails significant continuity" (Cartensen, 2011: 160). Actors change or reconfigure institutions from choices depending on existing institutional rules, norms, and practices. Therefore, the new institutions resemble the old ones since they contain elements from the past. It leads to evolutionary change since what is created is new but as a combination of already available elements and new ones, the result still resembles the past. Instead of a clear dichotomy between revolutionary and evolutionary change—for example, present in the concept of critical juncture—this conception of change is more complex as a matter of degree along a continuum. The newer elements become part of the recipe, the "more revolutionary and less evolutionary change becomes" (Campbell, 2005: 60). Nevertheless, bricolage and cooking are about change and not stability, depicted best by the concept of path dependence (Campbell, 2004). They are about incremental change: actors can change institutions by using multiple institutional legacies (Carstensen, 2011: 161).

[8] Cooking, like bricolage, shares affinities with the evolutionary theory of incremental change (Steeck & Thelen, 2005) and their typology by Mahoney and Thelen (2010) with drift, displacement, layering, and conversion.

Another advantage of the concept of cooking, like bricolage, is to consider the micro-level agency of actors working in political and institutional settings and in continuous reinterpretation. It adds to the macro-analysis processes of historical institutionalism, more individual mechanisms driving institutional changes (Carstensen, 2011: 160). Cooking, like bricolage, allow understanding institutional change "with a greater sense of agency, something that institutionalists have been criticized for neglecting" (Campbell, 2004: 71). Nevertheless, actors could not do what they want since the cooking concept insists that institutions are the ones that provide the tool kit and repertoires, as recipes, for institutional modification, and it is constraining because the number of elements in the recipe kit is finite.

The cooking mechanism will be helpful in understanding how CCT developments occurred in Brazil and Mexico. Mexican and Brazilian policymakers developed new recipes for social programs—the CCT—by blending old and new elements within their already existing institutions.

Standardization

For Ancelovici and Jenson (2013: 297), "standardization can be defined as a constitutive mechanism of the initial stage of the whole process [of transnational transfer], the chain linking the originators to the actors engaged in proposing and popularizing a standard model".[9] The focus is on exporters, to account for why some ideas, instruments, or policies, and not others, are identified and transformed to be suitable in other contexts. The selection is political since it depends not on the intrinsic superiority of the original practices and ideas but on the power and authority of the actors who transform these practices and ideas to construct the model (Ancelovici & Jenson, 2013: 296). These actors engage in the work of adaptation, interpretation, and repackaging. Ancelovici and Jenson (2013) underscored three mechanisms composing the process of standardization, itself a mechanism of the larger process of policy travel:

[9] In the same vein, Olivier de Sardan & Piccoli (2018) has built a theoretical framework about the "making of a traveling model" in development policies, analyzing the processes involved in the production of an international model. Olivier de Sardan & Piccoli (2018) identified the two processes of narrativization and theorizing social engineering in the construction of an international model. These two correspond broadly to what Ancelovici and Jenson (2013) pinpoint as certification, decontextualization, and framing that compose the process of standardization.

certification, decontextualization, and framing. All three processes are not linear but interconnected, overlapping, and involving a large range of local, national, international, and transnational actors.

The process of narrativization or certification refers to the construction of success stories about local practices or ideas. The role of international organizations and policy evaluations are central to legitimizing and building these success stories (Olivier de Sardan & Piccoli, 2018: 36). Certification implies asymmetrical power relationships where some actors have the power to certify sets of practices or ideas that thereby gain new authority and legitimacy (Ancelovici & Jenson, 2013: 298). The second process is decontextualization or theorizing social engineering (Olivier de Sardan & Piccoli, 2018). It involves the simplification and the distillation of the initial experiences. Complexity and diversity are stripped away, and treated as secondary elements so that local practices can be transformed into abstractions intended for export. This implies a deliberate effort on the part of institutional entrepreneurs to erase what they perceive as not exportable and involves "cognitive short-cuts" (Sugiyama, 2011: 265). In the decontextualization process, certifying actors downplay the failures, the mixed results, and the institutional, historical, cultural, political, and economic contexts of a given practice or idea and describe its success as due to its supposed intrinsic effectiveness (Olivier de Sardan & Piccoli, 2018: 37). They construct a thin recipe disembodied from its original context, although it is important to keep some links to the original stories, enabling the use of "the official genealogy of the standard [...] strategically" (Ancelovici & Jenson, 2013: 298). In the last process of framing, policy entrepreneurs work discursively to define situations and problems and suggest general solutions. They theorize simple and abstract solutions that specify causality correlations between model implementation and their outcomes by erasing dysfunctionalities and potential negative effects (Delpeuch, 2008: 16). They simplify events, connect issues, and could fold "key issues into others so as to make them more acceptable and thus rally the support of allies" (Ancelovici & Jenson, 2013: 298). The work of framing facilitates the introduction of the standard model of interest and values of potential supporters.

This causal mechanism of standardization will be very helpful in understanding how the World Bank and some Brazilian entrepreneurs turned the original CCT recipe into a standard basic recipe ready to be diffused throughout Latin America and beyond.

Translation

The causal mechanisms of translation complement standardization by providing analytical tools to understand, in the last sequence of diffusion processes, how the standard basic recipe changed as Peruvians and Bolivians adopted it.

As already noted, the literature on diffusion does not examine what happens when a set of external practices and ideas arrive in new contexts and assumes that the new practices and ideas are simply adopted in toto. In addition, this literature assumes that diffusion results in homogeneous outcomes (Campbell, 2004: 79; Delpeuch, 2008; Hassenteufel & Maillard, 2013; Stone, 2012). The causal mechanisms of the last stage of the diffusion process—translation—fill these gaps. This literature recognizes that ideas and practices are transformed when they travel, and even when they arrive at their final destination. The focus is more on national and local institutions that translate, adapt, and filter transnational sets of ideas and practices (Béland, 2009) even when countries are vulnerable to external pressures. Even in less developed countries, such as Peru and Bolivia, national entrepreneurs, as translators, must adapt and transform a model coming from abroad to secure its adoption and implementation (Orenstein, 2008).

The concept of translation theorizes the mechanisms involved in the final steps of diffusion when recipients implement ideas and practices coming from abroad in different ways depending on their context (Campbell, 2004; Stone, 2012). In public policy studies, translation is therefore never a replication but corresponds to a transformation and a new creation of the original involving actors, like translators, who have to build new orientations, norms, institutions, or instruments (Hasenteufel & Maillard, 2013: 388). Different processes of translation can take place from changing the language used but keeping the identical ideas and practices to altering them by creating something new in the mixing local and external elements (Béland, 2014: 13). Disturbances occur among the original model, the transmission, and the reception of policy innovation from abroad that should be interpreted nationally (Stone, 2012: 487). Translation implies the combination of new external elements with old local ones. International models must be transformed into culturally recognizable, and therefore understandable, norms and ideas (Zwingel, 2012: 125). In the translation processes, translators adopt and adapt ideas and practices from abroad to innovate and induce institutional policy change. At the same time, the more the new and external ideas and practices fit with local ones, the more readily they are accepted (Campbell, 2004: 87; Levitt & Merry, 2009: 458). To follow the analogy of kitchen work, translators adapted and sidelined the basic standard recipe to make it fit with local flavors and ingredients.

This mechanism will therefore be useful to explain how Peruvian and Bolivian translators adapted the standard model of CCTs to their gendered social policy legacies. The processes of translation depend on various local factors such as the institutional and ideational context, power struggles, and implementation capacities (Campbell, 2004: 80). The local institutional context and legacies constrain national institutional entrepreneurs to blend new recipes—ideas and practices—into local ones. Institutional capacities of the financial, human, and administrative kind are essential to ensuring translation (Campbell, 2004: 80–83). Political mobilization, support, and power struggle also affect the translation processes. These factors transform, modify, and alter traveling standard recipes. They influence the outcomes of the policy mechanism of translation that rely on the gendered configuration of institutions, actors, and ideas presented next.

The Why of Change: The Configuration of Institutions, Actors, and Ideas

Where does the impulse for change come from to drive the mechanisms of cooking, standardization, and translation? What are the factors shaping the direction of change in favor of or against including gender equality goals in CCT design? To answer these questions, I need to develop a comprehension of contexts that "are relevant aspects of a setting (analytical, temporal, spatial, or institutional) in which the analysis is embedded and has an impact on the constitutive parts of the mechanisms" (Beach & Pedersen, 2019: 78). I have conceptualized context as a configuration of institutional legacies and venues, strategic (gender equality) entrepreneurs and knowledge about gender. Their interactions are crucial to understanding why some prevailing gendered rules are or are not renegotiated during policy cooking, standardization, and translation (Staab, 2017: 34). This is coherent with historical institutionalism and gender analysis of social policies that "recognize that political explanation is about ideas, interests, and institutions, which are intertwined and mutually constituted" (Lovenduski, 2011: ix).

Social Policies as Institutions and the Products of Institutions

In the area of historical institutionalism and gender analysis of social policies, those last ones can be understood as gendering institutions since they constitute gender categories and have gendered effects. In Latin America, social policies have strong institutional legacies of maternalism. The analysis of the gendered origins of welfare regimes has shown that historically, in the segmented Latin American welfare regimes, women accessed entitlements by virtue of their being a mother or spouse (e.g., Blofield & Martínez Franzoni, 2015; Dore & Molyneux, 2000; Ewig, 2010; Gideon, 2014; Lopreite & Macdonald, 2013; Marino, 2019; Marques-Pereira, 2017; Molyneux, 2006, 2007). At the beginning of the twentieth century, social hygiene movements and women's movements achieved social policies regulating motherhood. Women received educational, medical, or financial benefits primarily because they were mothers (Molyneux, 2001: 13). For example, maternity leaves and legislations were to safeguard women's reproductive capacities or their moral virtue at risk in the workplace (Molyneux, 2007: 5). Women elites participated in these policies by the administration and dispensation of charitable activities to relieve poor families of their "degradation", by way of social hygiene and eugenics movements. Women become safeguards against the diseases of the social body caused by individualism (Molyneux, 2002: 178, 184). For example, one of the major premises of public health systems in many countries was to control the biological reproduction of rural, poor, and Indigenous women (Ewig, 2010; Nagels, 2018). Therefore, maternalism but also eugenics constitute strong institutional legacies of Latin American welfare regimes and social policies.

Social policies were based on deeply gendered conceptions of male breadwinners and female mother-dependents. Maternity was sacralized with such claims that mothers were authentically altruistic at the service of others in opposition to male liberal individualism. Even if these arguments were also present in other parts of the world, in Latin America, maternity and domesticity were endowed with moral importance. Maternalist social policies recognize the importance of motherhood and care but essentialize and exalt women's capacity to be mothers while excluding men (Ramm, 2020: 14, 15; Staab, 2012: 303). Maternalism sublimated motherhood as embodying distinctive sets of moral values and virtues such as care, affection, self-sacrifice, and altruism. Therefore, maternalism confers moral superiority onto women. According to Ramm (2020: 15), "by contrast, men—who by their own nature cannot bear children—are regarded as morally inferior". Maternalist social policy legacy made women responsible for the family and the community as the guarantors of morality and the traditional family.

Therefore, maternalist social policies "recognize and reward care as a female responsibility without seeking to reduce the gender gap per se" (Blofield & Martínez Franzoni, 2015: 47). These social policy legacies influence the integration or not of gender equality goals in CCT designs.

Social policies are also the product of institutions. I therefore look at multiple institutional venues including various ministries in the four states and different units of the World Bank that were involved in CCT design since they were mostly technocratic without strong links outside the state (Borges, 2022; De la O, 2015). Inside the state, I consider the institutional context in which strategic (gender equality) entrepreneurs wield political power and resources in processes of policy change and not only where women have gained representation. In the case of CCTs, these sites of power and resources can be found, for example, in executives and mostly in bureaucracies.

Institutional feminism (e.g., Haas, 2010; Kenny, 2007; Krook & Mackay, 2011; Mackay et al., 2010; MacRae & Weiner, 2017; Mazur, 2002, 2009) provides some helpful factors to understand CCT designs in relation to gender equality such as the role of critical actors or the structure of institutional opportunities. I complement this literature with a focus on bureaucracy as an institutional site creating opportunities or constraining gender equality policymaking; on the design building as a precise step of this policymaking; and on Latin America.

Gender relations shape formal and informal institutions as "rules of the game" and institutions shape gender relations and political behavior (Franceschet, 2011; Gains & Lowndes, 2014; Krook & Mackay, 2011). This understanding of gender as profoundly entangled in institutions enables us to analyze how power works in formal and informal institutions that are all gendered. Informal institutions, norms, and conventions interact with formal institutions and influence policy status quo or change in relation to gender equality (Waylen, 2014). For example, informal rules about masculinity and femininity that assign caring roles to women and decision-making to men have served to maintain male dominance in formal institutions. Informal rules about what makes a good leader, or a good expert have gendered effects because women are more likely to favor more low-key or collaborative styles. As we will see, these informal rules explain, in part, the difficulty or the possibility for women and gender experts or entrepreneurs to include gender equality goals in CCT designs in my different cases.

Strategic (Gender Equality) Entrepreneurs

Gender analysis in historical institutionalism underscores the gendered workings of institutions and how they are created and maintained but also altered through the agency of actors (Tripp, 2010: 197). Some scholars (Annesley, 2010; Beyeler & Annesley, 2011; Blofield & Martínez Franzoni, 2015; Staab, 2017) have documented the capacity of strategic actors in favor of greater gender equality, male or female, to shape and reform social policies. Their influence has varied dramatically across time, space, and issues and depends, as in other domains, on the strength of women's and feminist movements, access to the state, alliances inside and outside the state, policy process, institutional context, and the strength of progressive and redistributive political parties (Sainsbury, 2008: 112).

Who are these actors? In the early 1990s, feminist Australian scholars (e.g., Eisenstein, 1996) developed the term "femocrats" who are feminist actors inside different institutional sites of the state, as opposed to feminists outside of the state, and seek to promote a feminist agenda (Mazur & McBride, 2008: 249). They work in bureaucracies and participate in women's political agencies (WPA) or policies promoting gender equality (Chappell, 2000: 263). More recently, the notion of critical actors instead of a critical mass of women's representation has emerged as key to feminist success. This "moves away from essentialist portrayals of 'men' and 'women' as political actors, avoiding a priori expectations regarding what they 'should' do" (Childs & Krook, 2009: 126). These actors are gendered and "occupy male or female (or transexual) bodies" (Gains & Lowndes, 2014: 528) and hold ideas and values about gender relations and the possibilities to change them. Being female may matter less than holding "gender consciousness" (Childs & Krook, 2009). Female or male actors may adopt masculine type and pursue anti-feminist goals. Or, as critical or strategic actors (Childs & Krook, 2009), they may promote gender equality goals (Gains & Lowndes, 2014: 528, 529).

They could be bureaucrats working inside the state and can be policymakers, policy entrepreneurs, or "gender equity entrepreneurs" (Chapell, 2006), male or female, who support feminist causes but who do not necessarily officially represent women and feminist interests. In the case of

Latin America where small groups of bureaucrats and technocrats participated in CCT policymaking, the term strategic policy entrepreneurs is appropriate. They are individuals who can create support from the political elite and public opinion to initiate policies or participate in the implementation by making their designs and instruments (Paquet, 2015: 1821). They are cooks or bricoleurs who recombine institutional elements in innovative ways. More than their individual qualities, like talent or charisma, their capacity for creative institutional innovation depends on their strategic positions in social relations and in institutions. These actors should be positioned in institutional sites with resources and wield political power, such as core executives in the case of welfare reforms. In addition, the political-economic environment is also important for the opportunities open to strategic actors to introduce gender equality changes in welfare reforms that could be expansive (Annesley, 2010: 71). For example, the mid-1990 Mexican economic crisis and budgetary cuts provided a lot of resources and political power to the ministry of finance—convinced by gender equality goals—in comparison to social ministry. In contrast, Peruvian and Bolivian economic growth in the mid-2000s did not open greater opportunities to introduce gender equality goals in their CCTs.

Nevertheless, strategic (gender equality) entrepreneurs do not act alone, they work together in policy communities united by concern and knowledge about a policy area (Béland et al., 2018: 2; Mackay, 2011: 191). Different concepts—velvet triangle (Woodward, 2003), informal communities, policy network, advocacy coalitions (Sabatier, 1998), epistemic communities (Haas, 1992)—refer to complex informal and formal exchanges among state and non-state actors involved in policymaking from agenda-setting to policy evaluation. While various advocacy coalitions—a group of actors situated in key decision-making institutions sharing beliefs and perceptions about problem definitions and involved in political struggle to defend their causes—struggle to impose CCTs as the solution to poverty in Mexico and Brazil (Tomazini, 2016, 2022), the strategic (gender equality) entrepreneurs who won this battle and designed CCTs in the different sequences of their travels, gathered together within what I call intimate/informal instrument communities. I adapt the concept of Beland et al. (2018) of instrument constituencies that refer to spaces where "actors are united by their adherence to the design and promotion of specific policy instruments as the solutions to general sets of policy problems, usually in the abstract, which are then applied to real-world conditions" (Béland et al., 2018: 7). Unlike epistemic communities and advocacy coalitions, these entrepreneurs are not linked by core beliefs and a similarly defined policy problem. They are "networks of heterogeneous actors from academia, policy consulting, public policy and administration, business, and civil society, who become entangled as they engage with the articulation, development, implementation and dissemination of a particular technical model of governance" (Voß & Simons, 2014: 738 in Béland et al., 2018: 8). I prefer the term communities to constituencies because it better reflects the existence of strong interpersonal relationships within small groups where actors are bound by a policy instrument as a policy solution. In addition, in all the sequences analyzed in this book, personal and informal relations characterized the CCT design communities and in Mexico, in particular, these relationships were also intimate based on strong friendship or love.

Inside these instrument communities, international organizations[10] are important. Engaging in "building, expanding and spreading knowledge of the policy instrument to which they are bound [...] instrument constituencies are typically transnational in nature" (Foli et al., 2018: 110). Alongside local and national components, international and transnational actors are involved in instrument communities and policy transfer in that they move instruments as policy solutions from one context to another through knowledge sharing and diffusion—for example in international conferences and workshops that promote their preferred instrument. Interactions at local, national, and international levels occurred in instrument communities that are fundamental in policy transfer and policy development since "instruments are constantly adapted when they travel from one context to another" (Foli et al., 2018: 11).

Within instrument communities, making a clear difference between local, international, and transnational actors is difficult since the same actors are active in national and international arenas and each of those arenas provides them with legitimacy in the other (Campbell, 2004: 106; Hassenteufel & Maillard, 2013: 387). Orenstein (2008: 38, 39) has shown that in Latin America, local reformers may also be transnational

[10] Historical institutionalists explore the involvement of such actors in policymaking processes, including those using a gender lens to analyze international organizations, such as the United Nations bodies (Charlesworth, 2005), the International Criminal Court (Chappell et al., 2021), the World Bank (Bedford, 2007), the OCDE, and the UNICEF (Mahon, 2021) as well as the ECLAC (Mahon, 2024).

policy entrepreneurs.[11] In addition, International Financial Institutions (IFI) may co-opt these local reformers as one mode of influence offering them a high-paying career as policy analysts in other countries and opportunities to participate in instructional conferences. Therefore, we must study transnational actors' influence at the transnational and domestic levels (Orenstein, 2008: 39, 58). I will show that this phenomenon was present in the case of CCTs: some Mexican and Brazilian CCT cooks became CCT transnational entrepreneurs working in IFI and traveling throughout Latin America to advocate for CCTs.

Transnational proposal actors, such as the World Bank in the case of CCTs, may exercise influence on national policymaking by loan and membership conditionalities but mostly by advocacy and persuasion (Béland, 2019: 27). They deploy their ideas, expertise, and problem definitions by organizing publications, conferences, workshops, and policy travel (Orenstein, 2008: 56, 57). For example, the World Bank "has one of the largest budgets globally for norms creation and norms teaching" (Orenstein, 2008: 62). Then, it is a world leader in norm production and diffusion. As I will show in the case of CCTs, the World Bank was part of each instrument community in each sequence of CCT travel in Latin America. Mexican and Brazilian CCT designers were cautious to implement homegrown CCTs, but instead they relied upon technical data from the World Bank. The World Bank was much more active in the second sequence: CCT standardization but Brazilian CCT entrepreneurs were also active at this moment. During the translation of CCT processes in Peru and Bolivia, the World Bank was present to ensure "success stories" reforms by providing technical advice, and loans for the day-to-day technical implementation (Orenstein, 2008: 66, 67).

Based on these insights, this book asks, who were the actors initiating the proposal to include gender equality goals in the design of CCTs? Who acted on this proposal? With whom did they collaborate and who were the detractors? Did they archive policy change in favor of greater gender equality? Identifying the emergence or the absence of strategic gender equality entrepreneurs working within instrument communities and acting in different institutional venues at each sequence of CCT travel

[11] For example, Chilean reformers under the Pinochet government who privatized the pension system, worked closely with the World Bank and USAID providing policy advice in other countries (Orenstein, 2008).

helps to map where and why some CCT designs have included gender equality goals and others did not.

Knowledge on Gender

Gender analysis and historical institutionalism recognize that cognitive factors such as norms, paradigms, and repertoires serve to create, maintain, and alter the agency of political actors embedded in institutions (e.g., Béland, 2009; Béland & Cox, 2011; Hall, 1993; Muller, 2006; Jenson, 1989). All actions and interests of actors include a representation of that interest, and resulting actions involve the power to give meaning to these actions and interests (Jenson & Mérand, 2010: 85). Ideas are defined as claims about the description of the world, causal explanations, norms, cultural assumptions, and frames. Ideas provide experts and politicians with alternatives to solve problems (Hall, 1993).

Gender analysis scholars have long argued that the definition and framing of political problems, needs, and solutions are central mechanisms of power (Lovenduski, 2011: viii). Discursive struggles over the interpretation and representation of women's needs and identities are political conflicts. For example, the construction of the private as political with social problems as sites of political action is one of the key insights of the feminist movement and the famous claim that "the personal is political". Frames refer to how problems are defined and to the solutions offered up to fix them. For example, the World Bank's frame, or its instrumentalist ideas about gender used to build the CCT standard model, aligns more with Peruvian and Bolivian-style maternalism.

Gender norms enforce certain codes of behavior of masculinity and femininity. For example, women have to adapt their behavior in both the style and the substantive issues to the masculine norms and values that mostly dominate institutions. Then they may feel required to disavow different feminine and feminist concerns (Franceschet, 2011: 66). For example, in the World Bank, women gender experts have to behave like male economists to be heard. On the other hand, such norms can also empower women and feminist issues. For example, the 1995 *World Conference* on *Women* in Beijing set global norms for gender equality, empowerment, and feminist issues that influenced the inclusion of gender equality in *Progresa*'s design.

Since CCTs are evidence-based policies, evidence and knowledge about gender are key to understanding why gender equality was included in some CCT designs and not in others. The production of expertise is essential in complex contemporary societies. Policymakers see specialized knowledge as essential for the formulation and evaluation of policies (Béland, 2019: 36). Knowledge and expertise are ideational realities and relate directly to institutional processes that produce them.[12]

While state agencies are key providers of policy expertise and can exert a great influence on policymaking (Béland, 2019: 37), another source of policy expertise inside instrument communities comes from think tanks, mostly in states with a less developed bureaucracy, like Latin American states. Think tanks are nonprofit organizations, independent from governments providing expert analysis on public policy and lobbying (Campbell & Pederson, 2011: 171). They mostly simplify and disseminate the research of others rather than producing their own research to transmit ideas to policymakers through policy briefs (Campbell, 2004: 106). They have a key role in instrument communities since they spread cognitive material for policy reforms: ideas, discourses, problem definitions, and solutions. In policy travel, the use of statistical data enables the comparison of local and national contexts with the policy and its site of origin to help to convince domestic policymakers of reforms (Hassenteufel, 2005: 125). One interest in the relations between think tanks and policymaking is the politicization of expertise. Parkhurst has demonstrated how policymakers can use but also misuse evidence for political interests and how evidence-based policy influences policymaking (Parkhurst, 2017: summary). As I will show, the expertise produced and diffused by the think tank "International Food Policy Research Institute" (IFPRI) on poverty and gender has greatly influenced the Mexican CCT entrepreneurs and the World Bank's understanding of the links between gender inequalities and poverty. Based on this expertise and on its own, the World Bank—as a bank of knowledge—has a central role "in framing, labeling, and proposing solutions" (Noy, 2017: 6) to states about, in this case, CCTs. The World Bank diffused its standard CCT recipe and ideas about gender around the world by lobbying, networking, producing official reports, and organizing international conferences (Béland, 2019: 27).

[12] For example, in the analysis of gender mainstreaming strategies in Europe and in social policies in Canada, gender analysis scholars (e.g., Dobrowolsky & Saint-Martin, 2005; Walby, 2005; Woodward, 2004) have shown how gender knowledge, expertise, and information or their absence are key to the implementation of gender mainstreaming or childcare policies by officials.

Therefore, as I will demonstrate, the influence of the World Bank on CCTs in this instance was more ideational than material via loans (Noy, 2017).

From these insights, this book tracks the changing ideas and knowledge about gender at each step of CCT travel. What were the perceptions of women's needs and identities anchored in the policymaking of CCTs? But, overall, my questions turn around ideas about women and men embedded in the expertise and knowledge used to design CCTs. What evidence did policymakers and policy entrepreneurs select during the design process? How did those pieces of evidence frame and shape women's identities and the sexual division of labor? What were the cognitive links between gender (in)equality and poverty?

Conclusion

With this theoretical framework, the book speaks theoretically and empirically on the one hand to gender analysis of social policies and historical institutionalism and on the other hand to the literature on policy development and transfer. The combination of these literatures helps us to understand the causal mechanisms—cooking, standardization, and translation—to explain *how* CCT designs changed when they traveled in Latin America and the gendered configuration of institutional legacies and venues, strategic (gender equality) entrepreneurs acting in instrument communities, and knowledge on gender. Further, they explain *why* these mechanisms produced the outcomes they did about the inclusion or not of gender equality goals in CCT designs.

Mechanisms as deployed within specific sets of gendered configurations constitute my analytical framework to explain how, when, and why CCT policy designs, objectives, and meanings transform in (dis)favor of gender equality as CCTs traveled in Latin America. This theoretical framework provides the conceptual tools needed to answer the above questions linked to each step of CCT travel and cases studied in this book. On the one hand, the focus on mechanisms—cooking, standardization, and translation—helps us to understand the causal relationships between CCT designs and travel, in this case from Mexico and Brazil to Peru and Bolivia via the World Bank. These causal mechanisms enable us to explain the innovative cooking experiments in both Brazilian and Mexican CCT recipe standardization on the part of the World Bank, and the standard recipe translation of CCTs by Peruvian and Bolivian policymakers. On the other hand, the focus on gendered configuration—gendered institutional legacies and venues, strategic (gender equality) entrepreneurs acting in instrument communities, and knowledge on gender—allows us to explain more precisely why, at each stage of travel, CCT designs changed and what were their results for gender equality goals. Gendered configuration explains specific mechanisms' outcomes and the scope and direction of CCT changes. It explains why some CCT designs included gender equality goals—explicitly in Mexico and implicitly in Brazil—whereas others downplayed these goals—the World Bank—or replaced them by reproducing gender inequalities—Peru and Bolivia.

Bringing together concepts from policy development and transfer research and others from gender analysis and historical institutionalism, this theoretical framework stretches the analysis to include an international actor. In addition, the multi-level comparative analysis of CCT designs highlights the importance of knowledge mobilized by actors in motion and anchored in multi-level institutions. As I will demonstrate, the meaning of gender relations evolved as CCT traveled, and this evolution is political. Retaining only an economic and instrumental understanding of gender relations is highly political because it involves struggles and conflict where feminist knowledge and feminist actors have failed.

CHAPTER 3

Cooking from a New Recipe: Progresa and Bolsa Família with Gender Equality Goals

Introduction

This chapter presents the first sequence of CCT trajectory: their separate and yet almost simultaneous creation in Mexico and Brazil. It asks, how and why did Mexican and Brazilian CCT designs include explicit and implicit gender equality goals?

An analysis of the configuration of institutional legacies and venues, strategic (gender equality) entrepreneurs acting in instrument communities, and knowledge on gender, specific to each pioneer CCT, gives us an understanding of their respective gender equality goals. Mexico's *Progresa* (1997) was more favorable to gender equality than Brazil's *Bolsa Família* (created in 2003 at the federal level). Mexican strategic gender equality entrepreneurs eradicated much of what existed as social assistance programs and developed a new recipe including explicit gender equality goals while the *Bolsa Família* patchwork recipe of old subnational programs included implicit gender equality goals. Without analyzing the impacts of *Progresa* and *Bolsa Família* on gender—e.g., on the real lives of women recipients—this chapter argues that *Progresa* was more favorable to gender equality than *Bolsa Família* because its gender equality goals were explicit and not implicit. While *Progresa* explicitly promoted gender equality for example by transferring more cash to girls, implicitly, *Bolsa Família* policymakers decided to transfer the cash to women

N. Nagels, *Gender Equality in Conditional Cash Transfer Designs*, Studies of the Americas,
https://doi.org/10.1007/978-3-031-60871-1_3

as a means of improving women's financial autonomy and thus altering intra-household relations.

The chapter begins with a brief contextual and historical account of the social policy regimes and the positions of the center-right Mexican *Partido Revolucionario Institucional* (PRI) and the left-wing *Brazilian Partido dos Trabalhadores* (PT). In a second section, the chapter analyzes the gendered institutional legacies and venues and the strategic gender equality entrepreneurs who developed the recipe for *Progresa*, the first evidence-based policy linking poverty to gender inequalities. In a third section, I apply the same analysis to *Bolsa Família* within which strategic (gender equality) entrepreneurs built a recipe out of known ingredients—subnational CCT programs—to produce something new.

Institutional Legacies of Mexican and Brazilian Welfare Regimes

Historically, welfare regimes in Latin America were stratified and fragmented along class, gender, and ethnic lines. According to Mesa-Lago (1978: 6), the "social security system in Latin America has become a mirror that reflects the overall societal stratification". Military, civil servants, and judicial authorities have been the primary beneficiaries of existing social security systems. Welfare regimes never reached the entire population and "social policy provision remained unevenly distributed between the richer and the poorer states and within these, between rural and urban populations, as well as across sectors" (Molyneux, 2007: 3).

The literature on welfare regimes in Latin America (Barrientos, 2004; Filgueira, 1998; Huber & Stephens, 2005; Mesa-Lago, 1978, 2002, 2008) has built heterogeneous classifications that vary from historical approximations to more complex ones based on the interactions between state, markets, and families. However, Mexico and Brazil tend to fall into the same category, despite their substantial differences. For example, Filgueira (1998) identifies three groups of countries, focusing not only on the amount spent on well-being but also on the criteria with which it is made during the golden era of 1930–1970.[1] Filgueira's second group includes Brazil and Mexico, which are "dual regimes", with stratified

[1] This era is known as the first social incorporation of the popular sector in Latin America around class division and workers unions (Kapiszewski et al., 2021: 18, 19). For Collier and Collier (1991), it is a one-time-only event with enduring consequences. The

universalism in urban areas but with exclusionary policies in the countryside. Until the 1970s, primary education was almost universal, and the level of health coverage was significant but stratified. Territorial heterogeneity was pronounced. While formal and urban workers enjoyed a high level of social protection, rural and informal workers, then most of the population, were not incorporated either in the formal labor market or through the state. About only 17% of the total Mexican population in 1963 was covered by the social security system and 7.4% in Brazil (Garay, 2016: 87, 89). In addition, the Mexican and Brazilian states incorporated popular sectors through a combination of clientelism and patrimonialism in less developed regions and through vertical corporatism in more developed regions (Filgueira, 1998: 10).

Following the golden era of 1930–1970, Latin America experienced a lost decade in the 1980s following economic crises[2] and the coercive and punitive constraints of the debt crisis imposed by international financial institutions. The neoliberal economic model was oriented to trade opening, privatization, and marketization. Neoliberal states privatized much of the public sector (and licensing public workers) and parts of social protection in pension, health, and education and adopted more market-friendly social policies targeting the poor (Collier, 2021: xxxiv). However, this was also the period of democratic transition from military regimes. The new democratic regimes and their continuity led to social policy extension in the mid-1990s and the 2000s.[3] If the social insurance model inherited from the last period has eroded and corporatism has since broken down, social policies have expanded providing

incorporation of the working class into the state led to mass political parties, mass politics, and a fundamental change in the social structure (Collier, 2021: xxvii).

[2] This period marked the exhaustion of the import substitution industrialization model (ISI) that led the golden era. Given the state of the global economy, with foreign markets for domestic production, capital has viewed domestic labor only as a cost for production weakening unions and social policies oriented to workers.

[3] According to Kapiszewski et al. (2021: 1), since the 1990s, this democratic opening and its continuity created the conditions for an "inclusionary turn". This inclusion has formally recognized historically excluded citizens such as Indigenous or Afro-descendants, opened new channels of access to the state for the popular sector, and redistributed wealth via social policies. The resulting democracy is a fundamental break with a past known for extreme inequality. Efforts "to combat social and economic inequality – by left parties, social movement or guerrillas – have almost invariably triggered harsh conservative reactions, usually culminating in military coups" (Kapiszewski et al., 2021: 2).

unprecedented coverage to historically excluded sectors such as workers in the informal sector, women, and rural workers (Arza et al., 2022; Garay, 2016; Kapiszewski et al., 2021: 2).

During the neoliberal era, while Brazil had been a "reluctant adjuster", for example maintaining collective pension systems and not individual ones, Mexico might best be described as a strong neoliberal follower (Martínez Franzoni, 2008: 85). Faced with the economic collapse produced by the debt crisis in 1982 in Mexico, President Miguel de la Madrid (1982–1988) launched very strong state adjustments and harsh austerity measures. Social unrest grew against the *Partido Revolucionario Institutional* (PRI)—in office since 1929—because of the social cost of adjustment policies, its open use of fraud in the 1985 legislative elections, and its delayed response to the earthquake ravaging Mexico City the same year (Garay, 2016: 113, 114). The disaffection with the PRI led the PRI' politician Cuauhtémoc Cárdenas to form a new party, which becomes the Party of Democratic Revolution (PRD). The PRD then challenged the PRI in the 1988 presidential election and was the first party to adopt a pro-women agenda, including women within its platform and adopting a "voluntary gender quota" in 1993 (Hernández, 2018: 8).

Faced with the social challenges of the previous authoritarian regime rife with fraud, repression, and intimidation, the newly elected PRI president, Carlos Salinas de Gortari (1988–1994) launched a large social investment fund, the *Programa Nacional de Solidaridad* (PRONASOL). PRONASOL sought to alleviate poverty for the millions who fell into poverty after the adjustment that reduced the size of the state (Borges, 2022: 73). It financed social projects proposed by solidarity committees from local communities, but the PRI also absorbed the solidarity committee's leaders attributing resources according to clientelism and to their political support rather than according to programmatic eligibility rules (Garay, 2016: 114, 117, 118; Valencia Lomelí, 2000). PRONASOL targeted women, emphasizing their traditional role as mothers and caregivers, and was based on neoliberal ideas of self-help and individualism. It was a departure from the more state-dependent welfare regime created by the Revolution in 1910 (Hernández, 2018: 7).

By contrast, in the 1980s and the 1990s, during the transition to democracy from a military regime, Brazilian conservative governments adopted social policy innovations for those citizens that had been excluded from the social insurance system, a pattern that reflected a need to rethink one of the highest income inequality distributions in the world.

According to Garay (2016: 119, 120), mobilizations from below and electoral competition propelled presidents to launch social policies for health, pensions, and income transfers for informal and rural workers. Social movements, including feminist movements, were very active during the transition and the writing of the 1988 democratic Constitution (Bohn & Levy, 2019). Feminist movements fought to include labor legislation, health care, and daycare and put forward radical proposals to alter gender power and the gendered division of labor (Alvarez, 1990: 252, 253). Broadly, the 1988 National Constitution of Brazil embraced social inclusion as a social right and made the state responsible for the production and implementation of social policies to achieve social inclusion based on citizenship (Fenwick, 2009: 110).

These features of Mexican and Brazilian welfare regimes and the social policy legacy from the neoliberal era are key to understanding the institutional context in which CCT reforms took place. They constituted an environment for policy design and direction for policy change (Martínez Franzoni, 2008: 91). This chapter analyzes how these institutional legacies constrained the development of *Progresa* and *Bolsa Família* and why and how their designs partly overcame these legacies.

Mexico: Cooking from a New Recipe with Explicit Gender Equality Goals

Developed in 1997, *Progresa*[4] was the world's first federal Conditional Cash Transfer. Its designers did not rely upon old social programs such as PRONASOL but built a new program because they had the political power and the institutional space and resources to do it. *Progresa* was also the first evidence-based social policy in Mexico. Recipe development took place in the first institution that institutionalized gender and feminism knowledge inside the state in alliance with global feminism and the fourth International Conference in Beijing. *Progresa* cooks were

[4] The name of the program changed in each presidential six-year term: the Vicente Fox administration called it *Oportunidades* and that of Enrique Peña Nieto called it *Prospera*. The last administration of Andrés Manuel López Obrador did not give continuity to the program and instead created the *Benito Juárez* scholarships with the decree of May 31, 2019. These transfers are universal, reaching all children enrolled in school but without any conditions and without a health component. Therefore, this new set of transfers marked the end of the CCT in Mexico.

convinced by the links between poverty and gender inequalities. To fight poverty, they decided to reduce gender inequality by introducing explicit gender equality goals to the design of *Progresa*.

The first objective of *Progresa* was to reduce poverty and break the intergenerational cycle of poverty by investing in human capital. The central objective was never gender equality but poverty reduction. A less visible but nonetheless explicitly articulated objective was to promote gender equality, as one *Progresa* designer recounts:

> Rather, I think it was an issue that the designers themselves had in mind perhaps as a fundamental concern [for the gender approach] because they thought it was a way to also influence, not only a relevant objective for itself but because it was an essential purpose to achieve other relevant purposes, in other fields such as population increase. (Pablo)

Indeed, *Progresa*'s wording is such that it "recognizes that poverty acquires particular modalities given the social inequalities that prevail between men and women" (DOF, 1999, section 2.2.4). Strategic gender equality entrepreneurs operationalized this by transferring more resources to girls than to boys and by transferring subsidies to mothers, and not to fathers, to help modify relationships within the household and promote gender equality (DOF, 1999, sections 2.2.4 and 15.2). By Law (DOF, 1999), *Progresa* had as its objective "to improve the situation of women and strengthen the decisive role that they play in family and community with the aim of empowering them… for their full personal development [because] by empowering women and improving their opportunities and capabilities (potentialidades) the program w[ould] have a positive impact on the quality of life of all family members" (Federal Executive Power, 1997: 6, in Molyneux, 2007: 23). According to Molyneux (2007: 23), this design demonstrates the recognition of the importance of improving women's income-generating activities and their political integration.

How and why, this happened?

Historical and Institutional Context

The economic Tequila crisis of 1994–1995 and the political crisis caused by the Zapatista rebellion in 1994,[5] two important events as outlined by Falleti and Mahoney (2015), marked the presidential transition from Carlos Salinas de Gortari to Ernesto Zedillo (1994–2000) as a period of intense political debate on the welfare regime model and anti-poverty policies. Many people, inside and outside the government, strongly criticized the *Programa Nacional de Solidaridad* (PRONASOL) for being subject to clientelism and corruption. In addition, critics opposed the 15 general food subsidies, mostly for milk and tortillas, for being ineffective, used for corrupt purposes, and for not reaching the poorest people living in rural areas and not in cities where most of the food subsidies landed (Hevia de la Jarra, 2007; Levy, 2006; Tomazini, 2016). These critics of clientelism and corruption were in agreement about social policies inside Zedillo's government as well as the need for an effective anti-poverty program to alleviate the social consequence of the Tequila crisis.

During the first years of this government, two groups of actors who were public servants and public entrepreneurs agreed on the diagnosis but fought for competing changes in social policy. The first group, mainly coming from the *Secretariat de Desarrollo Social* (SEDESOL) and members of the "left" of the PRI, defended the idea of a PRONASOL-type program in which the community would have decisional power on the direction of support. The Social Development Minister, Carlos Rojas, the "father of PRONASOL", led this first group (Borges, 2022: 75). The second group, working in the Ministry of Finance[6] and led by its Undersecretary, the technocrat Santiago Levy,[7] was in favor of

[5] The economic crisis led to a 10% reduction in consumption, 30% of private investment, and with an inflation increase of 52%, 16 million people fell into poverty (De la O, 2015: 73).

[6] *Subsecretaria de Hacienda y Crédito Público.*

[7] With a Ph.D. and a master's degree in economics from Boston and Cambridge universities, Santiago Levy was a professor at Boston University where he published on poverty in Mexico. As of 1993, he became a "Chicago Boy" (Dezalay & Garth, 2002) as a technocrat inside the public Mexican administration firstly as director of the *Programa de Desregulación Económica* in the *Secretaría de Comercio y Fomento Industrial*, which promoted neoliberal reforms with state deregulation and public services liberalization. Santiago Levy had overseen the final evaluation of PRONASOL (Vite & Rico, 2001: 110) and identified negative results of inefficiency and clientelism. He made the same diagnostic in his evaluations of food subsidies (Levy, 2006, 2008).

a new kind of anti-poverty program: "better-targeted toward the poor, less costly in terms of administration, more transparent and less subject to corruption, based on the insights of academic research relating to the synergies among various forms of human resource investments, the nature of intra-household allocations, (…) and subject to systematic evaluations" (Behrman, 2010: 1474). This second team won the battle in the political and institutional context of fiscal adjustment, rationalization, and efficiency of public spending derived from the economic crisis. In the end, Levy, as the Minister of Finance since December 1994, had the last word on Roja's SEDESOL budget. The replacement of this last one by a Zedillo ally confirmed the definitive victory for the entrepreneurs from the Ministry of Finance over the SEDESOL (Borges, 2022: 75, 76). Indeed, at the end of 1994, President Zedillo asked Santiago Levy's team to develop a new social program to reduce the high poverty rate as the main social consequence of the economic crisis. Developing the *Progresa* recipe took three years (1994–1997) and due to the economic crisis, the budgetary conditions were met only in 1996 with a proposed launch in 1997 (Yaschine & Orozco, 2010: 63). The *Progresa* cooks offered up a new recipe with which to fight poverty with gender equality goals and its success can be attributed both to the close collaboration of key individuals forming what I call an intimate instrument community and to the institutional legacies of feminism that linked knowledge on gender and poverty.

Strategic Gender Equality Entrepreneurs in an Intimate Instrument Community

While politicians and political parties influenced the final design of *Progresa*, they were not the usual targets in recipe development that was essentially technocratic and led by entrepreneurs in favor of gender equality and working within an intimate instrument community. As shown by De la O (2015: 74–78), political parties intervened at the end of the development process when *Progresa* had essentially taken shape. Opposition parties PRD and PAN were initially set against the 1997 budget, demanding the elimination of presidential discretion and more stringent conditions and accountability. While the PRD remained opposed, the PRI and the PAN reached an agreement and approved the budget and *Progresa*'s design albeit with stringent conditions, strict means targeting and evaluation procedures. In the same vein, feminist activists in the PRI do not seem to have played a major role in the development of *Progresa*, although they were able to introduce a gender quota in the PRI in 1996 following pressure from the PRD and their feminist activists much more in favor of women rights and criticizing the other parties for their lack of involvement in these issues (Martínez, 2022: 136, 137).

The *Progresa* cooks did not come from political parties but from a pool of entrepreneurs, of which the most important were Santiago Levy and José Gómez de León.[8] During the entire period of zedillismo (1994–2000), Levy served as Undersecretary of Finance. Aside from his personal attributes or charisma, it was through this strategic institutional position (Campbell, 2004) that he became a powerful actor, overseeing budget adjustments during the economic crisis of 1994–1995. Therefore, by controlling the budget he was able to eliminate the budget for food subsidies and could argue from inside the administration for a program targeting people experiencing extreme poverty (first in rural areas) and with conditions (Yaschine & Orozco, 2010: 63), as he told me:

> So basically, all this analytical work on one side and the political opportunity on the other, and the two things came together in 95. And then I was in a position where I had the ability to really influence the programs because I controlled the budget. (Santiago Levy,[9] interview 2017)

In October 1995, Levy and his team created and launched a pilot program of conditional cash transfers to replace food subsidies and PRONASOL (Yaschine & Orozco, 2010: 63). It was the *Programa Alimentación, Salud y Educación* (PASE). A second group, led by José Gómez de León, director of the *Consejo Nacional de Población* (CONAPO), joined this first group to improve it. According to various sources (Bate, 2004; Borges, 2022; La Paz & Salles, 2006; Tomazini, 2016), these actors, as strategic gender equality entrepreneurs, were essential to integrating gender equality in what would become *Progresa*. It was only once José Gómez de León joined Santiago Levy's team that designers decided to transfer cash to women.

[8] Unfortunately, I was not able to interview him since he passed away in 2000.

[9] During the interview, Santiago Levy agreed to let his name appear in further publications and not being anonymized.

The PASE was launched in three cities in the southeastern state of Campeche in which bank cards, for the first time, distributed cash resources (Tomazini, 2016: 184). Levy chose Campeche because:

> It was far from Mexico, Mexico City, and because I convinced the governor [of Campeche] to let me do it without saying anything to anyone, neither to the press nor to anyone, and I offered him a highway [because] I was in control of the budget. So, I offered the governor a highway if he would let me do a pilot program in 3 cities without saying anything to anyone. [...] Yes, I did not want the press, I didn't want the Congress, I didn't want anyone. I did not even tell the president! (Levy, interview 2017)

This quote reveals the power and room to maneuver enjoyed by Santiago Levy as technocrat and political entrepreneur in the design and implementation of the pilot program and then *Progresa*. He was very powerful because he had the financial and political resources to eliminate food subsidies and to use this surplus for a new program.

Nevertheless, criticism was plentiful. The press heavily criticized PASE for being "pobrematic"—a contraction of the words "pobres" (poor) and "problematic" because the targeting and the use of bank cards did not work (Tomazini, 2016: 184, 185). Faced with these criticisms, the intervention of a powerful actor, President Zedillo,[10] was necessary to increase the legitimacy of Levy's team from the Ministry of Finance and involved institutions with experiences in poverty reduction programs other than SEDESOL—it too closely associated with PRONASOL and clientelism. President Zedillo asked José Gómez de León, the director of CONAPO, who had already worked informally with the subsecretary of Finance (Tomazzini, 2016: 180), to lead a team from his institution and collaborate formally with Santiago Levy's team and design what would become *Progresa*. As a researcher from CONAPO expressed:

> I think that something that we also had to see was when it was already clear that the PASE was not going to go and that the pilot program was

[10] Zedillo remained a powerful actor inside Progresa although the program had its own rules and staff. He unilaterally appointed the director (the first one was Gómez de León, an academic—an appointment that contrasted greatly with previous programs administrated by prominent politicians) and the ministries of Education, Health, and Social Development who formed the Progresa supervisory committee (De la O, 2015: 79).

> not going to work. Therefore, we were given the task, as CONAPO, to collaborate with everyone, but us as responsible. (Celina)

Personal relations gave *Progresa*'s cooks some room to maneuver in this development process. President Zedillo's request that Gómez de León be involved in *Progresa* was not arbitrary. In the 1970s, Levy, Zedillo, and Gómez de León met as researchers in the Bank of Mexico (Borges, 2022: 204). They kept in touch, with Gómez de León[11] pursuing a Ph.D. at Harvard and Ernesto Zedillo at Yale (Hevia de la Jarra, 2007: 90). In the 1980s, Gómez de León worked as Zedillo's assessor when he was budget Secretary in Salinas de Gortari's government. While Santiago Levy was building PASE, President Zedillo was asking Gómez de León to assess new anti-poverty policies. As recounted by a close person to him:

> I remember when Dr. Zedillo asked Pepe [Gómez de León] to make a note about, to see how we can really have something different to address the issue of rural poverty, right? (Beatriz)

In this note, Gómez de León cooked a draft outlining the features of what would become *Progresa*: a program transferring public resources to poor families channeled through women with the double aim of improving children as human capital and promoting gender equality and women's autonomy in their households (Yashime and Orozco: 63, 65).

While Levy's PASE team had decided to transfer cash (and not food) and that the transfers would be conditional (only in health and not in education at that time), it was with the addition of Gómez de León and CONAPO that the case was made for choosing women as recipients of transfers. The blending of Levy's team ingredients and Gómez de León's team led to the abandonment of PASE and to the development of *Progresa* with its gender equality goals. La Paz and Salles recalled in their book (2006: 9):

[11] Gómez de León studied demography and economics at the Catholic University of Leuven, Harvard University, and Princeton University. He had been the Director of the Mexican Population Council (Conapo) and had coordinated the Department of Demography of the Center for Economic and Demographic Studies at the *Colegio de Mexico* (De la O, 2015: 79).

> Dr. José Gómez de León, for whom progress in gender equality and women's social conditions were among his priorities like the expansion of women's freedoms and options, insisted on placing women at the center of the program [*Progresa*] and including transitory affirmative action mechanisms that would reduce inequalities between men and women, thus seeking to grant them greater opportunities to choose. Therefore, he left a special mark on this program.

Personal links among strategic actors were important in the cooking of *Progresa* and resulting in the formation of an intimate instrument community. The integration of both teams—one from the Minister of Finance and the other from CONAPO—was consensual and Levy and Gómez de León became friends, sharing as they did the same ideas about the adequacy of the CCT instrument. Gómez de León agreed with Santiago Levy regarding the ineffectiveness of general food subsidies and PRONASOL and shared his preference for monetary subsidies (Jenson & Nagels, 2018: 325). They both saw the need for a targeted policy (and not universal), for transfers in cash (and not in kind), and for conditions as co-responsibilities to improve human capital. As a very close colleague and friend of Gómez de Leon remembers:

> When Pepe arrived, the team gradually began to enrich each other and gradually they also reached a mutual consensus. Each one brought their ideas to the plan of the probable operation of an anti-poverty program [...] from there came a program that satisfied everyone, and that President Zedillo viewed very favorably [...]. So, it was much more a collective construction. (Pablo)

Personal links also fed *Progresa* cooks' feminist ideas and agenda. For example, demographer María de la Paz López[12] was clearly behind her husband Gómez de León's interest in gender equality and feminism institutionalization. As one *Progresa* designer recalls:

> Very mainly with Dr. Paz López, who is one of the highest authorities [in gender matters in Mexico], I would tell you now, in the case of *Progresa* that fortuitous reasons also influence policies. Well, then, Dr. Paz, was very insistent on gender and she is very knowledgeable about statistics because she had worked at INEGI[13] for a long time, and then her academic training in demography with a master's degree at the College (of Mexico), was a crucial component (in *Progresa*). (For her) we could not take a step if gender equality was not present. (Celina)

Personal and intimate links are essential to the making of *Progresa*: links among the cooks and the executive power, and also with feminist actors. As a *Progresa* cook underlines:

> My wife, she has also worked at UN Women, she studied sociology in Austin (...). We were about 10 friends who all had similar concerns and we are all convinced of their relevance. Whatever the reason. Women for being women, men because we are concerned about inequality, about expressions of inequality that required interventions to seek greater equality between men and women and so on. (Pablo)

For their strategic positions and their links to a gender agenda, Gómez de León and the members of the CONAPO team can be identified as strong allies of feminist claims and then can be qualified as strategic gender equality entrepreneurs. They introduced and institutionalized

[12] During the presidency of Peña Nieto (2012–2018), María de la Paz López Barajas was general director of gender institutionalization at the *Instituto Nacional de las Mujeres* (INMUJERES). She has also been regional advisor to UN Women and a consultant for various international organizations on gender issues such as the Inter-American Development Bank, UNDP, ECLAC, and UNICEF, among others. In the academic field, she has published in demography on gender, families, poverty, and health. She also has worked as an official of the federal public administration where she was responsible for various projects, many of them aimed at advancing gender equality. http://www.dane.gov.co/files/noticias/perfiles_Foro_tiempo.pdf, accessed August 2016. See also: http://integrantescciudadano.blogspot.ca/2010/02/maria-de-la-paz-lopez-barajas.html, accessed August 2016.

[13] *Instituto Nacional de Estadística y Geografía* (INEGI).

gender equality goals in *Progresa*'s design. As a future Coordinator of *Progresa* reports:

> Because there are male decision-makers who accept, or of course women, but who accept a gender perspective. What happened, was that Doctor Gómez de León had it [...] and I suppose he was surrounded [emphasis] by people, he surrounded himself by people with that perspective, it was wonderful [...] I mean, I was already literate in feminism before I entered the government. (Hector)

Nevertheless, institutions constrain and enable actors. As I will demonstrate in the next section, the institutional context and legacies explained how and why these strategic gender equality actors became convinced by the need for a feminist agenda.

Institutional Legacies of Feminism and Gender Institutionalization

More broadly, the incorporation of gender equality goals into *Progresa*'s design resulted from the long-term political work of collective feminist actors that archived to disseminate gender knowledge and to institutionalize gender analysis in the state, firstly in CONAPO. As a *Progresa* cook describes:

> Why does all this [*Progresa*] appears in '97? I believe that what lies behind it is a long history of the women's movement in Mexico. It seems to me that this is fundamental because it explains this adoption by the federal government of the gender perspective. (Maria)

The institutionalization of feminism in Mexico began indeed with CONAPO. In 1974, within the framework of the United Nations "World Population" year, the federal government enacted the General Law on population that created CONAPO to plan the country's demographic transition (Welti Chanes, 2014). Global feminism (Jenson et al., 2017) strongly influenced gender institutionalization in Mexico. Global feminism gained strength with the celebration of multiple international events that aimed to mandate the introduction of gender machinery and policies in favor of gender equality in government and state institutions. Mexican feminist movements were important in global feminism because, also in 1974, Mexico was the seat for the World Conference of the International Year of Women (Welti Chanes, 2014). Therefore, they succeeded, that same year, in reforming the 4th constitutional article that established legal equality between men and women and introduced the secular demographic perspective that was discussed in the international agenda (DOF, 1974; Nagels & Pozos, 2022). This strong institutional legacy allowed CONAPO to first institutionalize gender studies and a feminist agenda within the state. Five years after the First World Conference on Women, as early as 1980, CONAPO created and launched the first Programa Nacional de Integración de la Mujer al Desarrollo. Since its creation, an important part of CONAPO policies and strategies focused on the role of women inside the household and on their empowerment for improving family planning, always with very strong links to global feminism and international discussions (Cerva Cerna, 2006; Ulloa Pizarro, 2013; Welti Chanes, 2014).

Global feminist collective actors and the Fourth World Conference of Women in 1995 in Beijing established a watershed in the processes of gender institutionalization and had an important influence on the articulation of gender equality goals in *Progresa*'s design. Indeed, a significant portion of *Progresa* cooks worked in CONAPO as researchers or public servants like Gómez de León. And CONAPO, in alliance with feminist and feminine movements and organizations, was behind Mexican participation in the Beijing Conference.

Only two men participated in the Beijing Mexican delegation composed of 50 persons: Rodolfo Tuirán and José Gómez de León, both from CONAPO. Gómez de León oversaw the preparation process and led the Mexican delegation to Beijing. The feminist, academic, NGO, or social movement actors, part of the Mexican delegation, were able to convey their claims and demands to Gómez de León. As one *Progresa* cook relates:

> I think that it was definitely very important the fact that Dr. Gómez de León was leading the Mexican delegation at the Fourth World Conference and having been [involved] in the preparatory work for that entire agenda because [...] there was an opportunity [...] having been in discussions with many organizations. [...] They brought him a lot of clarity [about gender and feminist claims], I think that the fact that he was there at that moment was decisive [for the inclusion of gender equality goals in *Progresa*]. (Dolores)

According to Hernández (2018: 33), "the preparatory work for the fourth World Conference on Women in Beijing in 1995 allowed actors to underline in some spheres of the public function the relevance of introducing the gender perspective 'from the beginning' in the governmental policies". The link between poverty and gender inequality was central to the conference agenda. As a result of the preparatory talks for Beijing and the Conference itself, CONAPO created and coordinated the first *Programa Nacional de la Mujer* (PRONAM) in 1996 (Cerva Cerna, 2006, 2010; Welti Chanes, 2014). Several persons who participated in the elaboration of PRONAM prepared *Progresa* with its old ingredients. Cooking from an existing recipe left traces of the past: *Progresa*'s design included several components of the PRONAM. Before PRONAM, PRONASOL included a gender component targeting women and promoting productive opportunities for women (Cerna, 2006). PRONAM (1996–2000), however, was the first program to link gender equality with poverty reduction by investment in women's human capital, beyond productive projects, promoting, for example, girls' schooling. In this cooking process that blended together old ingredients with new ones, time matters. *Progresa* was taking shape shortly after the implementation of PRONAM and reproduced the main PRONAM objectives in terms of improving women's education, health, and job opportunities (Cerva Cerna, 2010).

Institutions constrain and also facilitate actor agency by introducing them to new ideas. In this case, the main cooks of gender equality had studied demography and sociology at a time when feminist studies and gender studies were first institutionalized (Caulier, 2011). It was this institutional element that further influenced the integration of gender equality goals in *Progresa*'s design. A *Progresa* cook confirms this:

> Now, consider that the 1980s approximately was the boom of gender studies [...]. The research professionals training in gender matters began. [...]. We were among the first to be trained in this matter. So, we are talking about a very short period, right? From the 80s to 97 (the creation of *Progresa*). [...] So, there was a very important movement from the academy, from civil social organizations [...] that have been pushing to include the issue of women on the public agenda. (Maria)

Gómez de León's studies brought him close to gender issues because sociology and demography were much more sensitive to gender knowledge than economic sciences, as related by one researcher in the CONAPO team:

> Gómez de León's concern for gender equality came out of his academic training, right? For his training in the areas of humanities [...] he was a sociologist and, also a demographer. [...] So, these issues (on gender) were very familiar in these disciplines [...]. In other words, [...] the issue of women's empowerment as control of their own bodies and the possibility of deciding their fertility were very familiar issues for him, right? Well, I tell you, these issues came from there and do not come from the economy. (Dolores)

This feminist-inflected gaze developed by way of a formal education and also through social contacts, his feminist friends, according to a very close person to him:

> Pepe was a person who read everything, everything, and had a very open mind to many things. So, when he went to Beijing it was because he already had [a concern for gender]. The issue is that when you study demography, you go through fertility studies and go through mortality studies. There is no way that one cannot see that in this world there are a lot of gender inequalities, there is no way [...] when he died and they did some ceremonies like, to remember him and so on, because my friends were there, and my not friends, now they are my feminist friends but first they were friends with him. (Beatriz)

Feminist and gender institutionalization in Mexico convinced *Progresa* cooks as to the importance of gender equality for social justice. As public entrepreneurs and technocrats, they integrated these ideas through evidence making *Progresa* the first evidence-based social policy in Mexico.

Knowledge on Gender and Poverty

Strategic gender equality entrepreneurs prepared *Progresa* by blending old ideational elements linking poverty and gender inequalities with new ones—the mandate of evidence-based policy—to integrate gender equality goals in its design. A key *Progresa* innovation was its focus on evidence and evaluations. Santiago Levy and Gómez de León's teams were persuaded to develop an anti-poverty program based on evidence—on poverty, malnutrition, school attendance, etc.—rather than by simply following a diagnosis. An evidence-based program evaluates its successes according to scientific proof and does not pander to electoral gains. Scientific knowledge and evaluations were a legal requirement of *Progresa* and became an institutional innovation to overthrow the strong social policy legacy of clientelism. As the first evidence-based policy in Mexico, *Progresa* aimed to guarantee its continuity beyond each presidency, to increase its legitimacy, and to rationalize public spending in a context of fiscal adjustments (Behrman, 2010: 474; Borges, 2022; De la O, 2015; DOF, 1999, section 15.2; Hernandez, 2018: 106). For example, strategic gender equality entrepreneurs, such as Gómez de León, were convinced that *Progresa* should use scientific evidence and they imposed this idea on the design team. As one of its members points out:

> Pepe (Gómez de León) was always convinced that it was the best way to guarantee that the program would survive, that the program would fulfill its purposes [...]. So, from the beginning, yes, many groups were invited, but above all from research and evaluation [...]. And that was a clear mentality [and] at that time it was something! [...] 20 years ago, in Mexico it was not the rule to use scientifically based information and knowledge to define interventions and programs. (Pablo)

Levy was also convinced by evaluation since his intention with the PASE was "to be ready with numbers when the time came to convince people" (Levy in De la O, 2015: 74). Levy and Gómez de León, who were very close to President Zedillo, convinced him of the importance of anti-poverty policy evaluations. As a CONAPO researcher relates:

> He [Gómez de León] had, like, a very close relationship with the President, well, and he wanted to show him results that allowed him (the President) room to maneuver for scaling up *Progresa* as a national strategy [...] who also heard him a lot (about evaluations) was Santiago Levy, right? The fact of being able to get to the deputies and show them and tell them, look, this is the result (was very important for scaling up the program). (Dolores)

Since the Ministry of Finance did not count on research traditions, CONAPO oversaw the production and collection of data to provide adequate indicators and to develop the program recipe. Indeed,

CONAPO members used their very precise socio-demographic data on households (and not on municipalities like in the PASE) to choose the beneficiary households according to their marginalization degree within a national comparable framework (Hernandez, 2018: 98). To design *Progresa*, the CONAPO team built and mobilized knowledge regarding poverty and social marginalization. As it is highlighted by a researcher from this team:

> Being in CONAPO [...] we worked on the strongest part of the design. I can assure you of that because [...] the design is finally based on what the evidence said, because we used all the evidence to make, with the available information, the best possible decisions. (Celina)

The CONAPO team created and collected data on poverty, social marginalization, and social inequality but also on nutrition, fertility, and gender relations. This production of knowledge on gender relations can be explained by CONAPO's reliance on demography that since the 1970s had established links between gender inequalities and poverty to propose policies reducing birth rate that was high in Mexico at that time (Welti Chanes, 2014). More precisely, CONAPO knowledge and data about intra-household power heterogeneity and the link between gender inequalities and poverty made it possible for them to argue for the transfer of money to women (Hernandez, 2008: 14; Tomazini, 2016: 185). Indeed, an important part in the CONAPO knowledge production related to *Progresa* cooking dealt with poverty, social, and gender inequalities, for example gender gaps in education (Hernandez, 2008: 59). As one CONAPO researcher reports:

> I was in charge of basically generating a very simple diagnosis that consisted of identifying the school absence of boys, girls, adolescents, and how that absence impacted [...] not only [...] social and economic inequalities but also gender inequalities [...]. We found that the differences were really very evident from the end of primary education and then, in response, what the design of the program should give higher scholarships for girls in secondary schools than those for boys. (Dolores)

Alongside their research, *Progresa* cooks relied on international evidence to justify both the instrumentalist rationale and women's empowerment for investing in women. As this quote from a researcher linked to *Progresa* design reveals:

> This group was also very aware […] because there was already a lot of evidence that investing in women early was a much more cost-effective means of achieving an impact, not just because women were the ones with the greatest gaps […], but […] because women spent money more wisely […] and in the case of girls, in addition, there was a larger gap (in schooling in comparison to boys) and it made a lot of sense because when these girls became mothers, they were going to have a much greater impact on the quality of life of their children's human capital, right? And that was from the beginning because, well, based on the international evidence that there was about that. (Manuel)

The influence of the World Bank and the international financial institutions was more ideational than financial or pragmatic. *Progresa* cooks "had long enjoyed close professional relationships" (Peck & Theodore, 2015, 67) with the World Bank and the Inter-American Development Bank (IADB). These relationships provided them with access to the bulk of information and knowledge accumulated by the World Bank on the operation of monetary transfers (Interview Progresa cook, Matias; Yashime & Orozco, 2010: 64). The World Bank also provided technical assistance during the process of developing *Progresa* and there was a "confluence of ideology between the actors dictating the international trend [IFIs] and the technocratic political elite that has ruled Mexico" (Borges, 2022: 124).

The international influence did not go beyond knowledge exchange. Santiago Levy refused the initial involvement of the IADB and the World Bank, in part to appease those critics who denounced the financial department's role in social policy affairs. His objective was to establish a Mexican-approved legitimacy for *Progresa*, far away from International Financial Institutions, seen as in part responsible for the Tequila crisis. As Santiago Levy remembers it:

> In Mexico, there was going to be significant political opposition to the program. First, it was taking away the tortilla subsidy. The last thing I wanted to be told was: "Ah, Mexico is doing that because the IDB told them to, or the World Bank told them to" […] They came to see me many times…. […] [It was] in 98, 99, When they already knew that I was working on it: everyone was like super interested, they came looking for me. […] And I took them out, I took them out because I expressly did not want them to be present. I did not want to contaminate the discussion in Mexico of what was already a very radical change […]. There was a

great deal of criticism in Mexico, people who disagreed with me [...]. In Congress, the deputies and senators stood up and criticized me and asked for my resignation and blah, blah, blah. So, the last thing I needed was... [...] Washington [involvement].

The ideational international influence was visible in the research led by main cooks Santiago Levy and Gómez de León on gender and poverty. For example, in the early 1990s, while a professor at Boston University and a visiting researcher at the World Bank,[14] Santiago published on poverty. In his 1991 publication,[15] he identified intra-household power relations as central to understanding poverty:

> And in this paper, there was a lot (...) about the importance of intra-household gender composition and the intra-household distribution of power does matter. So, it was clear that this dimension of strengthening the role of mothers and women was important for all these reasons. (Levy)

However, in this publication, Santiago Levy (1991: 68–70) related poverty, nutrition, and fertility from a neo-Malthusian perspective of birth control and not of women's emancipation (Riquer Fernández, 2000). Although this text affirmed that a declining birth rate releases women from their free domestic work, it limited women' social roles to reproduction and the raising of children. By contrast, Gómez de León's concern for gender relations was closer to the notions of autonomy and empowerment of women, as reflected in his publications on women's empowerment indicators. For example, in 1999 and 2000,[16] he wrote and published various articles with Susan Parker on poverty and female

[14] Santiago Levy was tenured professor at Boston University from September 1989 to May 1993 and a visiting researcher at the World Bank from September 1990 to January 1991 and from September 1991 to January 1992.

[15] The monograph summary was published in the Economic Studies journal: Santiago Levy (1991) "Extreme poverty in Mexico: A policy proposal", Economic Studies, vol. 6, issue 1, pages 47–89.

[16] See, for example, Gómez de León, José y Susan Parker (2000) "Bienestar y jefatura femenina en los hogares mexicanos", en María de la Paz López y Vania Salles, "Familia, género y pobreza", Porrúa Grupo Editorial, México; Gómez de León, José y Susan Parker (1999) El impacto de los programas de alivio a la pobreza en la participación de la fuerza laboral femenina y la condición de la mujer: el caso del Progresa en México. Documento preparado para la International Union of Scientific Study of Population, Conference on Women and the Labor Market, París.

heads of households in Mexico, in which they evaluated levels of women's empowerment (La Paz López & Salles, 2006: 76).

As part of their reading and writing on poverty, Santiago Levy and Gómez de León were familiar with international research on intra-household bargaining power. As one ex-researcher of IFPRI shares:

> They had read the papers of Richard Birdsall and others on the intra-household spheres of decision and the intra-household bargaining (power) [...]. I finished my Ph.D. and had read these papers and these guys had also read them [...]. They were guys who had understood that what happens inside the household is not neutral [...]. There was this notion of [...] female empowerment and about the fact that giving money to women in an environment like Mexico was not a bad idea because it allows women to better defend themselves in life. (Elizabeth)

The International Food Policy Research Institute (IFPRI)[17] was key to legitimizing *Progresa* as an evidence-based policy including gender equality goals. It participated in the design, the follow-up, and the technical approvals. As a researcher from this institute reports:

> I think the role of the institute was in part to just make sure the designs were right but also to really get [support] from the government [...] Well, I know that our researchers were involved in the design. (Shara)

IFPRI knowledge production was important to the making of *Progresa*.[18] As Behrman (2007: ix) pointed out, "IFPRI did not directly participate in the *Progresa* design [...]. Nevertheless, prior IFPRI research and research by IFPRI evaluation team members apparently directly (in the sense of direct citations) and indirectly (in the sense of contribution to evolving conventional wisdom) on topics including food subsidy programs, nutrition, health, gender, intrahousehold allocations, and related policies played some role in the design process". For example, in his 1991 publication for the World Bank, Levy cites 14 researchers from

[17] A think tank based in Washington, DC: https://www.ifpri.org/.

[18] The positive results of the first *Progresa*'s evaluation by the IFPRI convinced PAN's Vincente Fox administration, who broke the PRI's 70-year presidency, not only to save *Progresa* but also to extend it (Behrman, 2010: 1476; Borges, 2022: 77). In March 2002, Fox's administration renamed *Progresa* to *Oportunidades* and expanded it to urban areas (Borges, 2022: 77).

IFPRI on 71 references (Behrman, 2007: 17). Lastly, *Progresa* contracted the IFPRI for its first international evaluation (Adato et al., 2000) to improve its international and independent legitimacy and to distance itself from such social programs as PRONASOL and food subsidies evaluated as clientelist, ineffective, and used for corrupt purposes.

Regarding gender equality, one IFPRI central research axis was intra-household gender relations that influenced *Progresa*'s design. For example, Haddad (2007 cited in Behram, 2007: 16) recalled that Levy said that the IFPRI "work on women's income was influential in the decision to allocate to mothers". Similarly, Skoufias (2007 in Behram, 2007: 17) agreed that "from various conversations with/remarks by Jose Gómez de León (Pepe), the decision to give the benefits to women was significantly influenced by the previous IFPRI research on the intrafamily allocation of resources". An IFPRI researcher, who published a lot on intra-household gender relations, considered that this IFPRI literature (and hers) weighed on the *Progresa* design:

> (In) the policy documents written by Gómez de León and Susan Parker [...] they make a lot of references to the early intra-household literature, which shows that putting resources in the hands of women had better outcomes in terms of child health, nutrition, education. So, this was motivated by a lot of the intra-household literature, I would say, in the early 1990s [...] that research was very influential in the design of the program. (Eva)

Therefore, outside of the feminist movement, it was knowledge, data, and evidence about gender relations that influenced how and why gender equality became a *Progresa* objective. As one consultant and *Progresa* cook states:

> The data pointed out the lack of women compared to men in the dynamics including issues of marginalization or domestic violence. Women had to be empowered at home, yes? But not because we had feminist demonstrations, no, no, no, none of that. (Pedro)

Nevertheless, as shown, feminist movements and organizations were essential to institutionalizing gender ideas within the state and to convincing *Progresa* cooks to link poverty with gender inequalities. Therefore, the story of *Progresa* cooking revealed the success of the liberal feminist movement to institutionalize gender ideas inside the state, directly through administration such as the CONAPO or indirectly through gender studies programs followed by state staff. From these institutional legacies, strategic actors in powerful positions could cook a new social policy recipe blending new ingredients such as the mandatory evidence-based policy with older ideational ones such as the link between poverty and gender inequalities. In addition, time and circumstance mattered to *Progresa* development, occurring as it did during and following a significant feminist event, the Fourth International Conference on Women in Beijing (1995). By its explicit gender equality goals, *Progresa* takes some distance from the traditional gender division of labor.

Brazil: Cooking *Bolsa Família* from Old Subnational Recipes

In contrast to Mexico, in Brazil, strategic (gender equality) entrepreneurs, with the support of President Lula, cooked *Bolsa Família* with help from old recipes—subnational CCTs—designed for other uses—anti-poverty and education—that transferred the cash to mothers according to an instrumentalist rationale that mothers are better spenders than fathers as far as their children's well-being is concerned. This strong institutional legacy was one of the major institutional constraints impeding the development of *Bolsa Família* with explicit gender equality goals. Cooking from an old recipe left traces or tastes that dulled explicit gender equality goals, rendering them implicit.

Subnational CCTs as Strong Institutional Legacies

Cash transfers emerged first at the municipal level, where center-left governments were elected in the second half of the 1980s during the democratic transition. Thanks to the decentralization enshrined in the 1988 Constitution—a strong institutional legacy—these municipalities began to innovate in the area of social policy, implementing ideas that activists, scholars, and policymakers had been debating during the previous decade of widespread mobilizations (Lavinas, 2015: 12). The first two conditional cash transfers were introduced in 1995 at the municipal level to respond to significant social mobilizations (Fenwick, 2009: 111).

In 1995, the mayor of Campinas (in the wealthy state of São Paulo) took the ideas developed by PT senator Eduardo Suplicy around the minimum guaranteed income and launched the first cash transfer: the *Renda Minima* program (Garay, 2016: 141). It was based on the idea of citizenship rights and the redistribution of resources (Morais de Sá e Silva, 2017: 10, 11). The second experiment was the *Bolsa Escola*, a non-contributory transfer of income to poor families on the condition that children attend schools. This was implemented by Cristovam Buarque when he took office as Governor of Brasilia District in January 1995. Buarque however vigorously opposed Suplicy's idea of minimum income to the poor from the state without any conditions (Fenwick, 2009: 110) because he strongly believed in the importance of education as an investment in human capital to reduce poverty. There was no connection between the creation of these two programs because they are based on two distinct understandings of poverty and social inequality. While the *Renda Minima* program in Campinas was related to social assistance as citizenship rights, *Bolsa Escola* was conditional and linked to education and social investment (Morais de Sá e Silva, 2017: 12). Nevertheless, both anti-poverty program designs shared the same intention about gender relations: they transferred the cash to mothers based on the instrumentalist view that mothers are better at spending on their children than men (Lindert et al., 2007: 11). That could be explained because any strategic gender equality entrepreneurs or feminist actors—individual, experts, or collective—participated in the design of these municipal social policy innovations.

Such programs attracted attention in Brazil and in 1998, 23 subnational entities (3 states of 27 and 20 municipalities of 5564), mainly dominated by the leftist *Partido dos Trabalhadores* (PT), launched a non-contributory cash transfer, many conditional on school attendance. The federal government, under the Cardoso presidency (1995–2002), remained little involved in national non-contributory programs despite pressure from their promotors, such as Senator Suplicy and Governor Buarque. As recounted by one of them:

> Fernando Henrique (...) resisted. I spent four years trying to convince him, Dona Ruth [First Lady], and Paulo Renato [Minister of Education in the FHC government] but they didn't want to do it.

It was only in 2001 that the Cardoso government launched the first non-contributory national program: *Bolsa Escola Federal* (BEF). It was partly a response to his popularity decline after the 1998 elections when his rate of disapproval reached 73% and was implemented as a means of alleviating the social effects of devaluation for the poorest[19] (Garay, 2016: 149). Housed in the Ministry of Education, BEF focused on education, as did the first municipal *Bolsa Escola*, and not on redistribution as did *Renda Minima* (Morais de Sá e Silva, 2017: 13). Like its municipal social predecessor *Bolsa Escola*, it transferred cash to women according to an instrumentalist view of women as better spenders (Lindert et al., 2007: 11).

Before the 2002 election and with growing electoral competition from the leftist PT, Cardoso launched two other non-contributory transfers to alleviate the poverty of families without school-age children targeted by BEF. Created in 2002, *Auxílio Gás* provided a little monthly stipend to low-income families to assist in purchasing cooking gas. Created in 2001, the second one, *Bolsa Alimentação*, was administrated by the Ministry of Health and aimed to improve the health and nutrition of pregnant and breastfeeding mothers and children under the age of six (Fenwick, 2009: 113). In contrast to all previous subnational or federal non-contributory programs, *Bolsa Alimentação* included, for the first time, goals relating to women's empowerment. The Decreto n° 3.934/2001 creating *Bolsa Alimentação* indicated that one of its goals is to "improve women's status and her household bargaining power" (p. 3). This is a strong social policy legacy for *Bolsa Família* recipe development.

However, these programs faced many organizational and institutional challenges including weak coordination among the numerous ministries that managed them, bureaucratic conflicts, and clientelism (Fenwick, 2009: 113; Jenson & Nagels, 2022: 364). These and the ambiguity between the transfer to women as an instrumental rationale or with the aim of empowering women were important institutional legacies for the cooking of *Bolsa Família*.

Strategic (Gender Equality) Entrepreneurs Embedded in Institutional Venues

In October 2003, a technical team with the support of President Luiz Inácio Lula da Silva (known as Lula) created *Bolsa Família*, which became the largest CCT program in the world with 45 million beneficiaries

[19] External shocks led to the currency's devaluation in 1999 and a decrease in per capita income (Fenwick, 2009: 105).

or 25% of the total Brazilian population and 50% of the Northeast, who lived in the poorest circumstances (Lavinas, 2015: 28). As with *Progresa*, the first objectives of *Bolsa Família* were to fight poverty by increasing poor families' income and to break the intergenerational cycle of poverty by linking them to complementary services in health and education (Lindert et al., 2007: 15). A technocrat who participated in the *Bolsa Família* technical operation reiterated these objectives, stressing that other dimensions—such as gender equality—were peripheral:

> The goal of *Bolsa Família* is clear: to reduce poverty. In two ways. First, by transferring monetary income. Second, by improving the schooling and health of children and adolescents. [..] This is the basic objective of the *Bolsa Família*. You can say that *Bolsa Família* does much more, but everything else is peripheral next to that. (Carolina)

The Law nº 5.209/2004 regulating the *Bolsa Família* enacted that women should receive cash transfers because they are the head of the household. As in previous subnational and federal Brazilian CCTs, the female head of household continued to be the targeted beneficiary (Hall, 2008: 805) according to the instrumentalist belief that "women are more likely than men to invest additional income in improving the education, health, and welfare of their family, particularly their children" (Lindert et al., 2007: 17). In contrast to Mexico, the *Bolsa Família* design did not include any explicit gender equality among its objectives and did not aim to alter the gender division of labor. It was not a program with a feminist and gender alteration perspective, as one gender researcher explains:

> *Bolsa Família* lacked a feminist perspective. It had a social development perspective, a leftist perspective [...]. But it was not a feminist perspective. That is, patriarchal domination was not in check. Women's emancipation was not in question. (Marina)

To explain why *Bolsa Família* transferred the cash to women, a technocrat who participated in the technical operation of *Bolsa Família* tracked the genealogy from subnational programs and insisted on studies[20] about feminine financial behaviors:

[20] The next chapter explores this myth about women as better investors in children than men in greater detail.

> It was already in the *Bolsa Escola*. It was already in the *Bolsa Alimentação*. It was already in the *Auxílio gás*. It was already in the previous programs. [...] It was in the previous programs, and I know also that [these] studies had influence, these studies on women's behavior and the use of resources. (Carolina)

Developing *Bolsa Família* was about blending already existing recipes to create something new, as one BF operator explains:

> The idea was maturing. *Bolsa Família* was not a Big Bang. It was a result that amplified and improved and gave another format and transformed, creating coherence for several vectors that were forming there over time. But I think that it is not just an amalgam, it is a qualitative transformation when you put it all together. (Julián)

Bolsa Família is a blend of subnational CCTs with new anti-poverty instruments just created by Lula, as the first working-class President supported in large measure by less privileged people. During his first days in office, he created institutions to fight poverty and hunger: the Extraordinary Ministry of Food Security and Struggle against Hunger (MESA), another non-contributory cash transfer—*Programa do Cartão Alimentação*—and the Zero Hunger program that repacked this program and the other three Cardoso's previous conditional cash transfers under its umbrella without any change in their designs (Hall, 2008: 804).

Critics emerged from international and domestic technocrats and experts against these initiatives advocating for better integration and the reduction of ongoing possibilities of clientelism (Jenson & Nagels, 2022: 364). A high-level private meeting in March 2003 gathered President Lula, the World Bank President, James Wolfensohn, the Senior World Bank Economist for Latin America, David de Ferranti, the IADB President Enrique Iglesias, and Santiago Levy. They criticized the excessive number of CCT programs, their lack of coordination (Folha de São Paulo, 2003[21]), and convinced Lula to shift his strategy from Fome Zero and unify all the CCTs that he initially wanted to get rid of (Borges, 2022: 60, 61; Morais de Sá e Silva, 2017: 127).

[21] https://www1.folha.uol.com.br/folha/brasil/ult96u47524.shtml, accessed February 2024.

While discussions about gender equality goals or transferring cash to women were absent from the table, the meeting was nonetheless fruitful because soon after "President Lula formally requested that officials in the Ministry of Social Assistance prepare a proposal for an integrated program" (Linder et al., 2007: 13, 14). They created a technical team in which, except for some persons, any of the policy entrepreneurs or ministries representatives had a background in gender studies or some affinities and links with feminist and women's movements. The technical group did not include any representative of the new Secretariat of Public Policies for Women, just created in January 2003 (Bohn & Levy, 2019).

They were representatives of the Ministry of Social Assistance and Promotion (MAPS), Ministry of Planification and Presidency, and sectorial ministries such as education, and benefited from technical assistance from the World Bank[22] and Brazilian experts (Monteiro, 2011: 68). The persons who joined the technical team to design BF were technocrats and policy entrepreneurs but not politicians. It was the case, for example, of the representative of the MAPS, Ricardo Henriques.[23] According to the *Bolsa Família* cooks, he was key to the elaboration of *Bolsa Família*. As one such cook stresses:

> Ricardo Henriques [...] was one of the great mentors in fact of the conception of the program. At the time he was the executive secretary of the Ministry of Social Development and he was indeed the great mentor of this whole model of integration of the programs. (Irene)

Henriques is an economist and was a professor at the Economics Department of the Fluminense Federal University (UFF) for 30 years and had a high-ranking career in various Brazilian private and public institutions.[24] While he had no expertise in gender studies or links with

[22] The relations between the World Bank and the Brazilian administration have "become increasingly symbiotic and truly dialogic over time" (Peck & Theodore, 2015, 103). The relationships between the World Bank and the Lula administration were one of partnership in which the latter enjoyed the technical advice of the former.

[23] He became the first Executive Secretary for the Ministry of Social Development. The Ministry was created to host *Bolsa Família*.

[24] https://revistaperiferias.org/en/mini-bios/ricardo-henriques-2/, accessed February 2024.

the feminist agenda, Ana Fonseca,[25] another key entrepreneur technocrat of this group, did possess this expertise. She was a researcher in the *Núcleo de Estudos de Políticas Públicas da Universidade de Campinas* (Unicamp) and became the first executive secretary of *Bolsa Família* in 2003. Although, in this technical group, she represented the *Caixa Econômica Federal*, she had a sensitivity to and knowledge about gender relations. As one of her colleagues explains:

> Now don't forget that Ana Fonseca was a companion of Adriana Piscitelli, who is a great gender scholar. Sometimes things are not so explicit in public policies, but there are influences. Ana was Adriana's partner. She is a professor from Campinas and a gender specialist. And Ana Fonseca, who was the executive secretary responsible for setting up the program, was clearly a person sensitive to gender issues. (Carolina)

As in the Mexican case, personal relations were important to the *Bolsa Família* process and Ana Fonseca fought to include, even implicitly, gender equality concerns in *Bolsa Família*'s design.

One objective of this technical group was to overcome conflicts inside the PT and among ministries advocating for different priorities in the fight against poverty.[26] One *Bolsa Família* cook remembers these conflicts and the tense discussions:

> And there was a lot of resistance from the bureaucracies of the programs: *Bolsa alimentação*, *Bolsa Escola*, *Auxilio Gas*. They had a lot of resistance to opening up and merging with the others. [...] there were bureaucratic technical fights not easily won. There were arid discussions in this sense. And everything was difficult: the computer program, the way of putting the money in the caixa econômica, etc. (Sebastián)

[25] https://fpabramo.org.br/2018/03/26/morre-cearense-criadora-do-bolsa-familia-ana-fonseca/.

[26] For example, the Ministry of Education, Cristovam Buarque, advocated for Bolsa Escola Federal which was under his responsibility while the extraordinary Minister for food safety, Jose Graziano, in charge of *Fome Zero*, fought for this program since food security was a historical claim of the PT linked to powerful rural movements such as the MST (Borges, 2022: 60, 61; Monteiro, 2011: 68, 115).

Conflicts inside the PT and between various social ministries of the Lula government—mostly education, food security, and social assistance—that institutionalized strong political interests led *Bolsa Família* cooks to think simple and streamlined in their efforts. Therefore, if *Bolsa Família* cooks meant for *Bolsa Família* to contribute to gender equality, this goal could not be made explicit. As one of the *Bolsa Família* executive secretaries explains:

> But there was an intention of gender equality, but it is not... [...] it is not written. [...] I know that *Bolsa Família* was kind of minimalist, but it is only written attribution [of women as] responsible for the administration of the resource. [...] that actually at the time of the text, was totally intentional. It was absolutely fundamental to be minimalist. There were many waves of conversations and much resistance [...]. It certainly wasn't the opposite, it wasn't anti-gender [...] The tension within the government was very high, communicating in the simplest and most direct way was essential to reduce noise because we were taking away the income program from four ministries. [...] Taking away the *Auxiolio gas* was a huge fight. [...]. [In addition], we had just created a program with a transfer [fome zero] and took it out of the budget. (Filipe)

In addition, although *Bolsa Família* provoked vigorous debate within the government about education, hunger, or the national-subnational coordination, it was not the case for the matter of transferring cash to women, as one *Bolsa Família* cook stresses:

> This discussion didn't really generate further discussion. There was almost a consensus that the resource passed on was for the person in charge, primarily for the mother, the person who held the position of the mother in the family. [...] This was almost a consensual issue. (Sebastián)

To end these bureaucratic conflicts, President Lula had to intervene, recommending as he did that something new had to be made from old recipes: the existing CCTs unified and remade into *Bolsa Família*. This stewardship is demonstrated by Lula's statement that "if there's anything good in the drawer, let's open the drawer, give it another name and we go ahead" (an official *Bolsa Família* cook in Borges, 2022: 60). As in Mexico, the President had to intervene to cease conflicts but in contrast to Mexico where Zedillo had only to ask CONAPO to be involved, Lula was required to intervene more directly to end the BEF and Fome Zero.[27] Lula also had a marked influence on the decision to transfer cash to women, a sentiment that is supported by this *Bolsa Família* cook:

> The final word was given by President Lula, who had a very personal experience with his mother. [...]. In Lula's case, he has a lot of common sense and he is very intuitive, very perceptive. So I think that in his case he had the final word, and it was very much due to his personal experience, in relation to his mother, his family experience. (Juan)

Finally, the creation of a new institution was necessary to overcome conflicts inside the government and among its various executive institutions and following experts' preoccupation to make management more technocratic and less subject to clientelism (Jenson & Nagels, 2022: 365). In January 2004, the Ministry of Food Security merged with the Ministry of Social Welfare to create the Ministry of Social Development and Fight against Hunger (MDS). One of its high-ranking officials shared the instrumentalist belief that women are better investors in their children than men and based his argument on the vague notion that is common sense and on academic evaluations:

> I don't know, honestly, it was [...] an option based on common sense. Those who know the Brazilian reality of recent times know that family bonds are more and more around mothers. A question of fragility, social problems, unemployment [...] alcoholism problems [...]. The research started to show clearly the positive of this [the use of the money in favor of the family when the benefit was paid directly to the women] (...) Because women are also more attentive to the needs of their children, more present. (Juan)

Gender Equality as an Implicit Goal and an Informal Institution

Alongside the instrumentalist rationale behind the transfer of cash to women, the gender equality goal was implicitly present in *Bolsa Família*. By implicit, I mean that gender equality was not officially written into the

[27] While the administration continued to refer to *Bolsa Família* as the flagship program of a broader *Fome Zero* agenda, "in reality, as soon as the former was enacted, the latter ceased to exist" (Borges, 2022: 60, 61).

Law that ratified it. However, it was present as an informal and secondary objective, as is explained by one BF operator:

> The central objective was more the fight against poverty itself, and associated to that there were other things like the empowerment of women, the autonomy of all the people in the family [...]. Sometimes the programs are designed as they are implemented. (Julián)

Many politicians, policy entrepreneurs, and bureaucrats involved in the development of *Bolsa Família* and in its implementation claimed this implicit objective. According to them, *Bolsa Família* aimed also to contribute to women's self-esteem and empowerment by allowing them more material resources, increasing their household bargaining power and linking them to health services (Moreira et al., 2012 in Bohn & Levy, 2012: 254). For example, the PT senator Paulo Rocha underscored the fact that "the choice to make women beneficiaries was to facilitate their emancipation".[28] In the same vein, Rosani Cunha (2006), Secretary of *Bolsa Família* within MDS in 2005, emphasized that: "by selecting women as beneficiaries, *Bolsa Família* became a strong instrument for women's empowerment and autonomy. To them, this meant independence, autonomy, and citizenship [...]. With *Bolsa Família*, they (women) accessed credit, they could plan their budget, increase their self-esteem and reduce their dependence on their male counterpart, and this reduced household conflicts and gender violence". In the same vein, President Lula praised the program as one which reduced poverty by teaching poor women "how to fish rather than giving them fish" (Lula, 2003b, 2006).[29]

Although *Bolsa Família* cooks did not place gender equality at the center of their concern, they did not either exclusively reproduce an instrumentalist view of gender. For them, as for Mexican policymakers, transferring cash to women was also a means to empower them to improve their intra-household bargaining power and autonomy. One *Bolsa Família* cook shared this idea:

[28] https://www12.senado.leg.br/noticias/materias/2018/03/07/paulo-rocha-com para-os-governos-de-lula-e-temer-quanto-as-politicas-para-as-mulheres, accessed February 2024.

[29] http://www.biblioteca.presidencia.gov.br/presidencia/ex-presidentes/luiz-inacio-lula-da-silva/mensagens-ao-congresso/2008, accessed February 2024.

> It also had a sense of affirmative action explicit in an empowerment agenda. Because we had the conviction that it had a positive externality [...] that you will put some money at the disposal of women, it had a stronger empowerment intention. (Filipe)

As in Mexico, this rationale was also based on gender knowledge, as is explained by a high official of MDS:

> And also this, there are some studies too, there are some published works showing that this also contributed to empowering poor women. Giving them a little more dignity, of affirmation, even to eventually counteract problems of domestic violence, of aggressive husbands. She started to have the minimum conditions [...] that gives them a certain self-esteem and dignity. (Juan)

In addition, *Bolsa Família* institutional design characteristics such as the extended coverage, the social rights-based framing, the regular payments, and the effective coordination with other social programs and institutions facilitated women's empowerment and thus are implicit gender equality objectives (De Brauw et al., 2014; Moreira et al., 2012; Sugiyama & Hunter, 2020). For example, *Bolsa Família* was framed as a social right, based on the strong legacy of the 1998 Constitution in which the state is seen as responsible for social well-being, and involved "soft conditions" that were not stringent and not monitored prior to 2006 (Borges, 2022: 63). They served to gather information about why children were not able to go to school or to comply with health check-ups and to engage municipal social workers to help families to comply with them (Fenwick, 2017: 667; Morais de Sá e Silva, 2017: 136).

This rights-based idea institutionalized in the *Bolsa Família*'s design enabled women's empowerment. As highlighted by Hunter and Sugiyama, "governments that recognize all members of the national community as worthy enough to have their basic needs met and their life chances lifted can go far toward generating this sense [of belonging]" (2014: 830).

Moreover, the merging of various CCT programs and the coordination of *Bolsa Família* with other programs further participated in the empowerment of women experiencing poverty. As the Secretariat of Public Policies for Women explains:

> These other programs arrived [with *Bolsa Família*] to improve the quality of life for women. [...] There is not [only] *Bolsa Família*, they are infrastructure programs, but they benefit the same families [...] in a significant way for women [...] So the *Bolsa Família* is linked to other programs that reached the families and made women feel less dependent on men [...] the woman then feels less dependent, she feels more autonomous. (Daniela)

For example, *Bolsa Família* gave women access to already existing health services (for pregnancy follow-ups and medical check-ups for their children) where they interacted with other complementary programs such as the *Sistema Único de Saúde* (SUS) that offers free contraception. This access could imply that *Bolsa Família* recipients had more control over contraception decisions than other women (Brauw et al., 2014: 496).

The implicit *Bolsa Família* gender equality goals could also be attributed to the institutional context of women's political and institutional apparatuses. According to *Bolsa Família* cooks, *Bolsa Família* was intimately connected to the Brazilian national policy prioritizing women's empowerment (De Brauw et al., 2014: 488), as recalls by on BF cooks:

> Then comes the Women's Ministry, and finally *Bolsa* [...] served as an element to strengthen this agenda [of gender equality]. It contributed a lot in the sense that we need public policies geared towards women, this brings return and makes a difference. (Irene)

In January 2003, Lula's government[30] created the women's political agency, the Secretariat of Public Policies for Women[31] (Bohn &

[30] Historically, the PT was open to a feminist agenda but without being a feminist party and embracing all feminist claims. The PT, created in the 1980s, is a social movement party with strong organizational and external links with social movements (Anria, 2019: 9) including feminism and women's rights movements. Its internal functioning based on internal democracy and in dialogue with leftist organizations allowed feminist and women activists to create a strong women's cell within it. They could make gender claims and their agenda more and more visible in the party (Bohn & Levy, 2019: 249). For example, in its 2002 electoral campaign, Lula emphasized the need to implement "a political and cultural effort to affirm in the country the principle of equality. It is insufficient to combat only the economic causes of the multiple forms of inequality. It is necessary to undertake positive actions to put to an end the different forms of discrimination against women, Afro-Brazilians, native Brazilians, disabled individuals, and sexual minorities, just to cite a few" (da Silva, 2002 cited in Bohn & Levy, 2019: 249).

[31] This agency had autonomy of action, its budget, and the Presidency's Office housed and recruited gender experts from universities as well as leaders from the most recognized

Levy, 2019: 250). The Secretariat would elaborate public policies in all areas, including social assistance and thus *Bolsa Família*. It succeeded in enacting feminist policies and laws,[32] but its role was weaker in the areas of social policies. The Secretariat of Public Policies for Women, in alliance with women and feminist movements, in line with other social movements at the root of the PT—such as the unions and the MST—strongly supported, but did not participate in the elaboration of such social policies as *Bolsa Família* addressing women and poverty (2003)[33] (Bohn & Levy, 2019: 253, 254). As the first minister of the Secretariat of Public Policies for Women who was also president of the National Council for Women's Rights elucidates:

> We consider that it was a great victory for women at that moment that the entitlement of the *Bolsa Família* went to women. Why do we consider it? Because first of all, we have a large [poor] population, the majority of whom are women. If we look at the indexes of the families most affected by poverty and misery are usually families headed by women with children and especially those families headed by black women. (Daniela)

However, this *Conselho* did not have any influence on the design of *Bolsa Família*, as explained by one of its members:

> The National Council for Women's Rights had no way of influencing *Bolsa Família* from the inside. The person from MDS who was on the National Council for Women's Rights heard the demands there, as she also heard them at the National Conference on Policies for Women. The demands were placed there and somehow, we hoped that this would have repercussions inside [*Bolsa Família*]. (Marina)

Therefore, the *Bolsa Família* cooks were not strategic gender equality entrepreneurs, femocrats of feminist actors who brought their feminist

women's organizations. The Secretariat and women's movements discussed and agreed on common priorities of action in national conferences.

[32] Such as the *Maria da Penha* Law (2006) against violence against women and electoral quotas (2009): https://www.institutomariadapenha.org.br/quem-e-maria-da-penha.html, accessed February 2023.

[33] Nor in public housing for poor women *Minha casa, Minha vida* (2007, 2008), labor rights for domestic workers (2015).

ideas, debates, and agendas to the table. As a participating entrepreneur technocrat explains:

> About the gender discussion [...]. I would love to be able to say 'This program also existed because of the women's struggle, the gender issue, it is a product of the gender issue debate'. [...] I didn't feel this inside. [...] I wouldn't be honest with myself saying that the *Bolsa Família* is part of the fight for the emancipation of women, for gender equality. (Sebastián)

Inside this institutional context, time matters. *Bolsa Família* development, in contrast to Mexico, was a quick process during the first year of Lula's government and the Secretariat of Public Policies was created in January 2003 (and *Bolsa Família* only then months later in October 2003). Therefore, discussions about gender inequalities inside the PT government were in general embryonic and the short time to put together *Bolsa Família* had left few spaces for non-essential questions. Gender equality was considered to be one such non-essential question. As one of the few gender experts on the *Bolsa Família* team asserts:

> Basically, because time was short. [...]. Gender equity matters for *Bolsa Família*. But if you must put poor, hungry families on the registry, you basically have no way, no time to take care that social workers are trained in gender equity. [...] What I can say is that I imagine that it was not given much thought [...]. I think there was a concern with the women's issue, but the degree of maturity and elaboration you had in 2003 on the gender issue was far below what it is today. Certainly. What was discussed was not so complex. [...] It was much more embryonic. (Carolina)

Lastly, political and partisan conflicts stemming from a fragmented Brazilian political system constrained the articulation of more explicit gender equality goals in the writing of *Bolsa Família*. Strategic (gender equality) entrepreneurs saw *Bolsa Família* as contributing to gender equality and intended it to become a state policy that participated in much more radical goals. As one *Bolsa Família* cook recounts:

> *Bolsa Família* could be the pivot. Since there is a high correlation between gender discrimination and race discrimination and income, for me income was a pretext to make the *Bolsa Família* a pivot. But we didn't get there. We needed a much more cohesive government than the one we got. But that was the intention. (Filipe)

They could not "get there", mainly for political reasons and because the PT was a center-left party with economic propositions in line with the center-right and right parties with whom the part had formed a coalition (Fenwick, 2009). To win the 2002 elections and to govern, the first PT government formed a coalition with six other political parties including ones of conservative religious groups gathering in the caucus of Brazilian evangelicals.[34] This group supported Lula's presidential candidacy and Lula's social policies including *Bolsa Família* but was virulently opposed to the feminist and LGBTQI+ rights agenda (Dip, 2018; Coenga-Oliveira, 2019).[35] Their presence inside MDS and the absence of feminists inside this ministry could also explain the implicit gender equality goals of *Bolsa Família* and more broadly the absence of gender equality discussions inside the development of social policies. As one gender expert and *Bolsa Família* cook states:

> We were not in the National Council of Social Assistance, which was the council of MDS. It is a council full of church organizations, [...]. A lot of very conservative Church organizations in relation to women. Moreover, I think that at that moment [...] I don't think there were any feminist organizations there [...]. And there are very few until today because it is difficult to assume that women's rights are a question of social development. (Marina)

In contrast to the Mexican case, in Brazil, the institutional constraints of political fragmentation and the institutional context of the WPA delinked to social affairs explains why strategic gender equality entrepreneurs—*Bolsa Família* cooks concerned with gender equality—were not so successful in institutionalizing women's rights as social rights. In this context, *Bolsa Família*'s designers cooked an instrument with implicit gender equality goals, hoping that cash transfers to women would challenge the more instrumentalist views of gender relations.

[34] 25 años de CFEMEA: *Movimento e transformação*: http://www.cfemea.org.br/index.php/2016-04-24-18-10-44, accessed March 2019.

[35] For example, they strongly opposed abortion decriminalization and legalization and the same-sex union and therefore to policies explicitly in favor of greater gender equality (Dip, 2018).

Conclusion: Institutions Legacies and Venues, Strategic (Gender Equality) Entrepreneurs and Knowledge About Gender

The parallel analysis of the two cases demonstrates how strategic (gender equality) entrepreneurs were able to include gender equality goals in the design of *Progresa* while their Brazilian counterparts were not quite as successful because they did not consider gender equality goals to be an explicit priority. This chapter argues that *Progresa*'s design included gender equality goals in response to the strength of Mexican and international feminist actors who, rooted in long-standing Mexican institutions for promoting gender equality, convinced *Progresa* policy entrepreneurs, who became strategic gender equality entrepreneurs, to link gender inequalities with poverty. Institutional machinery for gender equality in place since the 1980s and the strength of feminism following the United Nations' 1995 Fourth World Conference on Women in Beijing ensured the incorporation of gender equality in a social policy not originally oriented toward reducing gender inequalities. *Progresa* designers were policy entrepreneurs who became male supporters of liberal feminist goals and promoted the incorporation of gender equality goals within social policy. Once they internalized the idea demonstrated by feminist activists and gender studies that poverty increases inequalities between men and women, they translated gender equality goals in two ways. First, *Progresa* allocated a larger cash incentive for girls' school attendance than for boys. Second, only women received the cash payments. Both approaches are means of altering intra-household gender relations and promoting gender equality by empowering women. The *Progresa* experiment reveals that strategic gender equality entrepreneurs, gendered institutional legacies, and knowledge about gender drove its results. Technocrats, that became gender equality entrepreneurs, embedded in institutions, and constrained by institutional legacies and context, developed a CCT design based on knowledge linking poverty to gender inequalities. These three elements are co-constitutive: strategic gender equality entrepreneurs are rooted in institutions that gave them constraints and resources for actions and institutionalized knowledge such as on gender equality.

In the Brazilian story of *Bolsa Família* cooking, political conflicts were more important than in Mexico. This story reveals that in Brazil the development of *Bolsa Família* produced a recipe mixing old subnational CCT programs and new ones. This process took place during Lula's first government and his center-left PT in which policymakers had to recombine various ideas and projects about development in a quest to reduce social inequalities in the most unequal country in the world. The political solution was to break the long-standing institutional legacy of clientelism and poor institutional coordination that characterized Brazilian social policies. A team of policy entrepreneurs—without links with social organizations and movements and in which gender experts were few—have cooked *Bolsa Família* as a patchwork of old CCTs. Therefore, *Bolsa Família* aimed to reduce poverty by transferring income to women on the strength of a limited idea that mothers are better spenders on their children than men. This followed an instrumentalist rationale of gender relations. However, the gendered process of *Bolsa Família* development shows that these entrepreneurs also decided to make women recipients as a means of empowering them and improving their intrahousehold bargaining power and their self-esteem. In doing so, they have not followed a strictly instrumentalist rationale. This latter was accepted because of the historical links between feminist and women's movements with the PT and led to the creation of a Secretariat of Public Policies for Women. However, the PT government did not open social and economic affairs to feminist organizations or knowledge. Nevertheless, their influence convinced *Bolsa Família* cooks to include implicit gender equality goals in its design by focusing on a rights-based program. They could not cook a more radical social policy because of political opposition from right and extreme right parties and conflicts inside the PT government. Cooking from old recipes still left traces of the past, making it difficult to have a whole new design and go from implicit to explicit gender equality goals. Nevertheless, this *Bolsa Família*'s implicit gender equality goals had the intention altering traditional gender roles somewhat by making women more autonomous, for example, concerning household budgets and health.

This chapter has shown that strategic gender equality entrepreneurs, institutional legacies and venues, as well as knowledge on gender are essential in directing change in the matter of equal gender relations. Their contextual combinations explain why *Bolsa Família* and *Progresa* designs integrated gender equality goals implicitly or explicitly.

While the literature that tracked the processes of *Bolsa Família* and *Progresa* elaboration focused mostly on social investment ideas, individual trajectories for Mexico (Hevia de la Torre, 2007; Teichman, 2008; Tomazini, 2016), and institutional legacies and conflicts in Brazil

(Fenwick, 2009; Hall, 2008; Jenson & Nagels, 2022), this chapter added a gender analysis to these processes. Tracking the cooking processes behind *Progresa* and *Bolsa Família* facilitated a gendered analysis of the political configurations that ultimately determined the degree of gender equality objectives integration.

In the case of Brazil, this gendered analysis showed that a rights-based program allowed strategic (gender equality) entrepreneurs to (at least partially) overcome the instrumentalist gender rationale of subnational CCT legacies and to integrate an implicit gender equality objective. Institutional constraints were harder here than in Mexico. Party system fragmentation and conflicts within Lula's first center-left government limited access to the social and economic affairs of the state to feminist actors and ideas. Therefore, *Bolsa Família*'s design only had an implicit gender equality objective. In the case of Mexico, this gendered analysis highlights the role of Gómez de León and the CONAPO—that institutionalized feminism in the state in alliance with Mexican and global feminism—in developing the *Progresa* recipe. This work had remained a blind spot in the general literature on *Progresa* that paid greater attention to the role of Santiago Levy and the Ministry of Finance (e.g., Hevia de la Torre, 2007; Teichman, 2008; Tomazini, 2016). In a context of economic and political crisis, institutional resources gave great power and autonomy to strategic gender equality entrepreneurs—allies of gender experts and participants in feminist movements—to include an explicit gender equality objective in *Progresa*. This analysis makes three contributions to the literature.

First, in line with historical institutionalism, this analysis reiterated that time matters (Béland & Cox, 2011; Hall, 2003; Pierson, 2004). In Brazil, the historical moment of Lula's first center-left government coming from the PT led to huge expectations regarding women's rights, social redistribution, and rights-based social policies. However, room to maneuver was smaller here than in Mexico, where the political and economic crisis gave opportunities to start from scratch. In addition, the contextual moment of *Progresa* cooking coincided with the preparation of the Fourth International Conference on Women in Beijing, of which the Mexican contingent was led by key *Progresa* cook Gómez de León.

Second, this processes tracking revealed that the interests and ideas of strategic entrepreneurs are framed and constrained by institutions. Historical and institutional contexts matter to understanding strategic entrepreneurs' actions and ideas. In Brazil, institutional legacies including subnational CCTs and party system fragmentation as well as institutional features such as the very new institutional gender machinery—the Secretariat of Public Policies for Women created in 2003, the same year of *Bolsa Família*—and conflict among bureaucracies and ministries on the matters of zero hunger, education, and social assistance constrained *Bolsa Família* cooks. They had to count on presidential support and to build a new Ministry—MDS—to overcome subnational power, clientelist legacies and to sideline other social ministries fighting for other social programs including *Bolsa Escola* and zero hunger. In Mexico, conflict between the SEDESOL versus the Ministry of Finance conflict was solved in favor of the latter, which gained strong autonomy and huge financial resources. However, its scarce knowledge resources and research traditions necessarily meant CONAPO involvement in developing the first evidence-based social policy in Mexico that integrated gender equality goals in its design.

Social policy entrepreneurs that were mostly technocrats in both cases, embedded in public institutions—with feminist legacies in the case of CONAPO in Mexico—became truly allies of feminism in the case of Mexico. In this case, individuals and intimate relations are key: Santiago Levy and José Gomez de Leon became friends and agreed on the direction of change. With personal links with President Zedillo, Gomez de León and his CONAPO team promoted an agenda in favor of gender equality without strong direct ties with feminist movements outside the state. However, institutional feminism had succeeded in institutionalizing gender ideas inside the state—in CONAPO and among academics where *Progresa* cooks worked and studied, in alliance with the powerful actor of global feminism. The institutional, academic, professional, and even personal trajectories of *Progresa* cooks involved the acquisition of gender knowledge and convinced them that gender inequalities are related to poverty. By contrast, surrounded by a lot of political noise, Brazilian policy entrepreneurs had little time to prepare a solution out of existing subnational CCTs—that were not part of the picture in Mexico—that only left room for consensual matters such as transferring cash to women (and not men). Subnational CCTs had already shown success in this matter. Faced with political conflicts about the nature of social change, Lula's first center-left government had to tread carefully in a way that was not necessary in Mexico. The solution was technocratic as in Mexico, but the technocrats were mostly men with diplomas in economics without strong ties to feminist actors inside and outside the state. If the feminist and women's movements were close to the PT and the new gender apparatus and participated in feminist public policies, they did not have direct access to the cooking of *Bolsa Família*. However, their presence led *Bolsa Família* cooks to introduce an implicit gender equality objective. The decision to transfer cash to women was more than instrumentalist. Cooks also sought to empower them, increasing their self-esteem and intra-household bargaining power.

Third, knowledge matters. In both cases, if social investment ideas implemented by technocratic tools were the solution to old social policy legacies of clientelism, ideas about poverty diverged. Whereas in Brazil structural thoughts about social inequalities emerged, in Mexico individual and neoliberal approaches to poverty remained. Therefore, while *Bolsa Família* cooks promoted a social rights-based program with soft conditions and large coverage, Mexican counterparts adhered to an evidence-based program strictly targeted the poorest with strict and punitive conditions. Both primarily followed an instrumentalist rationale legitimated by international evidence when they decided to transfer cash to women but they also institutionalized the idea of gender equality, whether implicitly or explicitly. In Brazil, the strong idea of a social rights-based program inside the PT and the 1988 Constitution led *Bolsa Família* cooks to the at least peripheral goal of reducing gender inequalities by empowering women. In Mexico, the *Progresa* requirement of evidence-based policy led its cooks—economists but also demographers and sociologists convinced by the scientific link between poverty and gender inequalities—to include an explicit gender equality goal in *Progresa*.

This analysis of the cooking process behind *Progresa* and *Bolsa Família* shows that direction of change in both countries was one of more gender equality but not to the same degree. While the *Progresa* design included an explicit gender equality goal, this goal was only implicit in *Bolsa Família*. Therefore, the *Progresa* design contained more potentially egalitarian intentions about gender than *Bolsa Família* because women's and girls' empowerment was clearly articulated in the operational rules. This is surprising: center-left governments are not always more in favor of women's advancements than center-right governments.

CHAPTER 4

Standardization of CCTs Without Gender Equality

Introduction

By 2004, CCTs had entered a second sequence, traveling from both Mexico and Brazil and entering the international level of policy design and promotion. This chapter demonstrates how in this second phase of what might best be described as standardization—mostly led by the World Bank—CCTs essentially lost their gender equality goals. Ancelovici and Jenson (2012) defined standardization as a mechanism whose working parts include decontextualization, certification, and framing. Therefore, this chapter demonstrates that the World Bank took up *Progresa* and *Bolsa Família*, certified them as the best instruments to reduce poverty, and by doing so decontextualized and reframed them into a standard CCT model. *Progresa*'s social investment perspective and its required impact evaluations held a certain appeal. Then, there was *Bolsa Família* with its softer conditions that were easier to enforce and its child outcomes that were easier to measure. Aspects of each iteration therefore were maintained and inserted into the standard model. While the World Bank—and to a lesser extend the IADB—standardized and promoted their CCT standard model, Brazilian President Lula actively promoted *Bolsa Família* as a basic income model, to left-wing governments in Latin America (Borges, 2022: 120) and in Portuguese-speaking African countries. This other model also lacked the investment in gender equality goals. As the World

N. Nagels, *Gender Equality in Conditional Cash Transfer Designs*, Studies of the Americas,
https://doi.org/10.1007/978-3-031-60871-1_4

Bank supported this Brazilian diplomatic mission export *Bolsa Família*, this institution, as I will show in this chapter, was the main purveyor of the standard model.[1]

The World Bank social protection unit (PREM) decontextualized both *Progresa* and *Bolsa Família* to treat them as pro-poor policy instruments. The World Bank then reframed and certified a "thin" standard CCT version, abandoning concern for gender equality or women's empowerment.[2] These processes involved the sidelining of gender experts—who had to mainstream gender concerns in all seventeen sectorial units—who were virtually powerless vis a vis the institutional, knowledge-based, and even financial resources being deployed by their economist and economically-focused colleagues who were the strategic entrepreneurs of the standard CCT. These policy entrepreneurs were not strategic gender equality entrepreneurs[3] since they reframed their interest in women, only retaining the instrumentalist rationale for transferring the benefits to mothers as a means of maximizing improved child outcomes.

Knowledge is key to certifying and legitimizing the standard model and framing it with this instrumentalist view of gender. Always concerned to argue from "evidence-based" positions, the World Bank only retained quantitative and econometric data that broadly demonstrated positive outcomes for CCT approaches to poverty, malnutrition, education, and health. However, the World Bank—which is not an anti-gender institution in so much as gender equality is part of its official mandate—remained blind to qualitative and intersectional, historical, and very context-specific findings showing negative or at best mixed CCT results on the matter of gender relations. The World Bank's "measurement obsession" (Liebowitz & Zwingel, 2014) as well as the institutional location of the

[1] This argument contrasts with that of Borges (2022) who argues for the diffusion of two CCT models in Latin America—one focused on human capital that the World Bank diffused vertically to right-wing governments and another one diffused horizontally from Brazil to left-wing governments because both were unconcerned about gender equality goals.

[2] It also abandoned the bottom-up process and the social mobilization that were at the root of Bolsa Escola in Brazil, of which we see traces in *Bolsa Família* with its widespread coverage and soft conditions.

[3] In the standardization process, they are neither innovators nor early adopters. Rather, they are intermediary actors: a complex mix of state and non-state actors working in policy communities and, increasingly, across international boundaries (Ancelovici & Jenson, 2013: 294).

policy design led to a standard CCT model that failed to target gender inequalities. The standard CCT model embedded and promoted gender relations other than traditional ones by excluding men as breadwinners but also reinforced the traditional gendered division of labor and with it gender inequalities because women were solely seen as mothers and sole caregivers of children.

In this chapter, I present this second sequence of the CCT trajectory, their standardization. After briefly explaining the historical and institutional context of the World Bank in the area of social development and gender, I demonstrate how and why the World Bank weakened gender equality goals. In the second section, I document the strategic entrepreneurs and the knowledge they used to certify the standard CCT model without any concern for women's empowerment and gender equality goals. The third section is about the decontextualization and framing of the standard model, including the exclusion of strategic gender equality entrepreneurs and their knowledge and expertise.

Gendered Institutional Legacies in the World Bank

In 1944, in the exceptional context of the end of World War II, the Bretton Wood Conference in New Hampshire created two new international institutions: the International Monetary Fund (IMF) and the World Bank.[4] Conceived as gender-neutral, they were gendered institutions addressing "real" problems in the international, read masculine, public sphere that includes war and finance and avoiding "private", read feminine, matters. The mission of the then International Bank for Reconstruction and Development (IBRD), which became known as the World Bank, was to promote economic development to rebuild European countries devasted by the war (Noy, 2017: 6).

In the 1950s, following the US Marshal Plan for the reconstruction of Europe, "the Bank oriented its activities and the "D" (development)

[4] The IMF and the World Bank are very close institutions because IMF membership is a prerequisite to membership in the World Bank (Hammer, 2013: 8). They are not the most democratic institutions because unlike the one-nation–one-vote rule of most international organizations, voting in the IMF and the World Bank is share-weighted. In the early years of the Bank, the USA controlled 37.2% of the votes (Noy, 2017: 7) and now 15.9%.

of the IBRD began to gain greater importance than the "R" (reconstruction)" (Hammer, 2013: 8). This move corresponded to the 1949 President Truman's inaugural speech that identified a new problem: underdevelopment that developed nations must resolve by "making the benefits of our scientific advances and industrial progress available [to] [...] underdeveloped areas". Since this period and the emergence of "development", the World Bank, other United Nations organizations, and national cooperation agencies have also singled out the equality between women and men as a development objective. For example, the United Nations Charter consecrated the equality between men and women in its preamble and in articles one and five (Martinez, 2008). Nevertheless, the World Bank was a latecomer to institutionalize and recognize gender equality in its loans and projects.

The World Bank is anchored by neoclassical economic theories of the benefit of comparative advantage, where trade is linked to economic growth and economic growth is the source of greater well-being (Hammer, 2013: 11). These mainstream economic approaches lacked any consideration for feminist and gender research and knowledge. However, the ways to pursue development have changed over time and have turned the World Bank's attention to women and gender relations.

During the first phase of its existence between the 1950s and 1980s, the World Bank relied on a modernization approach to development.[5] According to this approach, underdeveloped countries would follow the same economic steps as Western countries to modernize through trade, private markets, and strong state institutions (Beaudet et al., 2019). In this period, a gender equality agenda based on gender knowledge on development was absent from these projects. They mostly addressed problems in productive areas targeting men except for neo-Malthusian policies focusing on women solely as mothers and wives (Griffin, 2009: 117). These policies were gendering practices as they identified "traditional families" and demographic growth in underdeveloped countries as one of the main obstacles to development. The USA, as the largest shareholder of the Bank, was the leader in birth and population control-based policies (Gautier, 2000: 169).

Diverse economic knowledges cohabited within this modernization approach, especially during the McNamara presidency (1968–1981) that

[5] Rostow (1960) was one of its most important academic and promoter.

integrated new development ideas and themes such as rural development, human resources development, and the alleviation of poverty even if this latter, at the time, failed to gain its currently central position in the Bank (Hammer, 2013: 28–31). Despite changes to the Bank's perspective over the years, development projects remained blind to most dimensions of gender inequalities and addressed gender relations only through neo-Malthusian demography policies. Development policies did not consider woman's lives and work nor their impacts on women (Benería & Sen, 2021: 25). For example, in the 1970s, the World Bank incorporated health issues into its population projects, setting itself up as a powerful player in the health sector with its offerings of financial and institutional resources. And yet these resources were still steeped in neo-Malthusian notions of population control (Noy, 2017: 49). In this sector, the fear of demographic explosion in developing countries was such that the World Bank led family planning projects that ended, in some cases such as in India, with forced sterilization (Martinez, 2008).

In the 1980s, the World Bank and the IMF changed their policies and operations departing from modernization knowledge and theories to embrace neoliberalism. They responded to the debt crisis, Brazil's payment default, and Mexico's foreign debts through the institutionalization of structural adjustment policies (SAP). With Thatcher's and Reagan's administrations, the World Bank became a powerful actor in neoliberalism able to coercively impose privatization and state deregulation through conditional loans. World Bank President A.W. Clausen (1982–1987) was a strategic entrepreneur seeking to shift ideas about poverty and welfare. He championed anti-welfarism promoting the integration of the poor inside the market rather than promoting social and public provision (Noy, 2017: 50, 51). The World Bank emerged as the headquarters of the Washington Consensus and neo-orthodox knowledge on the development economy that sought to get rid of anyone with dissonant views. New strategic entrepreneurs gained power inside the Bank. Professional neoclassical economists with US or UK academic training, whose number increased considerably with pressure from the Bank's largest shareholder, the USA, controlled the Bank from top to bottom (Hammer, 2013: 34–36; Nay, 2020: 146).

During this period, noted for being slow, impermeable, and unresponsive to women's movements despite their increased visibility and influence on the United Nations from the 1970s, the World Bank only established a

Women in Development (WID)[6] division in 1987 (Bergeron, 2003: 405; Griffin, 2009: 125). The WID approach was based on knowledge developed by the Danish economist Esther Boserup (1970)[7] that "women had to be integrated into the process of development" (Benería & Sen, 2020: 26). The WID approach tried to connect gender equality issues and development concerns. According to Razavi et Miller (1995: 2) "WID hinges on economic efficiency arguments about what women can contribute to the development process". This approach had roots, politically and theoretically, in the so-called second wave, western, egalitarian, and liberal feminism. It produced knowledge such as sexual-specific statistics supporting the integration of women into the productive sphere and claimed legal and political equality, as well as sexual and reproductive rights (Griffin, 2009: 118). The World Bank could embrace WID because it was developed in concordance with the theme of modernization that equated the decrease of women's oppression with the transformation of the economic and social relations of so-called traditional societies to modern societies. Implicitly, WID assumed that the improvement of women's lives leads to the improvement of societies in general if development and modernization integrate women (McIlwaine & Datta, 2003: 370). The main drivers of the WID approach were education, access to credit, and agricultural techniques to increase women's productivity and improve their standard of living (Jacquette & Staudt, 2006; Kabeer, 1994; Martinez, 2008; Moser, 1993).

[6] Pushed by feminist liberal movements in the 1970s, mostly from the USA, the United Nations adopted the Women and Development (WID) approach that marked the International Conference on the Status of Women, held in Mexico City in 1975, which celebrated the International Women's Year and led to the United Nations Decade for Women (1976–1985). This conference drew attention to the need to develop strategies and actions for the promotion of women's rights, including civil and political rights. This is not surprising since most delegations present at the conference came from opponents to authoritarian regimes. During these international meetings, tensions arose amid Southern and Northern feminisms. For example, while feminists from the USA promoted a global feminist sisterhood, women from the South and the East rejected the feminist label believing that the exploitation of the North and capitalism and not patriarchy constituted their major source of oppression (Jacquette & Staudt 2006: 22).

[7] It was the first publication with international impact that challenged mainstream development theories. She demonstrated that colonization and not traditional agriculture had radically degraded women's roles and positions in Asian, Latin American, and African economies.

In the World Bank, the 1987 WID division's first objective was to invest in women as a means to achieving broader development goals, especially population control. This shows that in the World Bank, neo-Malthusian policies were very strong institutional legacies. However, in the 1980s the World Bank rarely concretized even this outdated and instrumentalist WID objective in policies and projects in the field (Bergeron, 2003: 405). The World Bank remained blind and deaf to feminist knowledge and agendas. For example, an Operational Policy on the gender dimension of development was only written in 1994. It was to become the World Bank's gender policy, which was revised in 2003 (Griffin, 2009: 129).

Since the end of the 1980s and the 1990s, the critics of SAPs were virulent and came from various actors, including UNICEF, feminist and ecological social movements, and NGOs.[8] Feminists vigorously denounced SAPs as generating and/or failing to address the marginalization and poverty of women. Feminist economists (e.g., Benería, 2003) criticized the masculine assumptions at the center of SAPs embedded in neoclassical economic theories. They show that SAPs were based on a male bias: the reduction in public social expenditure essentially increased the reproductive and community workload of women. In other words, unpaid female labor tends to absorb the social cost of SAPs (Moser, 1993: 71). Face with these criticisms, the Bank responded to an evaluation report of its projects. The 1992 Wapenhans report revealed the high failure rate of financed World Bank projects that generated shock waves at the highest level of the organization (Nay, 2021: 33).

As in Mexico and Brazil, conflicts and criticisms required the intervention of a strong external actor. In 1995, President Clinton designated James Wolfensohn as the new president of the World Bank with the mandate to change the main idea and knowledge driving the Bank and to give it a human face (Hammer, 2013: 1). This resonated with the success of the ideational and knowledge innovation in the United Nation Development Program (UNDP) that institutionalized the conceptual approach of "human development" with their Human Development

[8] UNICEF published a report (Cornia et al., 1987) demonstrating the negative effects of SAPs on health, education, sanitation, housing, and nutrition with disastrous impacts on children's vulnerability (Noy, 2017: 51). NGOs and social movements, mostly environmentalist, created a coalition to criticize SAPs and the World Bank became their main target (Nay, 2020: 142).

Index. This knowledge conceptualized poverty and development beyond the economic concepts promoted by the World Bank and the IMF. The Bank incorporated the critiques and shifted its idea of development to make it more inclusive, participatory and to empower the poor, including women. It institutionalized new methods to support bottom-up approaches by involving local communities in the design, implementation, and evaluation of development projects (Nay, 2020: 140, 152). This institutional context left more room for knowledge on gender and for gender equality concerns to be institutionalized in the World Bank.

Gender Knowledge Institutionalization in the World Bank in the Post-Washington Consensus

Under the presidency of James Wolfensohn (1995–2005),[9] the period during which the Bank standardized CCTs, the World Bank shifted from neoliberalist knowledge to human development promoting development projects that included bottom-up participation, social capital, and gender equality. After a study involving 60 000 participants to understand the "Voices of the Poor", development became not just about growth but included people's hopes, dreams, opportunities, and capabilities (Sen, 1999). In an institutional and ideational context very critical of the SAP and neoliberalism, Wolfensohn became an important strategic entrepreneur who influenced these changes in the Bank. One way of doing this was by hiring some dissidents of neoclassical economics such as Joseph Stiglitz as chief economist (1996–2000) who called for a post-Washington Consensus and blamed the IMF for the 1997–1998 East Asia crisis (Bedford, 2009: 203). Wolfensohn and Stiglitz wanted the institution to become a knowledge bank and to institutionalize poverty reduction as its first mandate (Hammer, 2013: 3). Strong strategic entrepreneurs could institutionalize new knowledge in which the market and the state were made complementary. This was archived in the World

[9] The president of the Bank, according to informal rules, has always been American—the USA being, the largest shareholder. The power he/she exercises has varied across time. Some presidents were merely figureheads and others influenced the development of the Bank. James Wolfensohn (1995–2005) belonged to the latter category. The Board of Governors—which includes member countries' elected ministers not paid by the Bank—elect the president. The Executive Directors serve the Board of Governors and oversee the day-to-day running of the Bank. They are elected or appointed by the countries' members and meet once or twice a week (Griffin, 2009: 91, 92).

Development Reports of 1999–2000 and 2000–2001, in which the Bank recognized that growth does not trickle down to the poor and embraced a comprehensive anti-poverty strategy including attention to the environment, HIV/AIDS, health, crime and violence, lack of freedom of choice, lack of self-confidence, and gender equality.[10]

Women and gender equality concerns became key in the World Bank's turn toward a more balanced development approach close to marginalized voices and lending social projects focused on poverty eradication "away from its traditional brick-and-mortar projects" (Bergeron, 2003: 405). This new approach carried a "feminist face" (Prügl, 2017, 2021). To mark this turn, Wolfensohn started his tenure by leading, for the first time, the World Bank delegation to the Fourth World Conference on Women, in Beijing in 1995 (Bedford, 2009: 11). As previously discussed, this conference was a watershed event for the promotion of gender equality and women's empowerment supported by global feminism. After the conference, the Bank increased spending on women's education to improve their market access, in line with the WID approach, but it also embraced the Gender and Development (GAD) approach targeting women as agents of development in, for example, microcredit lending programs (Bergeron, 2003: 405) and in CCTs.

Indeed, the Fourth International Conference on Women in Beijing institutionalized the GAD approach to development.[11] GAD promoted two strategies to tackle gender inequalities in development: women empowerment and gender mainstreaming. Development policies should empower women by providing them with resources so that they can have greater control over their own lives and determine the type of gender relations in which they want to live, and the strategies and alliances that enable them to achieve their goals (Kabeer, 1994: 97). Unlike the WID's exclusive focus on women, GAD aimed to integrate gender issues in all development policies through gender mainstreaming (Benería, 2003; Marques-Pereira, 2000). GAD was born in the1980s as a result of

[10] The Bank projects and loans also changed. While only 6% of Bank lending was in health, nutrition, and other services in the1980s, they reached 25% by the 2000s (Bedford, 2009: 6).

[11] For a critical examination of the institutionalization of GAD in international development organizations and agencies, see Marques-Pereira (2000), Calvès (2009), and Verschuur (2015).

postcolonial and Southern feminisms' criticisms of the WID approach[12] (McIlwaine & Datta, 2003: 371). GAD analyzed women and development in the context of social relations of gender, race, and class while taking into account the triple roles of Southern women accumulating productive, reproductive, and community work (Jaquette & Summerfield, 2006). GAD developed a more holistic perspective of social, political, and economic gender relations. In general, it has been less concerned with women than by the social construction of gender (Griffin, 2009: 122). However, the World Bank institutionalized GAD remaining close to WID.

Institutional and Organizational Changes to Include Gender Equality Concerns

Between 1995 and 2001, the institutionalization of GAD, and thus the attention paid to women and gender relations in the World Bank, saw an increase of 40% in project designs that included some considerations of gender equality (Bedford, 2009: 12). In addition, the Bank made internal institutional changes to recognize gender issues in its organization. In 1996, following the Fourth International Conference on Women, the gender policy created in 1994 became an "External Gender Consultative Board" and then a "Gender and Development Board" (known as the Gender Sector Board). Moreover, the Bank developed closer relations with feminist strategic gender equality entrepreneurs from NGOs and gender experts in academia (Bergeron, 2003). The institutionalization of GAD intensified in 1997 when the network Vice-Presidency "Poverty Reduction and Economic Management" (PREM), one of the most respected and credible vice-presidential units, made an institutional innovation by creating a GAD unit, despite being relatively tiny with

[12] DAWN (Development Alternative with Women for a New Era) network was the actor who articulated these critiques to WID. It was launched in 1984 by a group of women researchers and activists in Bangalore, India, to prepare the Third United Nations Conference on Women, to be held in Nairobi in 1985. They focused on the macroeconomic causes—famines, debt crises, militarism, and religious fundamentalism—as factors in the deterioration of the living conditions of women in Latin America, Asia, and Africa. DAWN represented feminist voices from the South and challenged the process of "othering" of so-called Third World women (Mohanty, 1984) and the colonialist views "deeply embedded within feminist and development epistemologies" (McIlwaine & Datta, 2003: 371). Influenced by intersectionality and postcolonialism studies, DAWN focused also on differences among women in the South in terms of class, nationality, and culture (Martinez, 2008: 79; Moser, 1993).

approximately ten staff members (Griffin, 2009: 130). Karen Mason, an economist recognized as a peer among Bank staff, was hired as the first director of this GAD unit in PREM from 1999 to 2005.[13]

The PREM was part of the Vice Presidencies Networks—substantive sectors of the World Bank—along with, for example, the Environmentally and Socially Sustainable Development Network (ESSD) (Griffin, 2009: 92). Their numbers have varied over time. Staff in these sectors have administrative, analytic, and operational activities and may have overlapping regional or cross-regional responsibilities (Hammer, 2013: 30). These operational staff—most of them economists or with a background in infrastructure, finance, energy, or nutrition—have research activities.[14] These details concerning the World Bank's administrative structure are important here because the PREM was the institutional site where CCTs were standardized.

Other dimensions of the World Bank's administrative organization institutionalized gender equality concerns. Alongside the substantive dimensions, the Bank is divided into geographic and hierarchical dimensions that are distinctive but overlapping. Six Regional Vice Presidencies correspond to six regions—Africa, Latin America and the Caribbean, Middle East and North Africa, and South Asia (Griffin, 2009: 93).[15] Each region appointed a gender coordinator to mainstream gender equality

[13] To trace this institutional evolution, see https://archivesholdings.worldbank.org/gender-and-development-sector, accessed July 2023.

[14] Other Vice Presidencies housed within the Bank include Chief Financial Officer, Finance and Private Sector, Controller and Development Economics (DEC). The DEC is of particular interest to me here because "the bulk (in budget, staff and output terms) of the research and data management activities of the Bank is conducted by the Development Economics (DEC) Vice Presidency" (Hammer, 2013: 30). Since 1980, the DEC has been the intellectual and epistemic center of neo-classically trained economists who have been the key writers of the *World Development Report* diffusing the bulk of Bank research on development. Social scientists are absent from the DEC. Economists control the main spaces of Bank intellectual production mainly in the DEC and are wary of social innovation (Hammer 2013: 30; Nay, 2020: 154; Nay, 2021: 42). According to Hammer (2013: 30), "ideas do not become part of the Bank establishment unless they can effectively penetrate the intellectual and organizational domain of the DEC".

[15] Wolfensohn's administration initiated this institutional innovation to concretize the shift to "participatory development" based on country ownership and knowledge sharing (Griffin, 2009: 93). Each country receiving loans from the World Bank has a Country Director who manages the loans and the Bank's projects in that country (Hammer, 2013: 30). All country offices operating in more than 100 countries employ approximately 3000 staff in which the majority are not hired locally (Griffin, 2009: 92, 93).

concerns throughout operational activities (Bedford, 2009: 12). In 1996, Wolfensohn announced a new matrix organization in which sectors and regions would intersect. Therefore, gender specialists were to work in the GAD Unit situated within the PREM Network but also in other networks such as the ESSD and also in sectors situated within the larger networks (e.g., the post-conflict sector situated within the ESSD). Gender specialists would also be active in country offices (Griffin, 2009: 92, 130). This was the first step to mainstreaming gender within the World Bank that implied an important workload on the shoulder of gender experts as strategic gender equality entrepreneurs in the World Bank.

The last but nonetheless important dimension of the Bank's administrative organization involved the functional and hierarchical aspects of each sector and country. The distance between Washington DC and the Bank's in-country operations could greatly limit the Bank's engagement with gender equality. Staff rewards are based on the volume of loans on offer and the size of projects brokered leading to standardized and scaled-up projects (e.g., in the case of CCTs). These requirements are not conducive to doing the kind of high-quality research work needed in gender policies that so depend on context. In addition, the Bank has tried to make its internal bureaucracy work like a competitive labor market. Staff must allocate their time to budget codes, a few of which they control. Then, they must sell their time like consultants do, without time to read new knowledge and information (Hammer, 2013: 31) about gender relations for example.

Lastly, the Bank has concretized its equal opportunities agenda by hiring more women. Between 1995 and 2004, the number of women in key professional grades increased from 31 to 42% and in key management and senior technical grades from 13 to 25% (Bedford, 2009: 12). Currently, the World Bank has approximately 10 000 employees and 120 offices in the World (Noy, 2017: 6). However, "nearly three-quarters of employees are based in Washington DC" (Hammer, 2013: 30) and most staff, if they are not Western nationals themselves, have studied in the highest major Western universities. In addition, approximately 80% of this staff hold a Ph.D., participating in the highly technocratic nature of the Bank. If more women and more non-Western nationals are working at the Bank than ever before, few of them occupy senior management positions with power (Griffin, 2009: 99, 100).

During Wolfensohn's era, in its policies and research activities, the Bank recognized that women paid high social costs for some of its programs along with other populations defined as vulnerable such as Indigenous and ethnic minorities. Therefore, gender equality became a major social factor to archiving growth and equity. In 2001, the Bank adopted a "gender mainstreaming strategy" defined as the inclusion of gender and women's needs in all aspects of the Bank's operations. Under Karen Mason's lead, the GAD unit in the PREM produced two publications[16] providing a detailed framework about how gender should be institutionalized into Bank operations at the level of country director, sector managers, and task teams.[17] The objective of this strategy was to make "the business case[18] for mainstreaming gender, contending that equality is an issue of development effectiveness" (Griffin, 2009: 126). In line with human development knowledge developed by Sen (1999) and appropriated and institutionalized by the Bank, women needed not just economic aid—as promoted by the WID approach—but also social opportunities, political rights, and the right to live without violence and to be able to shape their lives. Most of the Bank's research and knowledge production and policies focused on women at the micro-level as potential drivers of development. Whereas WID policies had given education, land rights, and seed to rural and poor women, in the GAD approach, the Bank ensured that the money was placed directly into women's hands in social situations where men, in general, controlled the income to increase women social capital and autonomy (Bergeron, 2003: 405–407). This was the case with microcredit and CCTs.

Even when the presidency changed from Wolfensohn to Paul Wolfowitz in 2006—who was a neoconservative and an architect of the USA's war in Iraq—the Bank saw few drastic institutional and ideational changes (Hammer, 2013). While the World Bank tried to institutionalize the GAD approach, it was difficult to get away from the WID ideas that resonated much more with its economist commitments. WID remained

[16] Mason, Andrew D. and Elizabeth M. King, 2001, Engendering development through gender equality in rights, resources, and voice, World Bank; PREM, 2002, Integrating Gender into the World Bank's Work: A Strategy for Action, strategy paper, World Bank.

[17] Gender and Development—World Bank Group Archives Catalog, accessed January 2023.

[18] Ferguson (2015: 380) testified to "the messy business of working as a gender expert in international development" that has to work inside the framework of a "business case" for gender equality. She underlined the feelings, contradictions, complexities, and tensions, as a feminist and "gender expert", to have to work in this paradigm.

a very strong institutional legacy in the World Bank that was difficult to overthrow. For example, in 2005, the new Head of the GAD unit, Mayra Buvinic, was known for her commitment to the WID approach in development. In 2006, the Bank produced its most comprehensive policy paper about gender, titled "Engendering Development", which positioned the Bank as a "knowledge bank" and "the disseminator of 'good practices' on gender in the development community" (Bedford, 2009: 13). In the same vein, in 2007, the World Bank launched the "Gender Action Plan" with the subtitle "Gender Equality as Smart Economics" (Griffin, 2009: 127, 129) in which the Bank developed and institutionalized its instrumentalist views of gender equality based on knowledge production: it is smart economics to invest in gender equality because it promotes shared growth and development for all. Gender equality as smart economy was the case for the World Bank when it standardized CCTs as the new model with which to fight poverty, as the next sections demonstrate.

CCTs and Gendered Standardization by the World Bank[19]

Based on Mexico's *Progresa* and Brazil's *Bolsa Família*, the World Bank has standardized CCTs as a model to be replicated worldwide (Leisering, 2019: 121–123). In this process, "the World Bank and its allies have been proactive, if not hyperactive, in promoting their versions of 'best practice' in the field of new-generation social policies" (Peck & Theodore, 2015: 91). Indeed, the World Bank turned "local ideas and practices into a 'standard model'" (Ancelovici & Jenson, 2013: 294). As seen in the theoretical chapter, the standardization of CCTs by the World Bank implied three subprocesses: certification, decontextualization, and framing that were interrelated, not linear, overlapping, and synchronized. In this section, I argue that strategic entrepreneurs, institutional legacies and venues, and knowledge contributed to gender equality goal erasure from the standard CCT model. First, strategic entrepreneurs involved in standardization were gendered humans, mostly socialized as men with economist training but without much knowledge about gender studies and gender equality. Second, they worked in an institutional site—the PREM—without strong coordination with the GAD unit despite this unit

[19] This section is a revision and an improvement of Nagels (2021).

being part of the PREM. Third, they used knowledge to certify, decontextualize, and frame CCTs as a model of poverty reduction strategy without the need for any gender equality goals. Constrained by a strong WID institutional legacy, strategic entrepreneurs in the World Bank framed the CCT standard model with causal correlations between transferring cash to mothers and the improved well-being of children and the reduction of poverty that are based on instrumentalist views of gender relations. The outcome of the standardization mechanism is therefore the exclusion of gender equality goals in the standard CCT model and the reinforcement of the traditional gendered division of labor. In this model, women were solely seen as mothers and sole caregivers of children.

CCT Certification Without Gender Equality Concerns

While, as I demonstrated in the previous chapter, *Progresa* and *Bolsa Família* were "homegrown" solutions to domestic problems, the World Bank played a key role in the expansion of CCTs, first in Latin America and after in the entire world (Brooks, 2015; Jenson & Nagels, 2018; Jenson, 2009; Leisering, 2019; Martínez Franzoni & Voorend, 2011; Osorio Gonnet, 2017; Peck & Theodore, 2015; Sugiyama, 2011; Teichman, 2007). One of *Progresa*'s designers emphasized the role played by the Banks:

> The World Bank and the IADB are transmission belts that, through their different frameworks, spread the word throughout the world and the truth is that they did it very well (...) And the truth is that it is an extraordinary success story that barely 20 years later, [CCTs] have become perhaps the most powerful intervention in social policy in developing countries or even in developed countries, in specific cities such as New York. (Pablo)

The first step of the standardization was to certify CCTs as the best tool with which to fight poverty and not as a means of reducing gender inequalities. The World Bank achieved this by promoting evidence showing that CCTs reduce poverty and improve long-term economic growth. The World Bank got access to this information because, as shown in the previous chapter, *Progresa* and *Bolsa Família* cooks had links and exchanged information with the World Bank (Ancelovici & Jenson, 2013; Peck & Theodore, 2015). As shown by the disparity in the number of references to *Progresa* and *Bolsa Família* in the World Bank website

(Borge, 2022: 123), the World Bank preferred the first to the second recipe for its strict conditions, its focus on human development, and its reliance on evaluations. Indeed, as seen in the previous chapter, evaluations of *Progresa*'s results were a requirement in *Progresa*'s design (DOF, 1999). The World Bank rapidly gave attention to this requirement and the first *Progresa* evaluations (Adato et al., 2000; SDS, 1999) but without attention to evaluations about *Progresa*'s negative impacts on gender relations (e.g., González de la Rocha, 2000).

Since 2004, the World Bank began to produce knowledge on CCTs through its publications of evaluations, relying on statistical evidence, that stressed their positive impacts on economic growth, education, health, and poverty but remained mostly silent about gender relations (Fiszbein & Schady, 2009; Rawlings, 2004; Skoufias, 2005).[20]

Evaluations became a trademark of CCTs, and the World Bank used it to literally certify CCTs as the standard model for reducing poverty, but around gender inequalities there is silence. The knowledge production aimed to prove to Latin American technocrats and policymakers that these programs were effective so that they could "identify them as the new professional norm within the development community" (Sugiyama, 2011: 262). This knowledge was essential in the legitimation and expansion of CCTs throughout Latin America and beyond (Foli et al., 2018: 8), as a high-ranking official at the IADB and former *Progresa*'s director confirms:

> Because it was growing, more people were doing evaluations, more people were participating. The academics, the academic people who participated in the program also helped a lot [...]. Paul Gertler,[21] for example – he helped a lot because he started writing papers in academic journals. (Victor)

Certification legitimized CCTs by giving them credibility and diffusing this knowledge. For that, the World Bank shaped CCT networks by

[20] As seen in the introduction, the academic research and policy-driven research have followed this trend of analyzing the scope and the effectiveness of these programs (e.g., Adato et al., 2000; Barrientos & Dejong, 2006; Lomeli, 2008; Villatoro, 2004).

[21] Paul Gertler is a professor of economics at the University of California, Berkeley, USA: [He] was Chief Economist of the Human Development Network of the World Bank from 2004–2007 and the Founding Chair of the Board of Directors of the International Initiative for Impact Evaluation (3ie) from 2009 to 2012. At the World Bank, he led an effort to institutionalize and scale up impact evaluation for learning what works in human development (Gertler, n.d.). https://www.paulgertler.com/bio--cv.html.

funding meetings, workshops, conferences, and trips that connected CCT policymakers throughout Latin America without any intention to include its GAD unit, gender experts, and feminist actors of women's institutional machineries from Latin America. One BF's operator explained that the World Bank was specifically, and not Brazilian policymakers, first to certify and promote *Bolsa Família* and CCTs:

> The World Bank supported a lot by providing credibility. That was not us wanting to say it's going well. We never said that everything is fine, things are going well. It was the World Bank promoting dialogue, bringing people from outside, inviting people out in international forums and, doing studies, presenting reports. That was an important contribution. (Julián)

The "objective of these events was to learn from past experiences, as they featured case studies from early adoption of a variety of CCT designs" (Brooks, 2015, 560). For example, the social protection division (PREM) of the World Bank organized three international conferences on CCTs without any attention (for example, a panel or two during the conferences) given to gender relations: in 2002 in Puebla, Mexico; in 2004 in Sao Paulo, Brazil; and in 2006 in Istanbul, Turkey. Around 200 people gathered at each event, from eight countries at the first event, 25 at the second one, and 40 at the third. Alongside national CCT directors, designers, and implementers, the World Bank repeatedly invited international experts on CCTs to these meetings such as Norbert Schady from the World Bank and gender experts such as Michelle Adato from the IFPRI (Osorio Gonnet, 2017: 90). Nevertheless, gender experts were marginal in these events and did not advocate for integrating gender equality goals in the standard model, since, as will be unpacked later in this chapter, they were not convinced by the CCT impacts on gender relations (e.g., Adato et al., 2000).

Finally, the WB funded "study trips" and "expert trips". It sent CCT newcomer policymakers from social affairs ministries and not gender institutional machineries to visit and learn about the first CCT programs in Mexico, Brazil, and Colombia, exchanging knowledge and generating trust. As one *Progresa* designer states:

> The multilateral was useful as a [promotion] mechanism [...] many times people from the World Bank or the IDB asked us if we would receive a

> mission from the government of Honduras, a mission from the government of Colombia, a mission from the government here [United States] [...]. They came to Mexico, and we explained to them, I came to Washington many times to the World Bank and the IDB, [...] to present *Progresa*. [...] Once the director of the Colombian Ministry of Planning, Mauricio Cardenas, came to see me [...] and I convinced him to implement *Famílias en Acción* in Colombia [the Colombian CCT]. And then I have talked, I mean I talked to many presidents in the region. I spoke with the president of Peru... [Therefore, the role of the banks was one of] information transmitters. [...] Honest advisors, honest brokers. (Victor)

The Bank also sent CCT international and national technocrats—but the most famous were not the ones who had pushed for gender equality goals in Mexico for example, such as Gómez de León or members of his CONAPO team—to support the design and/or the implementation of new CCT programs (Osorio Gonnet, 2017: 91). As another *Progresa* cook explains:

> I went to Argentina three times, the IDB took me, or the World Bank took me, I don't know which of the two, three times to Argentina to try to get this thing. (Matías)

The role of international organizations in CCT expansion has also played out through their staff but with none a gender expert or coming from the GAD unit. Some actors, such as Paul Gertler, Ariel Fizbein,[22]

[22] "Ariel Fizbein has a PhD in economics from the University of California, Berkeley. He joined the World Bank in 1991. He has held several positions [...]. In the latter position, he coordinated the Bank's Development Impact Evaluation (DIME) initiative for several years." http://blogs.worldbank.org/fr/team/ariel-fiszbein, accessed September 2018.

Norbert Schady,[23] Santiago Levy,[24] Rogelio Gómez Hermosillo,[25] Manuel Salazar,[26] Graziano da Silva,[27] Emmanuel Skoufias,[28] and Veronica Silva Villalobos,[29] are among the most important strategic CCT entrepreneurs in the Latin American CCT networks. They have spread the word around the continent about the effectiveness of CCTs. For example, Paul Gertler, an economist from Berkeley and without gender expertise, coordinated the first *Progresa* evaluation impact led by IFPRI and has since become an influential member of the CCT diffusion networks. Some of these individuals were among the designers of the first programs in Mexico, Brazil, Colombia, and Chile, and the World Bank hired them for their high profile and their knowledge of CCTs (Osorio Gonnet, 2017:

[23] "Norbert Schady is the Principal Economic Advisor for the Social Sector at the Inter-American Development Bank (IADB). He holds a bachelor's degree from Yale University and a Ph.D. from Princeton University. In addition to the IADB, Dr. Schady has worked at the World Bank." https://blogs.worldbank.org/fr/team/norbert-schady, accessed September 2018.

[24] "Mexican economist Santiago Levy Algazi became the Vice President for Sector and Knowledge on March 1, 2008. (...) From 1994 to 2000, Levy served as the Deputy Minister at the Ministry of Finance and Public Credit of Mexico, becoming the main architect of the renowned social program *Progresa-Oportunidades* that benefits the poor." https://www.iadb.org/en/about-us/departments/biographies/santiago-levy-algazi, accessed September 2018.

[25] Sociologist. National coordinator of *Oportunidades* between 2001 and 2006. From 2007 is international consultant for the World Bank. http://media.wix.com/ugd/6a289c_c2340fda24e04d35993ad9396cea528d.pdf, accessed 25 September 2018.

[26] Economist. Director of Família en Acción Colombia. World Bank staff from 2002 (Osorio Gonnet, 2017: 105).

[27] Agronomist. Between 2003 and 2004, he has been Extraordinary Minister of Food Security in Brazil and responsible for the implementation of the program "Hambre Zero", a precursor of Bolsa Família. Since 2011, he is General Director of Food and Agriculture Organization (FAO). http://www.fao.org/about/who-we-are/director-gen/biography/en/, accessed September 2018.

[28] Economist. "Emmanuel Skoufias is a Lead Economist at the Poverty Reduction Group of the World Bank. He specializes in impact evaluation, targeting, poverty measurement [...]. Other experience at the Bank includes a senior appointment at the Poverty and Gender Group in the Latin American and Caribbean Region. Prior to joining the Bank, Emmanuel worked at the Research Department of the Inter-American Development Bank (IADB) and at the International Food Policy Research Institute (IFPRI)." https://live.worldbank.org/experts/emmanuel-skoufias, accessed September 2018.

[29] Social worker. From 2001 on director of the Chilean program *Fondo de Solidaridad Social*. Following this, she entered the World Bank as an expert in social protection in Latin America (Osorio Gonnet, 2017: 105).

84, 85). Mexican *Progresa* cooks took an especially important role in the standardization process led by the World Bank because, as I showed in the previous chapter, lots of Mexican policymakers, policy entrepreneurs, and even presidents, such as Zedillo, studied at American universities (Borges, 2022: 123). For example, Santiago Levy was among the first to diffuse *Progresa*'s positive evaluation within and outside of Mexico. During the cooking sequence of the program, he was influenced by the World Bank where he had worked as a visiting researcher during the 1990s. In the CCT standardization sequence, he worked hand in hand with the World Bank and in 2007, the IADB hired him as the vice president of the Knowledge, Innovation and Communication Sector. The profile of these CCT strategic entrepreneurs as international organizations' experts and former CCT policymakers but without gender training has helped knowledge circulation and has improved CCT legitimacy for newcomers to CCT implementation (Osorio Gonnet, 2017: 88). Moreover, the World Bank established the name "CCT" as a brand "with global conferences and networks of experts designed to spread the concept of CCT" (Von Gliszczynski & Leisering, 2016: 335).

Lastly, to certify, legitimize, and promote CCT around the world, the World Bank supported Brazilian South–South cooperation in a bid for horizontal cooperation in which Brazil under Lula's administration (2003–2011) was very active (Ancelovici & Jenson, 2013; Leite et al., 2015). While Mexican cooks promoted *Progresa* on behalf of the World Bank and the IADB, Lula's administration made *Bolsa Família* a central part of his foreign policy. It provided technical cooperation for social policy in Africa and Latin America and the MDS created a department to promote *Bolsa Família* abroad and to address queries from foreign governments and international institutions (Borges, 2022: 128). Without involving Brazilian entrepreneurs or institutions that had advocated for implicit gender equality goals in *Bolsa Família*, the Lula administration and the Bank organized meetings and knowledge exchanges (Peck & Theodore, 2015: 111–122) by, for example, sponsoring events at which *Bolsa Família* representatives presented their experiences to other state officials in African countries speaking Portuguese (Leite et al., 2015: 1449, 1454).

Gendered Decontextualization and Framing

The World Bank certified the new instrument while decontextualizing it from the Brazilian and Mexican experiences and framed a standard model with a rationale that lacked gender equality goals and enforced an instrumentalist view of gender relations. This could be explained by (1) institutional legacies of gender-discriminatory norms in implementers' countries and (2) knowledge showing mixed results of CCTs on the matter of gender relations and (3) asymmetries among strategic entrepreneurs holding different knowledge and marginalizing gender research and gender equality entrepreneurs.

Institutional Legacies of Gender-Discriminatory Norms

Although *Progresa*'s design included explicit gender equality goals and the *Bolsa Família* design implicit ones, these goals were absent from the World Bank's standardized CCT model. This standardization implied the decontextualization of Mexican and Brazilian experiences. In this standard model, cash transfers served to enhance the well-being of children in general—and not in particular to girls as in Mexico—and to poor families—and not to empower women within them as in Mexico and Brazil. The first reason lies in the institutional legacies of gender-discriminatory norms in implementer countries that the World Bank had no intention of overthrowing. The World Bank bought the CCTs as a good "product" to sell to developing countries because the cash is invested in children and not just given to the poor (Osorio Gonnet, 2017: 84–85). In this they followed the social investment perspective according to which the investment in children leads to economic growth (Jenson & Mahon, 2022; Nagels, 2016; Von Gliszczynski & Leisering, 2016).

In line with the social investment perspective, the evaluations of *Progresa* have shown that investing in girls was more effective than investing in women. However, the World Bank eliminated both gender equality objectives—for girls and women—from the standard model. *Progresa*'s and *Bolsa Família*'s impact evaluations emphasized progress in children's education and health, and sometimes in adult women in the case of *Bolsa Família*. More precisely, positive discrimination toward girls in Mexico has proven to be effective in closing the gender educational gap and in enhancing girls' self-esteem (e.g., Levy, 2006: 63, 64), as underlined by a high-ranking official at the IADB and *Progresa* cook:

> [N]ow the expectations and aspirations of girls, this is very important. The expectations and aspirations of girls are now radically different. Now you have girls who aspire to be doctors, or girls who aspire to study at the university. In rural communities, when her mother did not finish primary school, that's [incredible]. (Victor)

CCT international entrepreneurs explained the elimination of positive discrimination toward girls and more broadly the erasure of gender equality goals in standard CCTs by way of institutional legacies of gender-discriminatory norms and priorities in countries where CCTs were to be implemented. While transferring more cash to girls than boys for schooling demonstrated positive impacts in terms of gender equality, CCT international entrepreneurs left the choice to national policymakers whether to include positive discrimination for girls in schools depending on the gender educational gap. As the same person underlined:

> [I]n general, what the programs do is increase school attendance. Sometimes more boys or more girls. Sometimes more in primary or secondary school. This depends a little bit from country to country and also depends a bit on the amounts of the scholarships. Because of the opportunity cost of the children, the opportunity cost of the girls differs in one or the other. So, here is a variation from country to country. (Victor)

A senior economist at the World Bank and author of leading CCT evaluations confirmed that the abandonment of the gender equality goal was not a World Bank strategy but rather it depends on certain countries, "I don't think it was a Bank sort of explicit strategy to do that, it was more a country specific choice not to do that" (Arthur).

According to Mexican *Progresa* cooks who have traveled to "sell" CCTs in Latin America to national translators, the gender component was a more difficult sell to national designers:

> [A]round the program there has been an interest in bringing these elements of gender equality into the design, but the countries do not buy them… [because] in the Central American countries [for example, they are] a bit more conservative in this matter. (Beatriz)

According to one of the first *Oportunidades* directors, who has promoted CCTs internationally, national CCT translators were reluctant to include a gender perspective because they are men whose primary concern was reinforcing discriminatory budget even if they could express gender awareness in their discourses:

> There are discourses but when it comes to money, it is not easy. In other words, to translate politics into something more than intentions and declarations and discourses, as far as I can remember, we have not achieved almost any program that has this focus [on gender].... We had separated data [for men and women, but] we did not understand, we are macho men. The issue is basically the budget. That is, if you offer them a gender perspective that does not cost, they will accept it but cervical cancer prevention and differentiated scholarships cost money. (Hector)

While evaluations have shown positive results for positive discrimination for girls in school in Mexico, the World Bank has not included this recipe's ingredient in its standard CCT model. According to the Bank, evaluations have not been sufficient to mandate this measure, and thus the World Bank left the choice to implement it to national translators. According to international CCT advocates, these national policymakers have rejected gender goals because of their institutional legacies of gender-discriminatory norms and priorities. While the World Bank alters countries' norms and priorities through the propagation of CCTs, with conditions and targeting for example, this has not extended to gender equality.

Knowledge: CCT Mixed Results on Gender Relations

In the main international evaluations of CCTs, there was skepticism as to whether the program led to changes in gender relations among adults even if some *Bolsa Família* international evaluations, mostly produced by the World Bank (2010), showed that the transfers to women increase their self-esteem, empowerment, and intra-household bargaining power. *Bolsa Família* seems to have better results on gender equality than other CCTs on account of its generosity, large coverage, and soft conditions (e.g., De Brauw et al., 2014; Hunter et al., 2021; Sugiyama & Hunter, 2014). However, these evaluations were residual and concentrated in *Bolsa Família* and did not concern *Progresa* and other CCTs. For example, the first randomized evaluation trial on *Progresa* led by the International Food Policy Research Institute in 2000 placed hopes for gender equality in the future, because existing evidence showed the limited impact of the gender equality mandate. Gender equality was "fostered, if at a low level, by a discourse within *Progresa* communities around gender issues" (Adato et al., 2000: xix).

Based on this evidence, the World Bank framed the standard CCT model erasing gender equality objectives that were present explicitly in *Progresa* and implicitly in *Bolsa Família*. Three important World Bank publications framed the standard model: Rawling (2004); Skoufias (2005); and Fiszbein and Schady (2009). Rawling (2004) was the Social Safety Primer on CCTs that expressed the official position of the World Bank. It is a summary of "consensus among the World Bank safety nets team and general practitioners on good practice and policy" (Rawling, 2004). It illustrates that the World Bank weakened gender equality objectives in the framing of CCTs as a model by the very fact of its limited references to gender and women's empowerment. Women's empowerment was only mentioned twice in *Progresa* by discussing recipient participation in community activities and managing the program (Rawlings, 2004: 11, 17). First, the document stresses that the "provision of the grants to mothers in the household (…) has introduced changes in empowerment dynamics that are playing out in the household and communities" (Rawlings, 2004: 11). Second, it claims that the CCT program, by setting up "channels through groups of mothers' representatives (…) has led to the empowerment of women" (Rawlings, 2004: 17). Thus, in this document, "agreement was clearly that gender empowerment was not a priority" (Jenson & Nagels, 2018: 329). The mixed results of CCTs on gender relations explained the elimination of gender equality objectives. The subsequent World Bank evaluation of *Progresa*—Skoufias (2005)—summarizes these mixed results:

> Because responses about girls' education were far stronger than statements about *Progresa*'s effect on women's position within the household, it is thought that *Progresa* will have a far stronger secondary effect on household relationships through the next generation than the program is having on this one. (Skoufias, 2005: 61)

Therefore, the much-cited 2009 Fiszbein and Schady's book institutionalized the instrumentalist rationale about gender relations. It expresses the official position of the World Bank about CCTs providing a strong rationale for CCT implementation with all the information and evidence on CCTs available at that time (Leisering, 2019: 122). It argues that "making payments to mothers also resonates with well-accepted beliefs (mostly supported by evidence, as shown above) that women will tend to put funds to better use than will men" (Fiszbein & Schady, 2009: 11). With Fiszbein and Schady's report of 2009 the World Bank framed the CCTs as a standard model. This report expressed the official position of the World Bank on CCTs: they are the best strategy for fighting poverty without concerns for gender inequalities. Since this report, CCTs became part of the World Bank's mandate, and the World Bank "was the main advocate of CCTs" (Leisering, 2019: 122). Fiszbein and Schady's report refuted gender equality goals because, in the foreword, they expressed their doubts as to whether transfers to mothers altered gender relations and increased women's bargaining power inside the household (Fiszbein et al., 2009: xii).

With CCT randomized evaluations showing mixed results on gender relations, CCT entrepreneurs in the World Bank abandoned larger concerns about reducing inequalities between women and men and between girls and boys. They framed a standard CCT model retaining only an instrumentalist perspective on gender recognizing only the rational and the causal correlations that transferring cash to mothers maximizes children's outcomes because mothers are better spenders than fathers when it comes to children (Holmes et al., 2010: 3). This resonates with the notion of gender as "smart economics" that is so profoundly rooted in the WID institutional legacy at the World Bank. As underlined by Chant (2016: 7), for CCT entrepreneurs, "women are expected to make sacrifices for future generations".

Interestingly, Brazilian policymakers reproduced the framing of the standard CCT model when they promoted *Bolsa Família* internationally, mostly in Portuguese-speaking African countries. Brazilian politicians and technocrats reproduced the confusion about gender equality goals and instrumentalist views of gender relations. For example, when promoting *Bolsa Família* in African countries, Antônio Claret as manager director of *Bolsa Família*, and Camile Mesquita as chief operator of MDS, pointed out that *Bolsa Família* has had "a direct impact on its first goal to reduce extreme poverty as well as on objectives linked to education, health, and gender equality because 93% of cash beneficiaries are women" (Tribuna PR, 2005). This Brazilian position shows that framing, certifying, and decontextualization processes are overlapping and simultaneous. When Brazilian CCT cooks became international CCT entrepreneurs, they promoted the CCT standard model framed by the World Bank in terms of gender and therefore repeated the instrumental view on gender relations and gender equality.[30] Gender equality goals were no more related to equality between girls and boys or to women's empowerment but concerned only with the simple fact of transferring cash to women. This transfer was framed and disseminated by the World Bank as a gender equality goal per se[31] (World Bank, 2010).

Asymmetries Among Policy Entrepreneurs and Their Knowledge

Faced with the mixed gender impacts of CCTs, international CCT entrepreneurs preferred to remove gender goals in the program design to avoid setting "program standards that would be likely only to 'fail'" (Jenson & Nagels, 2018: 328). In the process of framing, including decontextualization that involved shortcuts and simplification from the original experiences, the World Bank erased gender equality goals by marginalizing gender knowledge and experts.[32] In doing so, the Bank reproduced gender inequalities. The World Bank mainly published quantitative evidence that shares success stories while dismissing feminist and gender knowledge and research as unscientific. This selection in the process of publication is political since it depends not on the intrinsic superiority of one kind of knowledge over another but on power relations between institutional sites and actors producing this knowledge. Indeed, the World Bank's organizational structures allocate few human and financial resources to the cross-sectoral gender unit in comparison with economics-based networks.

[30] Although the version of *Bolsa Família* that they promoted was closer to a basic universal income, with its soft conditions and huge coverage (Borges, 2022).

[31] https://documents1.worldbank.org/curated/en/500031468015635584/pdf/IPP3820P1015041A1IPP1English0oct015.pdf, accessed February 2024.

[32] My argument is not about the intentions of the World Bank. I do not know if the World Bank intentionally excluded gender experts and their knowledge when standardizing CCTs, for example, without inviting them to the meetings debating on CCTs. However, this section shows that strategic gender equality entrepreneurs from the GAD unit in the PREM were absent from these meetings and that the huge amount of World Bank publications on CCTs did not make any references to feminist and gender knowledge. There is thus a correlation here between this persistent exclusion and the negative outcomes of CCTs on gender relations (e.g., Escobar Latapí & González de la Rocha, 2004; González de la Rocha, 2000, 2006; Molyneux, 2006; Tabbush, 2010).

Knowledge was crucial, not only to certify the standard CCT model and to legitimize it internationally but also to frame it without gender equality goals. Knowledge production was key to the process of decontextualization and framing by weakening the political and social dimensions that are central to the concept of gender and to understanding relations between women and men. Since measurement became an obsession (Liebowitz & Zwingel, 2014) in development policies led by the World Bank, the production of evidence was primordial. The evidence (or the absence of evidence) goes a long way to explaining the abandonment of the gender goal in the design of the standard CCTs model. The problem is the absence of "good" gender indicators, as a *Progresa* cook points out:

> Why have other countries not incorporated these aspects? It's because we have not built that information that sometimes leads us to make public policy, right? [...] I think that if we had had other tools, it would have been easier to sell the gender goal to other countries. (Beatriz)

In the framing of CCTs as a standard model, the World Bank retained specific forms of knowledge and not others: the evaluations establishing causal correlations between giving cash to women and the reduction of poverty. A former World Bank staff member and author of leading CCT evaluations outlined the role of economic and academic knowledge around the question of CCTs:

> What was influential was the fact that economists bought the idea of these programs and that has and has had influence in several ways. On the one hand, obviously, [it has influence] on the ministries of economy, finance... because... I think that the evaluation and the fact that it has an evaluation gave it a strong recognition... I think that the influence of the economist community was very important [in the dissemination]. (Gabriel)

A senior economist and author of leading CCT evaluations at the World Bank also attributed the success of CCTs to economic evaluations, and more precisely to the randomized studies led by Massachusetts Institute of Technology (MIT) with Esther Duflot and Abhijit Banerjee and their consultancy company, "the Abdul Latif Jameel Poverty Action Lab" evaluating poverty programs. *Progresa*, with its indicators and poverty lines, was their first experiment:

> The impacts of these programs were disseminated, but this was mostly at academic conferences [...] to provide supporting evidence or supporting information, like, "Look, these programs are doing what they're supposed to be doing so you can get the whole package here." [...] [O]ver the past 15–20 years, program evaluation has become very big – well, actually the main activity of professional economists. You have people like Esther Duflot, and famous economists at MIT [...] There are two pioneers [...]. Well, they sort of managed to shift the emphasis of the profession from doing what it was doing, mostly, to using randomized controlled trials for learning about what works or doesn't, especially about development [...]. And initially in the first few years – let's say between 2000 and 2008, 2009, 2010 – a lot of this work was done with CCTs because of *Progresa*'s example. (Arthur)

Despite evaluation and knowledge being crucial to the framing of the standard CCT, the World Bank did not attach the same value to all forms of knowledge. It valorized economic academics and quantitative evaluations over local or qualitative knowledge. However, the forms of mostly quantitative (numerical) measurement that are privileged lack "the detailed particulars of context and history" (Merry, 2011: 84) and thus have implications for power relations—including gender relations—that merit investigation. International evaluations based on quantitative indicators are widely accepted as "scientific" and "objective" even if their construction remains opaque. These indicators—such as in health or education in the case of CCTs—"rely on the magic of numbers and the appearance of certainty and objectivity that they convey. A key dimension of the power of indicators is their capacity to convert complicated contextually variable phenomena into unambiguous, clear, and impersonal measures" (Merry, 2011: 84). Gender analysis has pointed out that this simplification is particularly problematic to understanding gender relations because it "results from the exclusion of social dimensions that cannot easily be translated into categories, not because they are unimportant, but because they are complex and fluid" (Liebowitz & Zwingel, 2014: 365). Gender research has shown that gender relations are complex, multiple, and linked to other axes of domination such as class, race, sexuality, ethnicity, religion, and ability. Quantitative indicators do not adequately consider these complexities.

Therefore, researchers and publications on CCTs constructed "positive results" in which "gender objectives" have not been clearly distinguishable. The publication processes in the World Bank implied that selection and "findings have to be endlessly rewritten and reshaped to be published or adopted" (Cornwall et al., 2008: 8). For the World Bank, "success stories" are much more likely to be published and diffused than "mixed results", leading to a "one-size-fits-all" approach that fails to take into account national specificities. As a senior economist and researcher at the World Bank stresses:

> They are modes. [...] [A]ll of a sudden in the African region, for example, they make public works and conditional cash transfers – in every country, the same program! It's incredible! Ultimately, it's not based on something that says that it works better. [...] [because] there are publication biases. [...] [the program] must always have [positive] impacts. You never read a study that has no impact. In academic journals, it does not exist. And then, based on one or two studies that are published, the whole policy is based! [...] [There are biases in] what is selected, or even by the researchers, the researchers want to be well published, and then they want to have [studies showing positive] impacts. [...] The stuff like J-PAL. [...] Esther Duflot, blah blah. So, they do, I do not know, 10,000 assessments all the time! They have all the students and everything, but [...] most are thrown out! Because there are no impacts, because it did not work.... (Carol)

The World Bank positions itself as a "knowledge bank" (Hammer, 2013; Leisering, 2019) that frames its policies on the basis of evidence. However, biases permeate knowledge production at the Bank by promoting "success stories" and erasing all complexities, mixed or failed results. As the same researcher in the WB underlines:

> What comes out [of the publications], what we see, are [the evaluations] where the impacts are strong, where you can tell a success story... [T]hat's what the people who build policies...see. We do not know the number where it did not work. All we know is that it worked there [in one case]....[W]e are governed by what is published, and it is a big problem [...]. Ah, it's so irritating! [laughs] Because that determines the development and what we do [...] The problem is that sometimes we [the members of the Research Unit at the World Bank] have problems [because our publications] everything must be accepted by the operation [operational units of the World Bank]. So, I come out of a period where I have a paper that [...]. It took five months for them to accept. [...] And everything they do there, in the operations, is often something that we invented here [in the research unit] [...] after a while it will be necessary to say:

> "That's stupid to do that," but for now, people like me, we're persona non grata. (Carol)

Paradoxically, evidence-based policies so widely promoted by the World Bank are based on false evidence, or ignorance, because nothing is known of those policies or elements in them that failed or produced mixed results. Primarily, development policies have not emerged from a completely objective evaluation of the evidence; instead, they have been predominantly shaped by knowledge production that is deeply influenced by power dynamics. CCT evaluations have thus privileged neoclassical economics while they have ignored qualitative and gender knowledge—such as the focus on the added unpaid work burdens that conditionalities very often impose on mothers (González de la Rocha, 2000, 2006; Molyneux, 2006; Nagels, 2016; Tabbush, 2010). These are not referred to in the World Bank's huge repository of publications on CCTs. An illustration of this limited gaze can be found in Cookson's study (2018: 52–57), where Peruvian CCT evaluations portrayed the program as a success due to certain quantitative indicators showing improvements in school attendance and health check-ups for children. However, these assessments overlooked the significant shortcomings in the quality of health and education services provided. Additionally, they neglected to acknowledge the substantial burden of unpaid work imposed on women recipients expected to meet the program's conditions.

Understanding how the World Bank produces knowledge gives us clues as to why feminist knowledge and gender knowledge have been marginalized. Framing depends on political power and power asymmetries between actors, hierarchies between disciplines, and the organizational structures of the World Bank contributed to gender equality goal erasure in its standard CCT model. The following example highlights the lack of serious consideration for feminist research and knowledge on gender at the World Bank. As this senior economist and author of prominent CCT evaluations within the institution asserts:

> I mean, to some extent, it does [reproduce traditional gender roles], obviously you know, but…I haven't thought about it really. The least of my concern – as a conservative man actually, I've been excluded from the…program [laughs], like reverse discrimination [laughs]. I don't think that's something to take seriously, you know. (Arthur)

The power asymmetries at the World Bank between economists and gender researchers with humanities diplomas in academia determined the selection and production of knowledge for the CCT redesign and framing of a standard model. As observed earlier, the World Bank possessed the economic means and diverse political connections to enforce a specific narrative about CCTs, simplifying "gender" to merely providing cash to mothers. Consequently, gender knowledge and researchers have not received much legitimacy within the World Bank. A staff member from the institution's cross-sectoral gender unit acknowledges that the social protection unit (PREM)—which standardized CCTs—considered gender issues only recently:

> Discussions about gender in social protection [are] pfff... two or three years old, here. [...] I think that the gender units were quite marginal here... Ultimately, I can still allow myself to talk about gender in social protection since I come from social protection. But it's true that when I talk to the guys who do the transport of all that, they look at me [strangely]. And it's true... Ultimately in this unit, there are not really people who come from technical practices, where they are already technically credible. (Elizabeth)

This quote is surprising and shows the weakness of the gender unit in the World Bank even in the PREM where the first GAD Unit was born. Gender knowledge suffered from considerable underrepresentation in comparison with other academic and technical domains, resulting in gender staff facing a lack of credibility when it came to sectoral and operational matters like social protection or agriculture. As a senior economic researcher at the World Bank relates:

> Each sector has someone who represents gender perspectives. And often these people do not know anything [...]. There are many people who are gender specialists who do not know much else. They have not really had very serious academic training.... Yes, [they graduated], but in sociology [...] or in politics, [but] we are a bank here! Most people are economists [...] and I think that's a big problem for the gender perspective: there are a lot of people who have just studied women's studies, or I do not know what, but who do not know how to talk to economists, who cannot speak. And that's why it's not taken seriously [...] I think it helps if we speak the same language [...]. I think there are a lot of gender experts who have a lot of problems, who do not have enough training, and who do not know

how to convince and talk to other people who work at the Bank, and so [gender] is not taken seriously. (Elizabeth)

In addition to the confluence of diverse academic backgrounds, institutional and organizational structures have historically weakened gender equality concerns at the World Bank, as is stressed by the same person:

Well, it's not just that – there's certainly a lot of prejudices, sexism, and all that. [...] The people we hear all the time [...] are the men who shout all the time, and who [...] take a lot of space [laughs]. [...] Yes, [to convince colleagues of gender awareness] is difficult because (1) it's not taken seriously by so many people at the Bank, and (2) because XX [a high-ranking administrator of the cross-sectoral gender unit] is not from the Bank. It's her first job at the Bank, so it's been very hard for her because there is a lot of politics here. And she arrived when everything has been restructured, but obviously, it's full of people who were there before, who know exactly what to do to have budgets, all that, and for her it was very hard, and then she had to build that, and then she has no resources. (Elizabeth)

As seen before in this chapter, the Bank slowly and lastly implemented gender equality through GAD or gender mainstreaming in its operational sectors. Despite the fact that the PREM—that standardized CCTs as a model—saw the initial institutionalization of the GAD unit, it is one of the most conventional economics-based Vice Presidencies at the Bank. Therefore, even in this institutional site of the Bank, gender equality concerns were weak. Besides, without a strict mandate and policy with clear guidelines on how gender analysis should be included in all Bank's projects and loans, the strategic gender equality entrepreneurs inside the Bank must sell their services to attract the support of project designers who are mostly economists. Therefore, they must make the business case for gender equality as smart economics and avoid all gender social justice considerations (Griffin, 2009: 130–136). The organization of the work inside the Bank, close to consultancy firms, makes it such that Bank staff do not have any formal and very few informal incentives to include gender-related work. They are overburdened and have a lot of time constraints that do not encourage them to seek extra work for themselves in gender areas (Griffin, 2009: 100; Hammer, 2013).

The issue at the World Bank could stem from technical, personal, or organizational factors, as the above quotes indicate. They shed light on the stark asymmetry between the cross-sectoral gender unit, which faces resource constraints, and other well-resourced sectors. Consequently, gender equality concerns do not seem to be a priority for CCT international entrepreneurs. A senior economist at the IADB (formerly at the World Bank and an author of leading CCT evaluations) agrees:

> So, it is interesting because, to me, the gender aspect seems less important... There are outcomes in education and health, in which girls are worse off, but I do not think that in Latin America it is particularly important. (Marc)

One Griffin interviewee confirmed: "nobody really cares' about gender" in the Bank" (Griffin, 2009: 130). The Bank only accepted the gender "myth"[33] about giving cash to mothers to enhance the welfare of their children. Based on international publications (e.g., Adato et al., 2000; Quisumbing & McClafferty, 2006; Quisumbing, 2003; Skoufias & McClafferty, 2001; World Bank, 2001), this myth is founded on the belief that women are more likely than men to use their incomes to invest in the education and nutrition of their children. Consequently, CCTs that transfer the cash to women were investing to enhance the living conditions of children. However, this assumption oversimplifies behaviors that are deeply influenced by specific contexts[34] (Jackson, 2008). This powerful myth persists within the World Bank, upheld by dominant economists "for whom gender disaggregation and comparison is methodologically more tractable than researching the relational significance of gender" (Jackson, 2008, 107). They continue to view women as a separate category from men, neglecting the understanding that gender is rooted in complex social relations (Jackson, 2008, 107). A senior economist and author of leading CCT evaluations at the World Bank confirmed this delegitimizing of feminist knowledge and research, which he perceived as unscientific:

[33] Some authors argue that in development, actors have needed myths to orient their action to transform conditions of misery and inequality (Cornwall et al., 2008: 4).

[34] Blacken and Bhanu (1999) have shown in a technical report for the World Bank that the allocation of resources to women will significantly reduce poverty in sub-Saharan Africa. The World Bank has universalized this in its report "Engendering Development through Gender Equality in Rights, Resources and Voice" (2001). "The study is limited in focus and time-period, but the results are generalized to an unspecified and timeless geographic area" (O'Laughin, 2008: 23).

> Yes, exactly [I use a gender perspective], and to me that's natural in the sense that you always have a bigger and a more interesting story to tell because the results are different [laughs], and it gives me something to look at and talk about, as opposed to…I don't know what a feminist researcher is or does…. (Arthur)

Many Bank staff did not consider gender as a structural dynamic but as a concern for difference. Gender was reduced to gender-disaggregated data and measurement based on differences between the sexes. Therefore, gender is reduced to sex, and the evacuation of gendered structural dynamic knowledge "allows the Bank's macroeconomics to appear gender-free" (Berik, 2017; Griffin, 2009: 139).

Knowledge at the World Bank is shaped by a strong institutional legacy of neoclassical economics, which models gender relations within households (intra-household resource allocation) and produces statically quantitative findings (O'Laughlin, 2008: 23). Gender does not make sense to economists in the Bank, "except through a thinly superficial veneer of instrumentalism and economic efficiency, resulting in an instrumentalization and limited operationalization of gender that fit too poorly with how people actually function and develop to be useful" (Griffin, 2009: 133). It is much more challenging to produce and deliver data about relational aspects, "compared to the relative simplicity of gender category comparisons" (Jackson, 2008: 107). Feminist knowledge stands out as qualitative and context specific since women's behavior is intricately tied to gender relations rather than simply gender characteristics (Buss, 2015; Cookson, 2018; Liebowitz & Zwingel, 2014). Consequently, in the World Bank's evidence-based policies, such as CCTs, gender equality objectives that cannot be easily quantified with numerical data lose their strength and get reduced to instrumentalist interpretations of gender.

Conclusion

This chapter has documented the process of standardization leading to the retention of a merely instrumentalist view of gender: giving cash to mothers to maximize children's outcomes because mothers are seen as better spenders than men when it comes to children. First, it has underlined that the World Bank is not an anti-gender institution but to the contrary has incorporated gender analysis in its development policies, projects, and loans. For this bank, populated first by orthodox economists convinced by neoclassical economy knowledge and the virtues of the market, the WID approach has been much more seductive and has permeated the GAD approach (Calkin, 2015). Even during the more open era of Wolfensohn promoting bottom-up, participatory development and GAD approaches, the Bank picked up (critical) ideas, such as gender equality or participation, and instruments policies, such as CCTs, from outside to legitimize itself in the face of harsh criticisms of its SAP policies. It reframed these ideas, however, in accordance with its core institutional legacies of orthodox economical theory. Therefore, gender equality in the World Bank became smart economics rather than being seen as valuable in and of itself.

Second, the chapter has documented the standardization of CCTs including gendered certification, decontextualization, and framing. It demonstrated that because evaluations are a trademark of CCTs, the mixed results relating to gender following randomized trial evaluations are to blame. Due to this perceived lack of evidence, the World Bank's framing of the CCT standard model did not include gender equality objectives and did not challenge the institutional legacy of gender-discriminatory norms and priorities in countries that have adopted CCTs. The chapter has argued that knowledge production at the World Bank is informed by power relations characterized by the privileging of quantitative and economic knowledge and the marginalization of gender equality entrepreneurs and knowledge, which is both qualitative and quantitative. This is because, historically the World Bank did not prioritize gender equality and it was difficult to measure gender equality in a privileged way where "success stories" are more easily demonstrated. Therefore, the World Bank had taken gender equality goals off the table. Important biases affect knowledge production at the World Bank, as well as the impact evaluations of CCTs. Therefore, in a paradoxical way, evidence-based policies such as CCTs, that the World Bank, a "knowledge bank", widely promoted, were rooted in an ignorance of more complex stories. Framing the standard CCT model with measurement obsession had political and governance-centered implications (Buss, 2015; Merry, 2011). The pressure for quantitative results—measurable by metric indicators—has created social policy aimed at improving only these indicators (Liebowitz & Zwingel, 2014: 363). The measurement obsession is conspicuous in evidence-based policies such as CCTs, which not only failed to address structural problems, such as gender inequalities, but also managed to render unintended gender effects—both positive and negative—invisible (Cookson, 2018). Indeed, the obsession for quantitative impacts "may make it more difficult to secure funding for gender projects aimed at addressing the complex structural dimension of inequality not easily captured by quantifiable metrics" (Buss, 2015: 385).

More broadly, this chapter has shown that in the absence of institutional sites, legacies, and strategic gender equality entrepreneurs comparable to the Mexican and Brazilian experiences, the World Bank only retained an instrumentalist idea of gender relations and gender equality. Thus, this chapter has also demonstrated that alongside policy entrepreneurs and institutions, knowledge matters: gender equality in the World Bank mandate was lost as "smart economics" claimed to boost economic growth. Therefore, along with the literature on global social policies (Deacon, 2007; Mahon, 2021; Martens et al., 2021; Vetterlein, 2007), this chapter has reasserted the role played by the World Bank as a bank of knowledge. It is an influential driver even more ideationally than financially speaking. This chapter has shown how power relations at the World Bank ensured that gender equality entrepreneurs and knowledge remained thoroughly marginalized, despite the integration of gender equality into its mandate. Therefore, the outcome of standardization is the exclusion of gender equality goals in the CCT model. The standard recipe genders women as only mothers and sole caregivers of children and with it reinforces their traditional gender roles.

The World Bank's economic rationale for investing in women to reduce poverty is problematic because it occludes the structures—patriarchy and capitalism, for example—in which gender relations are embedded. In the standardization of CCTs, the marginalization of gender knowledge has resulted in a missed opportunity to mainstream gender equality goals within what the World Bank and the development community identified as the best strategy to reduce poverty. By ignoring gender knowledge because it is "unscientific", the World Bank did not consider the evidence proving that the first CCTs simply reproduced structural gender inequalities because they could only work at the cost of free reproductive and domestic work on the part of women (González de la Rocha, 2000; Molyneux, 2006). Consequently, the standard CCT model framed by the World Bank not only remained blind to gender inequalities but capitalized on the gender-discriminatory norms that led to them, thereby reproducing those same inequalities.

Therefore, as I will demonstrate in the next chapter, Peruvian and Bolivian policymakers translated the standard model without any concern for gender equality. Free to exclude gender equality goals in their CCT designs they thus reproduced strong social policy institutional legacies that reinforce gender inequalities.

CHAPTER 5

Juntos and the *Bonos*: Translation with Innovations Rooted in Exclusionary Institutional Legacies

In the last analytical chapter, I focus on a third phase of the CCT trajectory in Latin America: the translation and adoption of the World Bank's standard CCT model by latecomers Peru and Bolivia. I aim to understand how and why Peru and Bolivia were unconcerned about gender equality when translating the standard model and designing their programs. CCT translation processes occurred within two opposing political regimes. While the Peruvian political regime, under a center-right government, was still very neoliberal, the Bolivian political regime under Evo Morales's government promised radical change from the left to dismantle colonialism and neoliberalism. Nevertheless, these two political regimes adopted the same instrument as standardized by the World Bank adding innovations rooted in entrenched legacies of institutional gender exclusion.

Alejandro Toledo's center-right government (2001–2006) launched *Juntos* in Peru in 2005 and Evo Morales's left-wing government (2006–2019) translated the standard CCT model into the *Bono Juancito Pinto* (2006) and then *Bono Juana Azurduy* (2009). Without any gender equality goals in this thin standard CCT model, Peruvian and Bolivian policy entrepreneurs did not coordinate with either their state machinery or with strategic gender equality entrepreneurs inside or outside the state. Instead, they translated CCTs, adding ingredients to the recipe that were

N. Nagels, *Gender Equality in Conditional Cash Transfer Designs*, Studies of the Americas,
https://doi.org/10.1007/978-3-031-60871-1_5

heavily influenced by institutional legacies of gender exclusion. They thus managed to reproduce gender inequalities that intersected with the denigration of Indigenous mothering practices. Even though Mexico and Brazil also have diverse populations including Indigenous ones, it was only in Bolivia and Peru that translators explicitly described their goals of reinforcing traditional gender roles and changing the behaviors of Indigenous women. This approach was enacted in particular through extra-official conditions that CCT implementers enforced.

I begin the chapter by presenting the historical context of social policy legacies in Peru and Bolivia. After, I expose how CCT translation took place in these two countries in the first half of the 2000s. I demonstrate that the outcome of the translation mechanism was the exclusion of gender equality goals. CCT translators were not strategic gender equality entrepreneurs and they avoided women's political institutions. In the third part, I show that Bolivian and Peruvian CCT translators embedded intersectional inequalities in their CCT designs. The conclusion highlights the argument that Peru and Bolivia, which are not intrinsically more gender equality unfriendly than Mexico and Brazil, erased gender equality goals in the process of CCT translation and with it reinforced intersectional gender inequalities.

Institutional Legacies of Peruvian and Bolivian Welfare Regimes

Peru and Bolivia fall into the third group of Filgueira's Latin American welfare regime typology. They are "exclusionary regimes", defined as those countries that "exhibit elitist systems of social security and health care and dual systems in education" (Filgueira & Filgueira, 2002: 139). They also fall in the third group of "informal-familial" welfare regimes of Martínez's typology (2008) (along with Central American countries, Colombia, Ecuador, Paraguay, and Venezuela). In this group, the state is not the main provider of welfare, the labor force is less commodified and has minimal decommodified social protection. Therefore, families, and within them women, are the principally responsible for welfare.

During the incorporation period of 1930–1970 (Collier & Collier, 2002), in the exclusionary welfare regimes of Peru and Bolivia, the social security systems served the formal workers of the upper and middle classes—these made up of men, mestizo, and "wither" groups. In turn, the public assistance systems served the poor, Indigenous populations and informal workers with a concentration of women as heads of households (Ewig, 2010: 17). For these exclusionary regimes, social protection policies consisted of "elitist policies that grant[ed] additional privileges to [a] privileged population" (Filgueira & Filgueira, 2002: 139).

In Bolivia, in 1920, formal sector workers had to subscribe to a mandatory social insurance scheme (Wiebe, 2021: 210). The national revolution of 1952—led by the *Movimiento Nacionalista Revolutionario* (MNR) at the head of an alliance among middle-class nationalist intellectuals, peasants, and workers—allowed for the incorporation of marginalized groups into national political life. The MNR's government nationalized tin mines, implemented an ambitious land reform expropriating latifundia elites, expanded mass education, and established universal suffrage (e.g., Anria, 2019; Emmerij, 1998; Kaufmann et al., 2003). In 1956, after having nationalized the mines, the MNR enacted the first Social Security Code with pension insurance mainly for public sector workers, of which miners were among the majority. This series of amendments reinforced segmentation both between informal, mainly rural workers and women, and formal workers and among these latter according to their occupation (Carnes & Mares, 2016: 1653). While the economic structures changed little after 1952 with mining industries remaining the main source of the Gross Domestic Product (GDP), corporatist arrangements incorporated popular groups such as male workers and peasants through unions (Anria, 2019: 13). The nationalist ideology of the MNR underlined class identifications—peasants and workers—for social and political incorporation but masked racial divisions between Indigenous and non-Indigenous peoples, renaming Indigenous rural residents campesinos (peasants) (Ewig, 2018: 439). During the military-authoritarian governments (1964–78), rural syndicalist organizations remained crucial to the participation and mobilization of the peasantry (Anria, 2019: 13) and racism continued to be practiced against Indigenous people (Ewig, 2018: 439).

In Peru, the military government of Oscar Benavides (1933–1939) established the first compulsory social insurance program for blue-collar workers, and in 1947 the *Alianza Popular Revolucionaria Americana* (APRA) pushed compulsory social insurance for white-collar workers and their supporters (Mesa-Lago, 1978: 116–118). The incorporation of the male worker movement and more broadly of the popular sector reinforced corporatist relations between the labor movement and APRA as a populist party (Collier & Collier, 2002: 315). The leftist dictatorship under Juan Velasco (1968–1975) focused primarily on integrating the two social insurance systems, but without extending coverage (Haggard & Kaufman, 2008: 84). Following the restoration of democracy in 1980, there was an upswing in public spending on health care and education. However, the impact on social security was relatively limited. According to Haggard and Kaufman (2008: 96), "limited industrialization and the long-term exclusion of rural and Indigenous populations from the political system help to account for the limited spread of welfare benefits and basic social services, including schooling". Despite the emergence of unions, the limited level of industrialization hindered the integration of formal workers into a corporatist system. Additionally, the presence of ethnic and gender discrimination further contributed to the inadequate quality of public health and education services (Pribble, 2011: 209–210).

In the shift to neoliberalism, Bolivia, one of the poorest countries in Latin America, experienced a bout of "shock therapy", with social insurance privatization in health and pensions, the closure of the Ministry of Social Security (Ortiz, 2007: 54), and the privatization of public mining industries, weakening labor unions and deepening unemployment[1] (Anria, 2019: 14). Given the social cost of this shock therapy, Bolivia saw the arrival of the first social investment funds in 1986 intended to create employment and provide emergency food aid (Whitehead, 1995). In addition, decentralization, as in Brazil, was part of the neoliberal reform package. The Law of Popular Participation, enacted in 1994, led to the increased mobilization of mostly male peasant movements in which former miners became key players. Having been forced out of their mining jobs as a result of privatization, these players had turned to coca agriculture (Anria, 2019; Carnes & Mares, 2016; Yashar 2005). This Law encouraged political participation at the municipal level and encouraged the creation of new political parties such as the *Movimiento al Socialismo* (MAS). In the 2000s, the MAS rose as a movement-based party, in which popular movements, such as the female peasant and Indigenous union, *Bartolina Sisa*, were very active. Rurally anchored, the MAS as a left-wing party opposed to neoliberalism, was powerful during the "social wars"[2]

[1] In the second half of the 1980s, over 30,000 mineworkers lost their jobs (Carnes et Mares, 2016: 1654).

[2] The "water war" began in 2000 in Cochabamba to fight against the privatization of water supply and sanitation. The "gas conflict" began in El Alto in 2003 when powerful neighbor organizations of this city and peasant unions opposed the Bolivian gas exportation to Chile. This led to a crisis in the political system and President Gonzalo Sánchez

(Anria, 2019; Jenson & Nagels, 2022: 372). As I will demonstrate, the MAS and its leader Evo Morales, who became president in 2006, were the major translators of the standard CCT model into the *Bonos*. Their roots in social movements and mobilizations explain, in part, why they provided universal access to the *Bonos*.

In Peru, following the implementation of severe pro-market economic adjustment policies, Fujimori's "competitive authoritarianism" regime (Levitsky & Way, 2002) (1992–2000) expanded pro-poor programs to get political support but social security declined significantly (Segura-Ubiergo, 2012: 236–250). The "fujishock" implemented structural adjustment programs privatizing public enterprises,[3] pensions, and social protection and drastically reducing public expenditures. After the auto-coup of 1992 closed Congress, the 1993 neoliberal constitution concentrated the political power in the presidency and the executive branch. Nevertheless, Fujimori used social assistance policies as clientelist means to legitimize his authoritarian regime and gained support during the election. For example, the *Fondo de Cooperación para el Desarrollo Social* (FONCODES), created in 1991, attributed financial resources to infrastructure projects in the poorest provinces where the President wanted to gain popular votes (Degregori, 2000; Lavrard-Meyer, 2010; Schady, 2000). In the same vein, Fujimori coopted the women's popular vote with the institutional creation of the National Program for Food Assistance (PRONAA). In 1992, Fujimori undermined what had originally been self-managed women's local associations with *Comedores Populares*,[4] placing food distribution under the auspices of the presidency. Access to supplies depended on manifestations of political support for the president, by both women's organizations and individuals (Nagels, 2013: 42). In the Fujimori government, technocrats were protagonists in designing neoliberal pro-poor policies such as FONCODES and food aid. As I will

de Lozada—responsible for violent mass protest repression—resigned and went into exile (Do Alto, 2007: 90, 91).

[3] For example, the Supreme Decree 004 in 1991 allowed the government to lay off more than 155,000 public sector employees in 20 days, thereby reducing the active population from 14 to 10% (Bejar, 2001: 152).

[4] *A comedor populare* is a mixt between communitarian kitchen and popular canteen. They emerged in the 1950s and consolidated in the 1980s to cope with hungry by the collectivization of alimentary cost and women citizen auto-gestion.

show in the next section, they remained central to CCT translation, but the resulting *Juntos* was designed as a clientelist-free instrument.

In Peru and Bolivia, the historical legacy of social security segmentation marked the fragmentation of the Peruvian and Bolivian social policy architecture. Formal workers benefited from different social insurance funds and most of the population—informal workers, women, peasants, and Indigenous people—only had access to restricted public assistance services. Social policies have widened the gap between the upper and middle-class groups and "the majority of the population in the lower class" (Mesa-Lago, 1978: 8). In Peru and Bolivia, since services and transfers of social security are of better quality and more generous than those offered in the public system, social policies, such as institutions, reinforce existing racial, geographical, gender, and social inequalities between "white", urban, male, or mestizo citizens and women, rural, and Indigenous citizens. The health system illustrated the exclusionary character of these regimes (Nagels, 2018) because "social security health systems were an essentially male privilege and the public health systems were feminized" because "one of its major premises was to control women's biological reproduction" (Ewig, 2010: 17, 32).

Standard CCT Model Translation in Peru and Bolivia: *Juntos* and the *Bonos*

While the Peruvian political regime, under center-right governments, was still very neoliberal, the Bolivian political regime under the Evo Morales government promised radical change from the left to dismantle colonialism and neoliberalism. Nevertheless, these two political regimes adopted and translated the same instrument as standardized by the World Bank without any concerns for gender equality. They did, however, address different social problems or rather they framed them differently.

Peruvian Translation by Technocratic Entrepreneurs in a Fragmented State Without Gender Equality Concerns

At the end of Toledo's presidency, in 2005, the government created *Juntos* by supreme decree, as a translation of the standard CCT model with the same goal to break the intergenerational transmission of poverty through investment in human capital—and without any gender equality objectives (Vargas, 2010: 24). As in Mexico, *Juntos* was the achievement of entrepreneurs working in a small technocratic instrument community from the Ministry of Economics and Finance (MEF) who took control of social policies by overriding social ministry authority. Moreover, as in Mexico, *Juntos* was a cheap solution to a crisis, the internal war that pitted the state against the *Sendero Luminoso* (Shining Path)[5] and other insurgent groups between 1980 and 2000.

Juntos *as a Technocratic Solution to Clientelism*

The presidential announcement of *Juntos* and its creation by supreme decree[6] in April 2005 antagonized numerous actors. Civil society and the *Comedores Populares* complained because officials did not consult and include them in the design process. The *Comedores Populares* organizations wanted to have a hand in restructuring food policies and they wanted to share their long-standing contributions with *Juntos* (Nagels, 2013). Members of the opposition in Congress accused the unpopular government of using *Juntos* as an electoral strategy, arriving as it did a mere seven months before the election. They refused to approve the budget for the program and denounced the lack of criteria to select the recipients and demanded a transparent committee to oversee the implementation. As a concession, the President created a transparency board with representation from various ministries and various social sectors, including the church (De la O, 2015: 83–86).

Nevertheless, strategic entrepreneurs inside the MEF were decisive in shaping *Juntos*. They shared the concerns of the opposition in Congress, and like the controversy in Mexico in 1997, they feared clientelism and denounced the April 2005 Decree in which *Juntos* targeted urban and rural areas (Jones et al., 2008: 255, 256). They were powerful enough to succeed in changing the Supreme Decree establishing the MEF as

[5] This Maoist-inspired organization differed from other guerrilla revolutionary groups in the region with its violent methods. It did not tolerate any organizational form other than the armed one, destroying all organizations or networks that did not submit to it. It engaged in violent actions not only against state authorities, but also against peasant, Indigenous, or trade union organizations that did not show total allegiance (Yashar, 2005: 246–250).

[6] *Decreto Supremo* 032–2005 PCM.

responsible for determining the areas covered by the program. Strategic entrepreneurs in the MEF decided to target only rural regions with few voters but with most of the poorest population (Vergara & Encinas, 2016: 171). This shows that the strategic and technocratic entrepreneurs in the MEF became the most powerful *Juntos* designers. They succeeded in displacing political leaders from influencing the program using the *Sistema de Focalización por Hogar*[7] (SISFOH) and other statistical tools to identify *Juntos* recipients. Local and community authorities could not intervene in their selection. They could only validate the final list of recipients. This made the targeting more efficient and reduced administrative costs (Llanos & Rosas, 2010: 8; Vargas, 2010: 26).

The MEF's attempts to control the design process behind *Juntos* were part of a larger objective to combat clientelism, of which such institutional innovations as SISFOH emerged. Since the return to democracy in 2000,[8] during the transitional government of Paniagua (2000–2001) and the center-right Toledo's government (2001–2006), strategic entrepreneurs in the MEF strongly opposed Fujimori's social programs. They based their criticisms on studies conducted by the University of the Pacific (Monge et al., 2009; Vásquez Huamán,s 2005), that tracked the leaking of resources to non-poor beneficiaries in the operation of alimentary programs, including the milk program and the *Comedores Populares* (De la O, 2015: 86). They wanted to create evidence-based policies using technical tools that adhered to international norms, instead of relying on clientelism (Vargas, 2010: 25). Selection based on means-testing became the solution to block clientelism and thus overcome the technical flaws of social policies. With the SISFOH came an innovative technical tool with which to identify poor families as potential recipients of social programs.[9] Although an inter-ministerial committee oversaw it, the MEF gained influence over "social" ministries, such as the Ministry of Women and Development, that were obliged to embrace SISFOH in the design of their social policies. The MEF consolidated its influence, power, and control at the end of Fujimorism in a context where political parties remained weak and ephemeral. SISFOH generated resistance from

[7] Household System Targeting.

[8] In 2000, Fujimori exiled himself to Japan and announced his renouncement by fax.

[9] From large surveys about housing, personal assets, and family members' socio-demographic data, SISFOH classified households according to poverty quintile groups to determine their eligibility for social programs (Valderrama, 2009: 4).

social institutions and organizations, including municipal authorities, the *Comedores Populares*, run by women's voluntary groups, as well as from within central bureaucracies, such as the Social Ministry of Woman and Development, that the MEF had sidelined (Llanos & Rosas, 2010: 18, 19, 34).

Strategic entrepreneurs inside the MEF agreed that for social policies to be free of clientelism, they must be centrally conceived, and identify recipients technically (Jenson & Nagels, 2022: 367). *Juntos* was their first experiment to make use of the tool and apply it to the World Bank standard CCT model. MEF strategic entrepreneurs' choices reflected the international knowledge about CCTs available at this time about the need to "protect" them from political interferences, like in Mexico and Brazil. Nevertheless, unlike Brazil, *Juntos* did not generate a new ministry, but the central and powerful Presidential Council of Ministers oversaw it until it moved to the Ministry for Development and Social Inclusion under Humala's government 2011 (Nagels, 2016: 483). Lastly, unlike Mexico, *Juntos* entrepreneurs were not convinced by the link between poverty and gender inequalities. In this, they drew the same conclusions as the World Bank from which they translated its standard CCT model.

Juntos *as a Technocratic Solution to Social Crisis*

In addition, *Juntos* was the government's response to huge problems of social inclusion in a post-conflict context. Social conflicts were numerous and intense and discontent was widespread because economic growth was strong but without redistribution (Francke & Mendoza, 2006: 395, 399). In 2004, 51% of the population was poor, and 24% lived in extreme poverty (CEPAL, 2006: 74). Moreover, implementing the 2003 Truth and Reconciliation Commission (TRC) was difficult, particularly in the area of compensating victims of internal violence between 1980 and 2000. The Commission established that this violence meant the killing or disappearances of more than 69 280 persons and that the police and military were responsible for at least 37% and the rest was the responsibility of insurgent groups, *Sendero Luminoso* and the *Moviemento Revolucionario Tupac Amaru* (MRTA).[10] The TRC also established the gendered and racialized character of the violence: "Nearly 80% of the victims lived in

[10] It was a revolutionary movement, closer than the Shining Path to the Latin American revolutionary guerrillas inspired by the Cuban experience (Boutron, 2019).

the Andes or Amazon regions, where guerrilla groups and government forces killed with impunity. Most victims had Quechua or other Indigenous languages as their mother tongue. The geographic pattern of the violence closely followed the geography of marginalized rural communities" (International Center for Transitional Justice 2008).[11] The TRC's final report underscored the correlation between the probability of being a victim and social exclusion, poverty, and racialized identity documenting the racist, socio-economic, and neocolonial bases of the internal violence. Therefore, it recommended material and symbolic reparations for the victims-survivors, most of whom were Indigenous women (Laplante & Theidon, 2007: 234).

The Toledo government delayed the official response to this report for several months due to disagreements and conflicts inside and outside the government. On the one side, activists for transitional justice advocated for the construction of post-conflict and peace with the dismantlement of neocolonialism, racism, and social exclusion. On the other side, for strategic entrepreneurs and most of the elite, the major problem was just poverty and not one of justice, democracy, human rights, and transitional justice. The strategic entrepreneurs inside the MEF represented this latter position and "refused to allocate the necessary funds to support proposed reparations" (Laplante & Theidon, 2007: 247). However, with growing social unrest, the Toledo government needed to act and *Juntos* became an instrument of compromise to generate a coalition of support inside and outside the government. *Juntos* responded to the desire for efficacy and the desire to avoid clientelism through the use of the SISFOH registry. In addition, it addressed the TRC's concerns about the social inclusion of Indigenous families' victims-survivors of the internal conflict by prioritizing Peru's southern regions, the first to be affected by the violence, and home to the poorest citizens of the country (Jenson & Nagels, 2022). That was the institutional innovation in the translation of the standard CCT model. However, although Indigenous women were the primary victims-survivors of the internal conflict and the TRC included gender knowledge in its work, *Juntos*'s entrepreneurs did not include any gender equality goals in its design.

[11] https://www.ictj.org/publication/alberto-fujimori-trial, accessed February 2024.

Juntos *as a Translation of the World Bank's Standard CCT Recipe with Local Ingredients*

In contrast to Brazil and Mexico, in Peru, the key to legitimizing *Juntos* was its status as a standard model and the international certification of CCT effectiveness that went with it (Arroyo, 2010: 10). *Juntos*' entrepreneurs and members of the executive invoked the World Bank and other international studies to vaunt CCTs as the best instrument with which to fight poverty and avoid clientelism, for example over food and other in-kind programs (De la O, 2015: 88). *Juntos*' entrepreneurs climbed onto the international CCT bandwagon and enthusiastically embraced social investment in human capital as a solution to poverty. They had trans-American academic and work experience ties and adopted the standard version of CCTs. One *Juntos* strong expert supporter confirms this:

> It was literally imported from Washington and adapted from a combination of Mexican-Brazilian models. (Diego)

Therefore, influential MEF entrepreneurs counted on advice and counseling from the World Bank and Mexican and Brazilian cooks to translate the World Bank standard model into *Juntos*. To learn about the model, *Juntos* strategic entrepreneurs traveled to Mexico D.F. and Washington (Francke & Mendoza, 2006; Vargas Valente, 2010: 24; Levy's interview). The World Bank provided technical and institutional support—mostly with expert knowledge on means-test targeting—and produced frequent evaluation reports on *Juntos* (Perova & Vakis, 2009: 3).

The translation of the standard CCT implied appropriation processes in which strategic entrepreneurs added innovation to the *Juntos* design. In response to the TRC, the algorithm to target *Juntos* recipients would measure more than poverty including a "history of political violence" as a variable (Jones et al., 2008: 260). Therefore, the primary recipients of *Juntos* would be the Indigenous, poor, and rural populations first touched by the internal violence of the 1980s and 1990s. Moreover, recipients would be Indigenous women, one of the categories of the population most affected by the violence and with experiences of historical discrimination and lack of access to rights and justice. For example, during the Fujimori regime, the Ministry of Health organized the forced sterilization of approximately 346 219 poor, rural, and mostly

Indigenous women in the southern Peruvian regions. Also, the TRC established that sexual and reproductive violence was widespread during the internal conflict (Boesten, 2014; Tomasso, 2022). In recognition of these institutional legacies and because *Juntos* had a dual character as both reparation and anti-poverty instrument, the government made the important symbolic decision to launch *Juntos* in *Chuschi*, a municipality in Ayacucho department where the *Sendero Luminoso* had first attacked. During the ceremony, officials insisted that *Juntos* would not be politicized and would prioritize the population most affected by violence (De la O, 2015: 87).

While the Supreme Decree did not stipulate that mothers receive the cash transfer, all the communication about *Juntos*, for example on its website,[12] diffused the expectation that the mother would both receive the transfer and be responsible for ensuring that conditions be respected. This decision did not provoke controversy because, by 2005, it was a certified and standard international practice as was the idea, based on supposed knowledge, that mothers were more reliable in terms of "investing" in their children's health and education than fathers (Correa Aste & Roopnaraine, 2013: 6). Therefore, as the Peruvian translation of the World Bank standard CCT, *Juntos* reproduced instrumentalist views of gender: giving cash to women to invest in human capital: their children.

As seen, the World Bank decontextualized the CCT from the Mexican iteration, drawn up with a post-Beijing enthusiasm for the global gender equality paradigm and the Brazilian iteration with its implicit gender equality goals. Translating this standard model, *Juntos*, "was not explicitly designed as a mechanism for empowering women or transforming gender relations in society" (Vargas, 2010: 26). Gender equality goals were absent from the *Juntos* design. For example, it did not include any affirmative action for girls' education or the goal of women's empowerment, as in Mexico, or even implicit references to these, as in Brazil. And this was the case despite the Ministry of Women and Social Development's involvement in the first *Juntos* governing board (Molyneux & Thomson, 2011: 197) and the advocacy and pressure from feminist NGO *Moviemiento Manuela Ramos* as well as Congress woman *Rosario Sasieta*'s work tracking the gendered impacts of *Juntos* (Vargas, 2010: 27). The translation of the standard CCT model and the design of *Juntos*

[12] http://www.juntos.gob.pe/index.php/quienes-somos/vision-Y-mision, accessed October 2016.

occurred without any association with those institutions, social organizations, NGOs, and women's political agencies that were promoting the agenda of gender equality (Jenson et al., 2017).[13] Powerful strategic entrepreneurs from the MEF did not become strategic gender equality entrepreneurs as in Mexico and they did not collaborate with such entrepreneurs.

Instead, the translation of the standard CCT model into *Juntos* without any attention to gender equality left plenty of room for strong social policy legacies in Peru to reproduce gender inequalities.

Bolivia: Inclusive Top-down CCT Translation Without Gender Equality Concerns

At the beginning of its first administration, the bottom-up coalition and leftist MAS government launched the *Bono Juancito Pinto*[14] (BJP) in 2006, the *Bono Renta Dignidad* in 2008, and the *Bono Juana Azurduy*[15] (BJA) in 2009 as the pillars of new social policies aimed at redistributing the fruit of growth generated by the nationalization of hydrocarbon. This section does not include the *Renta Dignidad* in the analysis since it is a universal non-contributory pension for the elderly aged 65 years and older and not a CCT program. The objectives of the *Bono Juancito Pinto* (BJP) were to enhance school enrollment, decrease dropout rates, and mitigate the intergenerational cycle of poverty (*Ministerio de Planificación del Desarrollo* 2006). With the BJP, every child had the opportunity to receive an annual amount of Bolivianos 200 (approximately US$30) upon

[13] During the Fujimori regime, new legislations and policies promoted gender equality, for example, in the form of women's political representation with quotas (1997), the Law of protection from family violence (1992), and against rape (1997). Nonetheless, the authoritarian nature of the Fujimori regime, its top-down approach, and inadequate financing meant they were never effectively implemented (Jenson et al., 2017). At the return to democracy in the beginning of the 2000s, Toledo's government adopted a strict vision of family planning and limited contraceptive access (Vazquez del Aguila, 2006: 118). Close to the conservative Catholic Church, this sexual and reproductive policy focussed on natural strategies and intended to banish other contraceptive methods (Rousseau, 2007).

[14] Name of a 12-year-old child, a drummer in the army during the Pacific War where he died.

[15] During Bolivia's War of Independence, Juana Azurduy de Padilla (1780–1862) was a female fighter who became lieutenant colonel.

fulfilling two conditions: (1) enrollment in a public school and (2) maintaining a minimum attendance rate of 80% (Unidad Ejecutora, 2008). The *Bono Juana Azurduy* (BJA) targeted pregnant women, breastfeeding mothers, and those with children under the age of two who did not have any other healthcare insurance coverage (Vidal Fuertes et al., 2015: 14).

Institutional Legacies and Venues

The MAS government translated the standard CCT model without any attention to gender equality but included an important institutional innovation: the universal character of social rights to concretize the shift from neoliberalism to an "Indigenous and post-neoliberal" state (PND, 2006)—this is one of the most important shifts in Latin America. Elected in 2006 on a strong rhetoric of social inclusion and redistribution, Evo Morales promised two fundamental institutional changes to the Bolivian state. Following the main claims of social movements that brought the MAS, as a bottom-up coalition, to power, the first structural institutional reform was the nationalization of hydrocarbons[16] that would bring the state back into social redistribution while guaranteeing social rights (McGuire, 2013: 20). The nationalization of hydrocarbon ended the dependence on international aid and provided public funding for new public policies.[17]

Second, after a two-year Constituent Assembly, a new foundational institution emerged: the 2009 Plurinational Constitution, approved by referendum, that recognized and ensured the collective rights of Indigenous peoples. The Plurinational Constitution created a new category of political subjects: "Indigenous, native and peasant nation and people", who are a "whole human community that shares cultural identity, language, historical tradition, institutions, territoriality, and worldview, whose existence predated the Spanish colonial invasion" (Plurinational

[16] The July 30,558 Law made the national enterprise *Yacimentos Petrolíferos Fiscales Bolivianos* solely responsible for hydrocarbon commercialization and to increase taxes. Then, nationalization in this case was more of a negotiation on taxes with transnational corporations than a matter of expropriation (CEDLA, 2006; Gray Molina, 2007).

[17] The Bolivian state accounted for more than 80% of the industry's profit and with higher prices—due to the boom in global commodity prices—"the government intake from taxes and royalties rose from 28% of GDP in 2004 to 45% in 2010" (Borges, 2022: 149).

Constitution, 2009: art. 30). In addition, the Constitution created incentives for the *Bonos* because it guaranteed the right to education (arts. 77–90) and the right to health (arts. 35–39). The *Bonos* would transform these rights into realities (McGuire, 2013: 25). Although the new Constitution also institutionalized women's rights and a non-sexist language in the Plurinational state,[18] thanks to alliances between feminist organizations and Indigenous women in the Constituent Assembly (Nagels, 2013; Rousseau, 2011), the *Bonos* remained closed to them.

The *Bonos* were the major institutional innovations of Morales's government related to social policies but lacked gender equality goals despite the involvement of women's organizations in the Plurinational State (Anria, 2019). The elected MAS offered Indigenous and peasant strategic entrepreneurs and organizations unprecedented access to the state (Anria & Niedzwiecki, 2015), including powerful Indigenous women's peasant organizations, such as the *Bartolina Sisa*.[19] For example, Silvia Lazarte, an Indigenous woman and member of the Cocaleros movement, directed the *Constituent Assembly* and became a strategic entrepreneur for Indigenous rights.

Nevertheless, Indigenous and peasant women from the *Bartolina Sisa*, and the *Cocaleros* movement, were more convinced by Andean knowledge and the concept of *Chachawarmi*[20] than by feminist knowledge and the concept of gender equality that they considered as imported from NGOs during the neoliberalism era. Therefore, when Indigenous and peasant women gained access to the Morales government, they removed the "gender technocracy", as they named the Women's Political Agency of the 1990s, based on feminist NGOs and funded through

[18] The article 8, 9, 11, 14, 15, 26, 45, 47, 48, 56, 63, 64, 67, 79, 172, 179, 210, 338, 395 of this Constitution actively promoted women's economic, territorial, political, sexual, and reproductive rights (Rousseau, 2009: 156).

[19] Created in 1979 as the "female complementarity" of the powerful peasant unions, Unique Confederation of Rural Labourers of Bolivia (CSUTCB). They follow the complementary logic of gender relations in the Andes represented by the Chachawarmi.

[20] *Chachawarmi* is based on the Andean principles of duality and complementarity and constitutes the basic social, moral, and economic unit of society. Men and women share an equal and complimentary relationship and do not exist as separate being (Diaz, 2010: 13–14). Women and men, through the *Chachawarmi*, should be present in all spheres, including public decision making (Htun & Ossa, 2013: 11).

international cooperation[21] (Monasterios, 2007). They delegitimized institutional feminism[22] believing that it exploited them as recipients of policies and served feminist NGO interests more than their own. In 2010, they replaced the Women's Political Agency with a major institutional innovation to decolonize the state: the *Depatriacalización* Unit. Its aim was to implement decolonization policies rather than adhering to a strictly gender-oriented agenda. Strategic Indigenous women entrepreneurs and male officials in the government subsumed gender equality by decolonization with the premise that the eradication of colonialism would abolish patriarchal domination (Ybarnegaray Ortiz, 2011; Nagels, 2013).

Therefore, decolonization became central to the re-foundation of the state and not reducing gender inequalities per se, since decolonization's aim was also "de-patriarchialization" and with it the end of gender inequalities. In addition, social policies were important in this re-foundation of the state. With the *Bonos*, "the relations between redistribution, income, and social policies acquired a different political magnitude as they aimed to redefine the rules of the game underpinning the political system" (Riggirrozzi, 2010: 73). The government quickly developed the *Plan Nacional de Desarrollo Bolivia Digna, Soberana Productiva Democrática y para Vivir Bien* (National Development Plan for a Dignified, Sovereign, Productive and Democratic to Live Well, PND) that underlined that one of the first goals of the Morales administration was "to dismantle colonialism and neoliberalism to build a pluricultural and communitarian state" (Ministerio de Planificación del Desarrollo, 2006: xv–2). This ambitious National Plan aimed to build "a worthy, sovereign and democratic Bolivia to live well" and included a social protection

[21] Historically, women's organizations in Bolivia have been divided along ethnic and class lines. Feminist organizations are mostly NGOs composed of educated, middle class women and are financed by Western international cooperation, without any contact with rural, Indigenous, and peasant women (Monasterios, 2007). Feminist organizations accused Indigenous and peasant women's organizations of essentialism and conservatism, while the latter saw the former as racist, ethnocentric, and reproducing racial and social inequalities (Monasterios, 2007; Rousseau, 2011; Nagels, 2013).

[22] The typology of Latin American feminism differentiates between popular and Indigenous women's organizations, autonomous feminism, and institutional feminism. This latter refers, from the 1980s onward, to the development of institutional women's apparatuses promoting gender equality within state structures. United Nation International conferences on women (e.g., Mexico in 1975; Beijing in 1995) propelled the development of institutional feminism (Molyneux, 2002; Marques-Pereira, 2000; Vargas, 2002; Perea Ozerin, 2020).

policy and integral communitarian development (Nagels, 2016: 884). However, the institutional innovation of social protection for communities was difficult to launch because of constitutional and institutional uncertainty about the definition of "Indigenous communities" and their legal status for receiving fiscal transfers (Morales Escoffier, 2009: 23). Huge debates in the Ministry of Development Planning (MPD) centered on the role of local authorities—municipalities or Indigenous communities—in social policy design and delivery. The MPD also faced institutional and organizational instability with frequent changes of ministry, each with a different vision of social policies, roles, and functions, and different projects to pursue (Jenson & Nagels, 2022: 373).

The **Bono Juancito Pinto**: *Strategic Entrepreneurs with Presidential Interferences*

Faced with such institutional and organizational blockages and conflicts inside state institutions and with huge social expectations created by years of political and social mobilization, as in Brazil, Mexico, and the World Bank, the intervention of a strong actor was necessary. President Morales decided to create new policies—the *Bonos*—to redistribute the resources resulting from the nationalization of hydrocarbon. However, the MAS had never before embraced such an instrument. This idea emerged in the 2002 election campaign in the party platform of a conservative candidate[23] who promised to provide a CCT for school-age girls from low-income families in both rural and urban areas (McGuire, 2013: 9). The *Bono Esperanza* was another experiment that inspired the President. Launched by the mayor[24] of El Alto, this CCT provided a small monthly stipend to every child in El Alto's public schools (McGuire, 2013: 10).

President Morales assigned four policy entrepreneurs with international experience in consulting and social policy, the task of designing the BJP. Borges confirmed that "neither legislators nor representatives

[23] Sánchez de Lozada from the party *Movimento Nacionalista Revolucionario* won the elections but did not have time to implement this CCT because he was forced to resign in October 2003 after the "gas conflict" in which dozens of protectors died as a result of government repression (Do Alto, 2007).

[24] José Luis Paredes with the *Moviemto de Izquierda Revolutionaria* (MIR), which despite its leftist origins had been since the late 1980s a conservative party, and placing second at the 2005 election won by Morales (McGuire, 2013: 10).

of civil society were consulted [and that is] surprising given the close links between MAS and social movements" (Borges, 2022: 149, 208). The President was more involved in the development of this program than those of Mexico, Brazil, and Peru. Morales explicitly expressed that he wanted the BJP to be ready for his birthday,[25] 20 days later; its administrative cost should not be higher than 6% of the BJP budget, and that school-aged children in their first five years at public school on all the national territory would be the recipients. In the beginning, the policy entrepreneurs working in a very close policy community, following international CCT experiences and the World Bank's standard model, preferred selection based on means-testing and opposed to universality.

Nevertheless, Evo Morales intervened, and given his ideology and longtime criticism of the World Bank, he rejected the targeting proposal from policy entrepreneurs. For practical reasons, with only 20 days to translate the standard CCT model, BJP entrepreneurs eventually decided to imitate the *Bono Esperanza* and to broaden it to the entire territory (Interview with Alan, one of the first BJP responsible). They used school registration and attendance records, held by the Ministry of Education, to select the recipients. It was the simplest design solution. Meanwhile, time was running out in a low-capability state (Borges, 2022: 151) without reliable income data and with fluctuation in the policies led by the MPD. Therefore, the Ministry of Education—and not the MPD—was made responsible for the program (Marco Navarro, 2012: 25). An institutional innovation absent in the other cases was that the army, the sole institution with access to all the territory that Morales needed by his side (Borges, 2022: 151), became the entity in charge of biannual payment distribution in a country where roads and financial institutions were not everywhere. It was only in the following years that the operational and executive BJP team anchored it to the other Latin American CCTs when they made it one of the axes of the three *Bonos* (with the BJA and the *Renta Dignidad*) to fight poverty (UE, 2008: 53; Interview with Alan).

[25] This was the prelude to the use of the *Bonos* for electoral ends (De la O, 2015).

Bono Juana Azurduy: *Top-down Design with Resistance to the World Bank*

The BJA was the second standard CCT model translation and a pillar of Bolivia's wealth redistribution plan resulting from the nationalization of hydrocarbons. Two factors explained its creation: the international standard CCT model supported by the international community and high infant and maternal mortality rates. Most projects were created but were not concretized by policy entrepreneurs and civil servants inside the MPD. The National Development Plan included a maternal and early childhood component aimed at reducing maternal mortality and children's malnutrition. In addition, the World Bank provided US$ 30 million in 2009 to finance a "mother–child" pilot CCT program in the 53 poorest municipalities of the country. Breaking with the standard international CCT model and the international rules of program design about evidence-based policy, Evo Morales decided unilaterally to broaden this pilot program without waiting for the impact evaluation planned by the World Bank (Borges, 2022: 208).

Once again, in contrast to the other three cases analyzed in this book, like the BJP, the BJA design was top-down, and the President took the initiative. According to Morales's vice president, García Linera, the idea emerged during a conversation in which both concluded that, "single mothers are the most vulnerable, neglected and marginalized of all [...] and the state must help support these women" (McGuire, 2013: 18). However, unlike with the BJP, international organizations were involved in providing technical advice, credits,[26] and evaluations for the BJA. Instead of evaluating the pilot program, the World Bank and the Inter-American Development Bank co-financed a non-randomized evaluation of the BJA. In addition, the World Bank promoted its standard model by organizing meetings with Bolivian BJA designers and CCT designers from Brazil and Mexico. According to McGuire (2013: 20), "Mexican experts persuaded the Bolivian Ministry of Planning to introduce into the *Bono Juana Azurduy* monitoring and evaluation techniques similar to those used in *Oportunidades*, Mexico's flagship program".

[26] In 2011 and 2012, the World Bank and the IADB provided external credit to partly finance the BJA (McGuire, 2013: 19).

The Bonos*: Translation with Universalism as Its Institutional Innovation*

Despite the involvement of the World Bank in the translation of the standard CCT model, Bolivia added a major institutional innovation to the standard model in its decision to make the *Bonos* universal. As in Brazil, CCTs in Bolivia were part of a larger inclusionary project that displaced exclusionary neoliberal practices of neoliberal economic and social policy institutional legacies. Although there is no direct evidence of Brazilian involvement in the design of the *Bonos* (Borges, 2022: 166), as with *Bolsa Família*, Bolivians saw CCTs as an "acquired human right" or a citizenship right (Morales Escoffier, 2009: 23). Out of this belief came the major institutional innovation of a universal program. Indeed, all children enrolled in a public school and all mothers without healthcare insurance could benefit from the *Bonos*. *Bonos* did not base their eligibility criteria on clientelist considerations or poverty levels but on transparent and easily verifiable criteria. Categorical targeting became the norm. The recipient's selection was based on age for the *Bono Juancito Pinto* and *Renta Dignidad* or on status relating to social insurance—not having access to private insurance—for the *Bono Juancita Azurduy* (Wiebe, 2021: 213). For the government, this trend toward universalization of social policies has made the *Bonos* more in line with the processes of social justice. As a BJA entrepreneur highlights:

> Being universal, the *Bonos* led to a more equitable distribution of income (…) in line with certain concepts of universality and justice that the government wants to implement. Unlike others [CCTs] that are much more targeted. (Jimena)

Morales, who was deeply skeptical of means-tested targeting programs, justified universalism because the natural resources (hydrocarbon) behind this funding belonged to all Bolivians, and not only to the poorest (Borges, 2022: 145). According to the *Bonos* entrepreneurs, notions of social justice and the eradication of the causes of extreme poverty anchored in deep social inequalities are very strong in the *Bonos*. One such entrepreneur explains:

> We are trying to put in place a structural change for the real eradication of extreme poverty, a level of social justice. (Martín)

> This idea was enacted in the first paragraph of the Supreme Decree creating the BJP, underlining its "objective of eradicating extreme poverty and the exclusion of people, families and communities." (Presidencia de Bolivia, 2006)

According to the *Bonos* entrepreneurs, one of the primary achievements of Evo Morales's government has been the restoration of collective self-esteem among Indigenous and peasant communities including women, empowering them to exercise meaningful citizenship. Universal *Bonos* funded through the nationalization of hydrocarbons became central to the government's plan to reset this plurinational and socialist state and imbue it with a shared sense of national identity (Borges, 2022: 151). The goal was that all Bolivian citizens become aware of their rights and gain the ability to assert them. This boost in self-esteem within the lower segments of society has played a role in fostering increased social cohesion. As a deputy minister of equality of opportunity reports:

> I believe that one of the most important impacts of this process of change is precisely the fact that we have succeeded in recovering the collective self-esteem of the Indigenous peoples and the popular sectors of our country, and the substantive exercise of citizenship. (...) I believe that much has been done to recognize all Bolivians as citizens, with increasing opportunities in our country. (Alejandra)

The introduction of universal access to *Bonos* demonstrates that translation is never simply the adoption and the imitation of international standards but implies mixing ingredients from abroad—with such conditions as schooling and attending medical check-ups—with new ones, dependent upon national contexts and forces. In Bolivia, the re-foundation of the state with the 2009 Constitution and the nationalization of hydrocarbon allowed for the innovation of universality.

However, this trend toward universalization must be nuanced because universal social policies must "reach the entire population with similar generous transfers and high-quality services, making the resort to markets strictly subject to preferences" (Martínez Franzoni & Sanchez-Ancochea, 2014: 3–4). The education and healthcare sectors in Bolivia faced significant challenges in terms of both availability and quality. As a result, families, including those with lower incomes, have been inclined to rely on private services (McGuire, 2013: 28). Although the selection criteria for the *Bonos* no longer solely relied on poverty levels, the *Bonos* had not succeeded in reducing dependence on the private sector due to the limited improvement in the quality of public health care and education. The population covered by the *Bonos* program remained poor, making it difficult for them to afford private education and healthcare insurance. According to Hunter and Sugiyama, "a large share of the population [benefiting from the *Bonos*] would pass a poverty means test if required to do so" (Hunter & Sugiyama, 2014: 841). As a result, the division between the impoverished population who rely on public social policies and the rest of society who have access to private social protection systems remains intact (Nagels, 2014b, 2019).

In addition, the top-down approach to designing the *Bonos* and the translation of the standard CCT model saw *Bonos* entrepreneurs working in a close instrument community. They sidelined the gender equality agenda both inside and outside of the state. Although the design of the *Bonos* shows that Morales's government was certainly more inclusive, it also reinforced executive power to confront its domestic and international antagonists. According to Anria (2016: 104–105), "it has concentrated power in the executive at the expense of the national legislature, the courts, and the nonpartisan oversight agencies". The heterogeneity and conflicts among different executive branches of the government and the legislative during the *Bonos* design period are worth noting. Indeed, during the Constituent Assembly, Indigenous women—working within Indigenous and peasant organizations—and urban middle-income women—participants of feminist movements and organizations—demonstrated that they could and did cooperate. They succeeded in ratifying the gender parity law in 2009 and the gender violence law in 2013. Nevertheless, *Bonos* entrepreneurs did not include women's agencies, the *Depatricalizacion* Unit, or either Indigenous or not Indigenous Congresswomen in the *Bonos* design process with the result that the focus was more on maternal health than on women's rights and gender equality (Molyneux & Thomson, 2011).

Therefore, as in Peru, without any links to gender equality goals institutions, organizations, and strategic gender equality entrepreneurs, the *Bonos* translated the standard CCT model with strong social policy legacies rooted in intersectional gender inequalities.

Translation with Innovations Rooted in the Institutional Social Policy Legacy of Maternalism

Despite differences in translation, Peruvian and Bolivian CCT translators used the words "gender" and "empowerment" but not in the sense of the social construction of differentiated roles attributed to femininity and masculinity. They did not presume that providing resources for women would generate important changes in gender dynamics, and potentially leading toward real equality and/or women's empowerment. Gender and empowerment in these translations had more to do with rhetoric than action and the meaning attached to those concepts reveals a simplistic understanding of gender (Jenson & Nagels, 2018). For *Juntos* and *Bonos* entrepreneurs (the majority of whom were male), gender was synonymous with women, as a senior (and male) *Juntos* entrepreneur states:

> *Juntos* has a strong gender perspective because it is directly transferred to women, as heads of the household. (David)

Peruvian and Bolivian CCT translators shared an instrumentalist definition of women's participation in the programs while making a passing reference to the keyword "empowerment". For example, a *Juntos* entrepreneur and ex-director explains:

> In a country like ours, the poverty and illiteracy rates are much higher (...) for women, and so it is obvious that we want to empower [empoderar] them, work with them to overcome the main factor accounting for poverty in Peru. This is malnutrition and it is the objective of the *Juntos* program. (Jorge)

In the same vein, in Bolivia, the improvement of women's nutrition was understood as women's empowerment. As a BJA entrepreneur asserts:

> We have noticed that with the increase in nutritional training, the mother is in the process of taking on much more empowerment [*empoderamiento*]. (Maité)

Despite these brief references to gender and women's empowerment, CCT translators relied on an instrumentalist understanding of gender when they designed *Juntos* and the *Bonos*. In the translation process, they reproduced the international instrumentalist definition of women's roles as standardized by the World Bank. These terms are thin, proposing as they do that women's sole social role is that of mother, and that men have no responsibility for childrearing. Therefore, the mother must receive the cash to enhance their children's well-being. The translators assumed a clear dichotomy between male and female social roles that they expressed in two ways.

Translation of Essentialist and Instrumental Views of Gender Based on Various Forms of Knowledge

First, as with the international standard model, Peruvian and Bolivian CCT translators insisted on differential relations between parents and their children, their children's health, care and education, and their human capital. They relied on evidence from various international academics and experts emphasizing the "cost-effectiveness" of transferring cash to mothers. As an academic and prominent *Juntos* supporter and entrepreneur summarizes:

> This kind of program exists in 120 countries and there are studies that demonstrate the cost-effective results when resources pass through the women if the money is transferred to a mother with children. For example, in Bangladesh, Pakistan, and elsewhere, it is an accepted truth. (Diego)

In Bolivia, *Bonos* entrepreneurs also relied on international knowledge to assert the choice to transfer money to mothers and not fathers:

> Not just here but in different countries, [it turns out] that the one that best manages the money in the household is the wife (…) the wife knows best [the state] of the child if he is in recovering or not when he was sick. (Patricio)

Similar instrumentalist approaches were also based on another form of knowledge, more common. For example, as one former *Juntos* director and entrepreneur explains:

> [During the development of] the *Juntos* program it clearly seemed that the money should go to the women because they know how to manage much more responsibly. In the collective unconscious, we all know that the

> woman is the soul of the house. It is because of women that households work. They are good workers, loving and responsible. (Emilio)

In Bolivia also, *Bonos* entrepreneurs subscribed to this belief in the cost-effectiveness of transferring cash to mothers and not fathers. For example, a researcher who participated in the BJA design comes to the same conclusion:

> Women get money because they manage money better than men. (Nadia)

By prioritizing mothers as primary agents in securing opportunities for their children, both the *Bonos* and *Juntos* programs emphasize women's reproductive roles in the pursuit of effectiveness. However, this narrow focus tends to disregard any other aspects of women's health or broader life experiences. *Bonos* and *Juntos* entrepreneurs deployed the classic argument of nature and science to justify their instrumentalist representation of gender. As a senior official and *Juntos* entrepreneur asserts:

> During early childhood, when the mother–child bond is almost inevitable and natural, this is the moment that decides the life and future of children. (Alfonso)

Significantly, the *Juntos* and the *Bonos*'s reliance on women's reproductive, caregiving, and domestic responsibilities was rooted in the assumption that women possess an innate inclination to fulfill these roles for their families and others.

Differences in Values Between Men and Women

Second, *Juntos* and *Bonos* entrepreneurs rationalized their instrumentalist understanding of gender relations by assuming the existence of a clear dichotomy of values between men and women, as well as fathers and mothers. That was an innovative departure from the gender relations promoted by the standard CCT international model. Peruvian and Bolivian CCT entrepreneurs associated men with vice and women with virtue in a way that I did not encounter in the Brazilian and Mexican interviews. For them, women are better household managers, whereas men are likely to spend the subsidy for personal ends or on perceived failings, such as alcohol. In this discourse, there was then a clear justification for excluding men, who were represented as focused on leisure. For example, in Peru, one CCT entrepreneur proposes:

> The benefit should be transferred to the women because they are more responsible and because (...) men spend it on other activities, such as alcohol or other vices. (David)

In Bolivia, a BJA entrepreneur and ex-director shares this negative perception of men:

> You can't be 100% sure that the father [won't use] the money ... for drinking or to celebrate on the famous Singles' Friday, which is a tradition throughout the country. (Maité)

Such views of men as irresponsible and selfish sustained a complex of policy practices excluding men from CCTs that targeted women instead. Therefore, the translated CCTs include intentions about gender relations that reinforce social norms and strong institutional social policy legacies and assign women sole responsibility for managing and caring for the household. While those designs placed men in a negative light, they most importantly reinforced social policy legacy that assigned women responsibility for care and maintaining the household. They disempowered men as breadwinners as well as excused them from any responsibility for care and children, but without empower women to make claims for gender equality. They did not systematically advance the equality agenda, an agenda that ironically, as I have shown, other branches of the Peruvian and Bolivian states and nongovernmental associations promoted simultaneously (Jenson & Nagels, 2018: 333; Nagels, 2016: 488).

Therefore, *Juntos* and *Bonos* designs drew on the long-standing social policy legacy of Latin American maternalism. Moreover, as being a woman is assimilated into being a mother, the social policy legacy of maternalism is one that embraces a differential and essentialist sense of femininity and underscores gender differences. Differences between men and women are perceived as inherent to people and not built by contextualized and historicized social relations resulting, among other things, from the gendered division of labor. Social gender roles are then ahistorical and linked to normative values (Nagels, 2011). Reinforcing the strong institutional legacy of maternalist social policies, *Bonos* and *Juntos* equated women's contributions, as mothers, with contributions to the well-being of society (Jenson, 2011). The improvement of the living conditions of children, and therefore of families and, by extension, of communities and the country rested on their shoulders. Therefore, the *Bonos* and *Juntos* designs instrumentalized women's reproductive role as mothers to invest in their children's human capital to the detriment of the gender equality agenda (Jenson, 2009; Molyneux, 2007).

Translation with Innovations Rooted in Exclusionary Institutional Social Policy Legacies of Denigration of Indigenous Women

Bolivian and Peruvian entrepreneurs translated the instrumentalist views of gender embedded in the standard CCT model and added innovations rooted in strong social policy legacies denigrating Indigenous women. In Peru and Bolivia, gender interacts with race and class to produce institutional legacies of social policy exclusion (Ewig, 2018; Nagels, 2018). Unlike CCTs in Mexico and Brazil, the Peruvian and Bolivian CCT recipients were primarily poor Indigenous women. In both cases, most poor people are Indigenous; in Peru, *Juntos* targeted only rural areas where most of the Indigenous population live and in Bolivia, most of the population is Indigenous.[27] In both countries, poor Indigenous women had historically experienced serious exclusion, discrimination, violence, and lack of access to social rights and social justice (Boesten, 2009; Ewig, 2010; Nagels, 2018).

Translation with the Innovation of Extra-official Conditions

In addition to endorsing conditionality, certain local promoters and entrepreneurs embraced an educational approach that prompted them to utilize the cash transfer as a means to enforce extra-official conditions (Cookson, 2018; Correa & Roopnaraine, 2013; Nagels, 2014; Piccoli, 2014). I encountered these extra-official conditions in Peru and Bolivia but not in Brazil and Mexico. Since they are "extra-official", they are not

[27] According to the 2001 census, 62% of the population aged 15 and over declared themselves to belong to one of the native or Indigenous populations of Bolivia (Molina, 2005).

written on any official CCT documents but are enforced in the implementation process by local promoters and entrepreneurs. This section is thus largely informed by interviews, by which personal experiences of these unwritten conditions were shared. Recipients understood these extra-official conditions to be as binding as the official conditions linked to education and health care. In Peru, these informal conditions included giving birth in an institution, cultivating a garden, adopting a smokeless stove (known as a *cocina mejorada*), attending workshops, participating in parades, painting the *Juntos* flag on their house, covering the travel expenses of local managers, compensating teachers for filling out school attendance forms, sewing blankets and vests in *Juntos* colors, and wearing the vests during public parades or events. While certain informal conditions, such as engaging in activities like growing a garden or attending workshops, can be beneficial to recipients, others, such as participating in parades or covering the travel expenses of local managers, can be viewed as instances of patronage and corruption, ultimately benefiting the *Juntos* officials involved (Nagels, 2018: 423). In Bolivia, extra-official conditions concerned biomedical childbirth, home visits, and children's nutrition status.

In Peru and Bolivia, one such informal condition involved conducting home visits. Nurses and local promoters would visit the homes of recipients to assess their cleanliness and household management practices. A Peruvian local promoter in an Indigenous community explains the advantages of such home visits:

> When you visit you see what she will cook, how [the] space is organized, if salt is missing or there is too much of it, check the utensils. Starting with this, you can then explain what should be done before the next visit. (Aurelia)

In Bolivia, BJA doctors also expected to visit the homes of recipient. As a BJA official explains:

> In the case of *bono*, the doctor goes to the mother's aid and makes a home visit. It's community health. (Maité)

This incorporation of private space into public programs mirrored and intersected other Peruvian policy initiatives intended to "modernize" Indigenous practices. For example, the Ministry of Health policies included the promotion of kitchen gardens[28] and kitchens outside the main dwelling[29] where women would cook standing up rather than crouched down and surrounded by domestic animals. For example, a municipal official in San Miguel insists that recipients "agreed" to participate in these two projects:

> So, there's a tacit agreement that they have to improve their cooking, the organic vegetable garden. (Leonardo)

These initiatives "correspond to a hygienic vision of domestic space and rejects a vision of the interrelation between humans and animals" (Piccoli, 2014: 7). The belief in the necessity of intervening in household behavior largely stemmed from a reluctance to acknowledge the knowledge acquired through experience and cultural practices (Jenson & Nagels, 2018: 335). In addition, in Bolivia, extra-official conditions concerned children's nutritional status. For example, a doctor in charge of the BJA explains that she intimidated recipients by threatening to withdraw them from the program if their children did not gain weight:

> [Children] who are decreasing [in weight], let's put it this way, so we tell them, 'Ma'am, if your child doesn't gain weight next month, you won't get the *bono*.' (Milena)

Another extra-official condition in both countries concerned childbirth. A significant number of Indigenous women expressed a preference for giving birth at home rather than in a health center because at home they can practice "traditional childbirth". This last refers to a series of rituals and manipulations existing among the Aymara and Quechua populations and corresponds to holistic representations of bodies, health, and individuals (Platt, 2006; Rozée, 2007).[30] However, *Juntos* and BJA local entrepreneurs dismissed traditional births in favor of institutional

[28] This program promoted the construction of private vegetable gardens grown on people's land to vary their diet. The visibility of extra-official conditions meant that *Juntos* was more closely associated with the Ministry of Health than with the MIMDES or the Ministry of Education (Huber et al., 2009: 68).

[29] This program aimed to build a stove, a wood-burning stove, and a "kitchen" room separate from the rest of the dwelling. It was promoted by the Ministry of Health.

[30] During childbirth, woman must "push down", toward the earth, in relation with the Pachamama. Hence the vertical positions. A midwife, the future father, and other people

births. For instance, a doctor in the Ayacucho Department attempted to convince pregnant women of the advantages of institutional births, emphasizing the presence of trained biomedical staff and dismissing traditional practices:

> The people in this area are very attached to their beliefs. What often happens is that the person caring for the woman is another woman or her husband. We explain that here we have professionals trained for this, people who have studied and have certificates. (Luis)

In Bolivia, institutional childbirth was an official BJA condition that included an acknowledgment of and respect for traditional Indigenous practices of childbirth.[31] Nevertheless, vertical childbirth was not practiced. An extra-official BJA condition was therefore to impose horizontal biomedical childbirth without respecting Indigenous practices. As a doctor affiliated with the BJA confirms:

> That, at the center, we don't respect yet. As I said, to begin with, the infrastructure we have is not adequate. (Lucas)

A researcher at the *Unidad de Análisis de Políticas Sociales y Económicas* (UDAPE), who participated in the design of BJA, repeats here that traditional childbirth was not widespread in BJA institutional health centers:

> The traditional (birthing) positions of the Aymara and Quechua cultures are not that respected. (Nadia)

In Peru, if some cultural practices (such as vertical labor) could be accommodated in health centers (Ministerio de Salud, 2005), others were dismissed. One horrified male doctor declared:

> These rituals are unacceptable. They do not take place in a sterile environment, which would involve both the personnel and the patient wearing

that the expectant mother trusts accompany her. Hence, this childbirth is identified as collective (Patt, 2006; Rozée, 2007).

[31] In the National Development Plan (2006), a chapter was dedicated to the decolonization of health (NDP, 2006: 37–43) and articles 35, 37, and 39 of the Plurinational Constitution of 2009 recognized the traditional childbirth principles.

> medical gowns. We cannot allow these rituals which put the mother and the newborn at risk. (...) During the birthing ceremony at a woman's house, the ritual takes place in a closed room without the least bit of sunshine, lit with candles. The pregnant woman is seated on a cowhide and with her is her mother-in-law, who chews coca and drinks liquor. That's why I said we could not allow that here. (Monica)

The imposition of such extra-official conditions revealed the prominent eugenic institutional legacies of Peruvian and Bolivian health policy (Boesten, 2009; Ewig, 2010). As seen, most *Bonos* and *Juntos* recipients are classified as extremely poor and belong to Indigenous communities. The imposition of extra-official conditions and the expectation that recipients adhere to certain standards of hygiene, and education as prerequisites for receiving cash transfers reiterate long-established moral and racial narratives. In such narratives, Indigenous women are depicted as idle, unclean, and destitute (Meltzer, 2013: 649). As one finds in eugenic discourse, the responsibility for improving and modernizing "the race" falls upon women as mothers and carriers of genetic reproduction (Ewig, 2010; Molyneux, 2002). The *Bonos* and *Juntos* reproduced a strong eugenic institutional legacy in health policy that sought to modernize childrearing practices by targeting motherhood, thereby reinforcing traditional gender roles, and failing to promote gender equality (Nagels, 2018: 423).

Translation with the Innovation of Denigration of Indigenous Motherhood

The *Bonos* and *Juntos* conditions—extra-official but also official—were imbued with normative prescriptions of maternal roles that were derived from institutional social policy legacies dismissing Indigenous reproductive and family practices. In Peru, to be eligible to receive bi-monthly cash transfers of 200 Nuevos Soles (US$70), mothers with children under the age of 19 were required to fulfill three conditions: (i) ensuring their children attend school, (ii) attending prenatal check-ups and nutrition workshops, and (iii) ensuring regular health check-ups for their children. Local managers, who were primarily educated female professionals from universities or technical institutes, oversaw recipients' compliance with these conditions in each municipality. They collected certificates to verify that mothers had fulfilled the requirements and organized meetings with them (Molyneux & Thomson, 2011: 200). In Bolivia, to receive the BJA benefit, which amounted to US$260 in 2009 and was distributed over thirty-three months, mothers had to possess a valid form of identification. Additionally, they were required to attend prenatal health check-ups, choose to give birth in a medical facility, and complete postnatal check-ups (Vidal Fuertes et al., 2015: 14). Without any gender equality goals in their design, the enforcement of *Bonos* and *Juntos*' conditions, official or not, left plenty of space for the reproduction of these legacies. Their designs relied on implicit goals to create "good" and "modern" mothers who would invest in their children to prepare them for the "modern" world.

The design rationalization of extra-official conditions but also official ones relied on normative, prescriptive notions about what constitutes adequate maternal behavior. Few Peruvian and Bolivian CCT entrepreneurs explicitly denigrated Indigenous persons or made references to ethnicity or Indigeneity. However, the derogatory use of such terms as "community", "people", "myths", and "beliefs" served as code for these issues. These codes expressed veiled cultural and ethnic hierarchies. The majority of the Bolivian and Peruvian CCT entrepreneurs were male and identified or self-identified as "white" or métis, while the recipients were either identified or self-identified as Indigenous women. The *Bonos* and *Juntos* entrepreneurs saw Indigenous mothers as problematic mothers (Radcliffe, 2002: 153) because they were ignorant and were thus perpetuating "bad practices". In Bolivia, for example, a BJA national entrepreneur considers that recipients did not understand the BJA conditions:

> They don't understand that they have to go to the control. Many moms think that just being registered is enough. That they only had to register and then we would pay them. (Guillermo)

In the same vein, a female *Juntos* promoter in an Indigenous community complains:

> What they lack is maturity (…) but also a level of knowledge, of education. Many do not understand!. (Isabel)

The perceived "ignorance" of the recipients was attributed to their Indigenous origins, which was seen as necessitating intervention due to the assumption that Indigenous individuals exhibited poor mothering skills and engaged in unhygienic practices. An ex-national director of *Juntos* publicly criticizes Indigenous care practices:

> You must educate mothers to demonstrate kindness, affection [...] [because] when you study the Indigenous world you realize [...] that children are seen as one of the family's assets [...] and so the problem is that these children do not grow up in a happy environment [...]. In these areas, mothers often beat their children. (Emilio)

In Bolivia, *Bonos* entrepreneurs also perceived "myths" as obstacles to accessing health services, as a doctor in charge of the BJA explains:

> So maybe that's why [women don't go to health centers]: the myths: that doctors don't attend to you, they treat you badly or make you suffer even more. (Hernán)

These views on Indigenous women gave way to contempt. An illustration of this can be seen in the case of a nurse who oversaw *Juntos* in a rural Indigenous community:

> The mother from the field when her child is sick with diarrhea, she thinks that it is because the land has hurt him and not because he ate something bad. She still thinks like that! So, they take him first to be healed by a Shaman. (Isaac)

A doctor in charge of the BJA also resorted to Indigenous idiosyncrasy to explain the low spread of vaccines among the infant population:

> It's that they have this idiosyncratic of saying that vaccines can kill children, that 'you've come to kill my child because I have several children and you want to kill my child'. So, it's very difficult to reach these ladies. (Milena)

In Peru, a doctor of *Juntos* expressed a broader condemnation:

> We must understand that in some populations, where health is poor, it is not a priority: sometimes a person worries more about his animals' health or his land rather than his children's. (Luis)

These quotes revealed the ignorance, the dismissal, and the stigmatization of Andean ontology. In the Andes, there exists a blending of natural and animal elements with the human and supernatural realms. Mountains, rocks, streams, valleys, and the land itself are imbued with spiritual essences and agency (De la Cadena, 2010). According to Andean ontology, humans are not seen as separate or superior; animals, lands, and children hold equal significance (Hall, 2020; Mathez-Stiefel et al., 2007). Unfortunately, institutional actors involved in the design and implementation of *Juntos* and *Bonos* disregarded or failed to understand this ontology, leading to the perpetuation of stereotypes anchored in strong institutional legacies that labeled Indigenous mothers as inadequate caregivers. *Juntos* and *Bonos* entrepreneurs associated the intersection of Indigeneity and femininity with a lack of modernity. This was also the case in Bolivia despite a powerful Indigenous discourse at the head of the Bolivian Plurinational state.

Innovation: Using Conditions for Changing Indigenous Maternity Practices

When faced with what they perceived as ignorance, *Juntos* and *Bonos* entrepreneurs used the importance of the program's conditions, believing that their implementation would lead to a transformation in mindsets and behaviors. They aimed to replace current maternity practices—which are considered "inadequate", "archaic", and "Indigenous"—with practices deemed "superior" because they are considered "scientific" and "modern". A doctor in a rural health center stresses the recipient's ignorance to explain the educational mission of *Juntos*:

> [When] *Juntos* first started... their mindset didn't include the need to improve health or prevent problems. Thus, in the beginning, the health workers had to make a great effort to educate them, to orient them in the right direction. (Monica)

In Bolivia, the BJA's aim was also to change the mentality of women recipients through education:

> Here we change their mentality, we inform them, we educate them (...) through the talks and the care we give (...) we have to make them understand the importance of going to the check-up. And that, as I tell you, that means changing the mentality of those who come to the center'. (Lucas)

A provincial *Juntos* employee clarifies that, in her view, the primary challenge lay in altering behavior and aligning it with the expectations inherent in the "modern" policy instrument of a CCT:

> Actually, this is all a process of change that is necessary to activate in these communities and it is difficult to break their old habits. (Norma)

Even in Bolivia, where, as seen, the heart of the new model of development lay in the Indigenous community, some of *Bonos* designers believed that they also aimed to educate mothers to be "good mothers":

> That's been the hardest part: educating the population. We educate them, we teach them. (Hernán)

Another promoter of *Juntos* in a rural Indigenous community explains:

> What we want for them is a change of lifestyle. Poverty is a disease that needs to be removed from their heads, right? They cannot have that feeling all their lives, right?. (Isabel)

In Bolivia, the aim was also to change the habits of the poor, according to a researcher involved in the BJA design process:

> The idea is to create habits in the population. In other words, even when they no longer receive money, they continue to turn up. The idea is to generate a habit and to do that we educate the mother. So, she knows that bringing her child to the check-up brings her a benefit; whether she's given money or not. It's a benefit for her health and her family. (Jimena)

These perspectives regarding poverty, which attribute its origins more to beliefs, attitudes, and mentalities rather than material conditions and the unequal structures within which the lower classes are situated, reflect a particular interpretation of "responsibility" that serves as a justification for upholding conditionality (Jenson & Nagels, 2018: 334). In conjunction with maternalism, *Juntos* and the *Bonos* entrepreneurs in the translation and implementation processes used the conditions as leverage for modernity making the CCT an instrument to modernize and improve the behavior of poor Indigenous mothers. This translation of the CCT international standard added an innovation rooted in long-standing institutional legacies that denigrate Indigenous women.

Conclusion

In this chapter, I argued that the World Bank standard CCT model translation in Peru and Bolivia, which were not intrinsically worse in matters of gender equality than Mexico and Brazil, involved the innovation of introducing maternalism and the denigration of Indigenous women in their CCT design and implementation. Since the standard CCT model promoted by the World Bank did not include any gender equality goals, Peruvian and Bolivian translators did not include any gender equality entrepreneurs from inside or outside the state. Instead, they embedded strong exclusionary institutional social policy legacies into the new CCT programs. CCT entrepreneurs in both countries gathered in very small communities with international academic and professional ties, translated and designed the new CCT programs without any consideration for gender equality or contact with strategic gender equality entrepreneurs. That they should adopt such similar approaches is interesting given the marked difference in political regimes involved. In Peru, these processes occurred within the powerful neoliberalist MEF, where entrepreneurs were convinced by the efficacity of means-test targeting while in Bolivia, these processes took place inside the MPD where entrepreneurs followed the ambitious post-neoliberal and Indigenous project of decolonizing the state and universalizing social policies. This result contradicts in part the research sustaining the tendency of leftist political ideology to design and implement class-based gender equality policies (e.g., Htun & Weldon, 2018; Staab, 2017). However, following this literature, it shows the importance of inter-sectorial alliances among WPA and social ministries inside the government and the influence of feminist and women's organizations outside the state in the decision-making processes. All these elements were absent in Peru and Bolivia.

Bonos and *Juntos* translators reproduced those exclusionary institutional legacies in their modern instruments. The resulting *Bonos* and *Juntos* designs reinforced gender inequalities, traditional gender roles, and the gendered division of labor by discouraging men from taking up care responsibilities and imposing the respect for the conditions on women. By promoting maternalism and women's assumed virtues as primary caregivers within families, these programs could place increased burdens on their time. The time dedicated to meeting the conditions of the *Bonos* and *Juntos* would detract them from income-generating activities, reducing opportunities for women to escape poverty (Holmes & Jones, 2013: 73, 84; Molyneux, 2007).

In addition, I have demonstrated in this chapter that translation processes involve innovation and creativity that depend on the institutional and political context. *Juntos* innovations meant including victims of political violence that were principally rural, poor, and Indigenous women as recipients in response to TRC's recommendations and unravel social protests. Strongly influenced by President Evo Morales, *Bonos* entrepreneurs decided to universalize the program and redistribute the resources of hydrocarbon nationalization. Nevertheless, in both cases, these innovations could not overthrow the strong institutional social policy legacies that denigrate Indigenous women.

In both cases, CCT translation encouraged further denigration of the mothering practices of Indigenous women. The enforcement of conditions and extra-official conditions reinforced strong social policy legacies of dismissal, depreciation, and stigmatization of Indigenous mothers who were the first Peruvian and Bolivian CCT clientele. This is more surprising in the case of Bolivia given the strong Indigenous discourse of the Morales administration. While the government advocated for the decolonization of the state including the healthcare system, in practice the *Bonos* reproduced social policy legacies that institutionalized strong hierarchies between Indigenous and non-Indigenous people. According to Jhonson (2010: 142), "this asymmetry of social, political, economic, linguistic, cognitive and gender power persists in Bolivia and prevents genuine 'respect' and 'dialogue' [because] the structure itself remains intolerant". It shows that in Bolivia, the rhetoric in favor of ethnic recognition did not reach BJA and the BJP entrepreneurs and implementers. These actors reproduced strong social policy legacies and continued to hold Indigenous women responsible for poverty and considered Andean ontology as a barrier to accessing biomedical and "modern" institutional services and acquiring "good" health. Popular and Indigenous knowledge and practices were still associated with "beliefs" and "myths" and were even seen as harmful to people's health. As in Peru, Andean ontology was either held responsible for all ills or ignored (Ewig, 2018; Rozée, 2007).

CHAPTER 6

Lessons for Gender Equality and Social Policies

In this chapter, I place the conclusion of the book highlighting the theoretical and policy lessons that can be learned from the empirical cases presented. It then explores the differentiated explanations and variations built out of the theoretical framework and compares them to the empirical findings. In doing so, it lays open the implications of the inclusion or not of gender equality goals in social policies, stressing the limits and the potential of each sequence as well as discussing their implications for the study of social policies with a gender lens. After, the chapter discusses the theoretical implications and contributions of the findings for the gender study of social policies, historical institutionalism, and policy transfer. Finally, it unpacks the significance of this study for policymakers, politicians, and feminist activists who lead or advocate for such social policies throughout Latin America and beyond.

This book aimed to understand the "fading goal of gender equality" as CCTs traveled through the World Bank and throughout Latin America. My main conclusions underscore the importance of multi-level analysis, the agency of strategic gender equality entrepreneurs, as well as the knowledge they used that should take a step back from positivism and consider everyday life of women recipients of the policies they design.

In tracking these disappearing gender equality goals, I rely on a mechanistic approach situated in historical institutionalism and gender analysis.

N. Nagels, *Gender Equality in Conditional Cash Transfer Designs*, Studies of the Americas,
https://doi.org/10.1007/978-3-031-60871-1_6

The mechanisms of cooking, standardization, and translation are key to explaining how changes occurred. And an eye to the political configuration populated by strategic (gender equality) entrepreneurs, institutional legacies and venues and knowledge on gender gives us a sense of the evolving or devolving presence of gender equality goals.

Mechanisms: How Changes Occur

Cooking, standardization, and translation were causal mechanisms and account for how CCT policy designs—as a key instrument in social investment policies—transformed, from the beginning to the end of policy development and the transfer processes in between. While cooking refers to the first sequence of CCT development, the subsequent phases of standardization and translation occurred when CCTs traveled out of their origins.

Pioneer CCT *Progresa* seems to be an entirely new dish and is more of a departure in the area of gender equality than *Bolsa Família*. *Bolsa Família* cooks blended known ingredients—or subnational CCT programs designed for other uses—to make something new. What is new to this recipe is its attempt to alter intra-household relations in favor of women's financial autonomy. But flavors of its old constituent parts render implicit what could have been made explicit.

In the second sequence, I tracked the standardization process as CCTs traveled from Mexico and Brazil passing through the World Bank—that bought, transformed, and promoted them as the "best instruments to fight poverty"—and beyond standardization was an active process that implied certification, decontextualization, and framing. The World Bank began certifying and legitimizing CCTs using huge amounts of evidence to prove that they effectively achieved their social objectives. In this process, the World Bank social protection unit decontextualized both *Progresa* and *Bolsa Família*, lifting them out of their feminist and gender-sensitive contexts to treat them as pro-poor policy instruments. Therefore, the Bank reframed a "thin" CCT standard version, abandoning concern for gender equality or women's empowerment and only retaining an instrumentalist rationale for transferring benefits to mothers, and this to maximize improved child outcomes. The analysis highlighted that certification, decontextualization, and framing—constituting standardization—were not linear but overlapping and inter-connected.

In the third and last sequence of CCT travel, I traced the translation of the World Bank standard model by latecomers Peru and Bolivia. Translation implied innovations, adaptation, and filtration and not adoption in toto. In Peru and Bolivia, the standard model underwent interpretations and innovations depending on national context. While Toledo's center-right government targeted only rural poor people and included victims of the internal war as recipients, Evo Morales's left-wing government added the innovation of universalization. However, the analysis showed that the lack of gender equality goals in the thin standard model were reproduced by Peruvian and Bolivian translators. They took this lack one step further by incorporating gender relations based on exclusionary social policy legacies.

Context: Why Changes Occur

Why did *Progresa* and *Bolsa Família* include gender equality goals while the World Bank's standard CCT model and the Peruvian and Bolivian CCT translations excluded them? Using a mechanistic approach (Falleti & Lynch, 2009), I argue that context drives the direction of change. Institutional legacies and venues, strategic (gender equality) entrepreneurs and knowledge on gender are mutually constituted and intertwined and their particular configurations are what determines the presence or absence of gender equality goals.

My main conclusion is that only strong strategic gender equality entrepreneurs—convinced by feminist knowledge, embedded in institutions and venues and making claims for gender equality—could develop a new recipe that included gender equality goals. The book's best-case scenario was Mexico. There, such actors were technocrat entrepreneurs that became strategic gender equality entrepreneurs convinced of the link between poverty and gender inequalities. They were embedded in institutional sites—CONAPO—with strong gender and feminist institutional legacies, supported by a powerful and resourceful institution—the Ministry of Finance—and surrounded by the strong presence of Mexican and global feminism in the context of the Fourth International Conference on Women. In Brazil, institutional legacies and venues—the PT social right-based program, the progressive 1988 Constitution, and the new institutional gender machinery—led strategic entrepreneurs to develop the *Bolsa Família* recipe with implicit gender equality goals. They could not do more because they were constrained by subnational

CCTs, party system fragmentation, as well as conflicts among bureaucracies and ministries. Weak institutional legacies at the World Bank—here taking the form of the WID approach—meant the exclusion of strategic gender equality entrepreneurs and a resulting recipe that retained only an instrumentalist conception of gender. Following standardization, latecomer translators—Peru and Bolivia—were free to ignore gender equality and to add local ingredients to their recipes, inherited from institutional social policies rooted in gender and racial inequalities.

Agency, Mechanisms, Multi-Level Analysis, and Knowledge

Using a historical institutionalist approach and drawing from the literature on mechanisms, gender and social policies, I assert that CCT cooks, standardizers, and translators were essential to the presence or absence of gender equality goals. They are not "institutional automatons" (Gains & Lowndes, 2014: 528), but more than their charisma, talent, or individual characteristics, their power depends on their social and institutional positions (Campbell, 2004). Contributing to the literature on gender and social policies, I also stress the importance of strategic gender equality entrepreneurs gathered in informal or intimate instrument communities. The outlier case of Mexico showed that *Progresa* included gender equality goals because liberal feminism in alliance with the powerful actor of global feminism had succeeded in institutionalizing gender knowledge inside the state. I also demonstrated the importance of informal and even intimate links—based on love or friendship—inside instrument communities allowing for the circulation of feminist knowledge. In Brazil, feminist and women's movements were close to the PT and feminist actors indirectly influenced *Bolsa Família* in the form of implicit gender equality goals. Their absence was salient in the other cases. The World Bank CCT standardization and Peruvian and Bolivian CCT translation efforts took place without any strategic gender equality entrepreneur or representative of gender institutional machinery and their knowledge, despite the fact that they were simultaneously promoting a gender equality agenda elsewhere. This result confirms the importance of inter-sectorial alliances among women's institutional agencies and social ministries within the government and the ability of feminist and women's organizations outside the state to influence decision-making processes (e.g., Htun & Weldon,

2018). All these elements were absent from the World Bank, Peru, and Bolivia.

In addition, I contribute to the literature on mechanisms and historical institutionalism by adding a multi-level analysis to research that has been mostly state-centered (e.g., Béland y Cox, 2011; Falleti & Lynch, 2009; Hall, 1993; Pierson, 2004). I showed that the sequence of mechanisms was key to explaining the eradication of gender equality goals in CCT designs and that these mechanisms occurred at domestic and international levels. Cooking precedes standardization, which precedes translation. Standardization in and of itself did not lead to the exclusion of gender equality goals, but it was the particular configuration of, and the interactions between, strategic (gender equality) entrepreneurs, institutional legacies and venues, as well as knowledge on gender. This result partly contradicts the research sustaining the importance of left-wing political ideology to the design and implementation of class-based gender equality policies (e.g., Htun & Weldon, 2018). Since mechanism's outcomes are highly sensitive to context, the ability to generalize is weak. However, the presence of those mechanisms could be found in other cases with other mechanisms since I recognize that in the social sciences, most outcomes have multiple causes and do not depend on variables. Together, cooking, standardization, and translation could be useful to analyze other objects that travel, such as public policies, norms, or organizations. Researchers might look to their initial innovation, their translation in new places while take into account changes in time, space, and level of implementation—from the local to the international. In addition, while cooking and standardization could be useful for those researchers interested in the early stages of policy development and travel, translation might be a useful lens through which to examine the late stages of travel.

The third takeaway is that social policies are gendering practices in which domestic and international levels intertwine. Comparative social policy research on the expansionary era of social policies in Latin America looks mainly to domestic factors such as policy legacy and left–right cleavages (e.g., Arza et al., 2022; Borges, 2022; Garay, 2016; Huber & Stephen, 2012; Staab, 2017). I argue, however, that international and transnational factors are equally important to understanding this expansionary era, particularly as it crosses paths with the neoliberal era. The interactions among international and domestic factors are key to understanding the strategic (gender equality) entrepreneurs and the work that they do at different levels. This attention to multi-level interactions might usefully be applied to other social policies in the region. For instance, the influence of international organization such as the Economic Commission for Latin America and the Caribbean was influential during the expansionary era, but this international organization's sway has been mostly overlooked in the research (with exception, e.g., Jenson, 2020; Mahon, 2024; Razavi, 2020). I argue that multi-level interactions help us to explain how and why social policies, such as CCTs, make men and women equal subjects, or not, as the case may be, shaped as they are by other subordination processes such as racialization and class construction. This approach contributes to the research on policy transfer by stressing that what moves changes during travel, especially during its second phase—standardization—and the last one—translation. The current research on policy transfer partly overlooks this mutability. The focus on standardization mostly led by the World Bank explains why Latin American CCT designs have not included gender equality goals even as they followed the Mexican model and targeted women as recipients. Therefore, the contributions presented here reaffirm the centrality of multi-level institutional design to gender relations. Understanding how and why CCTs lost their gender equality goals helps this book to avoid the pitfalls of romanticizing the CCT as "the best instrument to fight poverty".

The fourth takeaway of this book is that knowledge on gender is crucial to designing social policies that promote gender equality. As with historical institutionalism and gender analysis, I have stressed that knowledge, produced through conflicts and institutionalized, influences policy design—because knowledge and expertise provide alternative solutions to public problems. Knowledge about women and gender relations are objects of political conflicts over such matters as, for instance, ways to frame gender equality. Since CCTs were the first evidence-based social policies in Latin America, I showed that knowledge and expertise about gender constitute an important piece of the puzzle that is altered gender equality goals in CCT design as these traveled in Latin America. In Mexico, liberal feminist knowledge linking poverty and gender inequality led to the integration of gender equality goals in *Progresa*. The quantitative and economic knowledge privileged by the World Bank led this Bank of knowledge to retain only an instrumentalist rational of gender and with it erase gender equality goals in its standard CCT model. Excluding feminist knowledge that stresses intersectional, historical, and very context-specific gender relations has led, paradoxically, to evidence-based policies such as CCTs. And these are characterized by thin narratives rooted in ignorance. The story about the "fabulous destiny of CCTs" that the World Bank has circulated with its instrumentalist views of gender has shaped decision making and policy designs—to the detriment of the knowledge shared by its female recipients. For example, in Peru and Bolivia, CCT translators were free to exclude gender equality goals and therefore had plenty of space to design programs rooted in exclusionary social policy legacies reinforcing gender and racial inequalities.

In addition, the taking into account of the different forms of knowledge involved in developing social policies has methodological implications that support the interpretative turn in social policy analysis, and more generally in political science. This manuscript is the first book-length work based on extensive empirical research and in-depth multi-level case analysis covering gender equality goals in the design of a policy that travels. Few studies analyze policy travel through in-depth fieldwork in domestic cases with an eye to international organizations and based on more than just quantitative data and discourse analysis. The book fills this gap with qualitative methods tracing the shape and reach of mechanisms by way of the careful analysis of empirical records from academic and specialized literature as well as from interviews. The latter allow us to uncover the micro-foundation of the cooking, standardization, and translation processes and to consider the meaning that strategic (gender equality) entrepreneurs assign to their actions. They give us access to the intentions about gender in policy design. Qualitative methods are better suited to understanding intersectional, historical, and very context-specific gender relations at work not only in the cooking, standardization, and translation processes, but also in the knowledge production upon which these processes hang.

These contributions show the importance of studying CCTs and more broadly social policies through gender and multi-level lenses. The recent development of social policies in Latin America have shown the crucial role played by cash transfers during the COVID-19 pandemic. The strongest cash transfer responses to the pandemic came from countries, like Brazil and its *Bolsa Família*, with established policy legacies to that effect. Faced with the opposition from the President Bolsonaro, political and social opposition as well as pressures from state governors led legislators nonetheless to pass a bill to expand the coverage and the generosity of *Bolsa Família* and to use its institution venues to create new transfers. In contrast, the elimination in 2018 of the highly institutionalized *Progesa/*

Oportunidades/Prospera by President López Obrador dramatically weakened these legacies and there was therefore no response of this kind to COVID-19 (Blofield et al., 2023). However, cash transfers, no matter how generous they could be, were insufficient to mitigate the crisis of care revealed by the pandemic. Without gender equality goals or a feminist agenda, these transfers did not recognize how essential nonmarket goods, services, and productive activities are to market economies. For example, these transfers did not finance or recognize women's unpaid and paid work to absorb the crisis through the care of children, elderly, and sick persons at home and the long-term deficiencies of care systems. They did not value or reward women's paid and unpaid work that is the direct result of gender, racial, and other inequalities (Heintz et al., 2021). Parts of the answer to the invisibility of care work in social policy lie in the data used by multi-level social policymakers as they cook, standardize, or translate social policies. Far from feminist knowledge close to intersectional and contextual everyday experiences, these data do not capture the realities of women's and men's lives, including care work and the gendered division of labor. Since data drive policy problems and solutions, social policies relying on quantitative data that do not capture the root causes and structural aspects of gender inequalities could reinforce these inequalities without questioning capitalism and patriarchy as the sources of poverty and the crisis of care (Fuentes & Cookson, 2020).

New questions emerge from this research. How and why do feminist social policies, such as family policies, work to better redistribute care? How are these policies informed by multi-level gendering practices and what does this imply for the feminist agenda? How do international organizations, the state, and women at the local level, who participate in the implementation of these policies by way of their paid or unpaid work, bring policies and practices promoting gender equality and the redistribution of care to the fore? More precisely, how do international organization, such as the World Bank or the ECLAC, gender women and men through their policies? How do the gendering practices and knowledge at work within international organizations explain these results? How do states navigate local and international influences and knowledge to cook social policies in favor of gender equality? How do women negotiate gender relations when they implement these policies by their paid and unpaid work and on what type of local, national, and international practices and knowledge do they rely? Finally, how do feminist researchers bottom-up women's everyday life experiences and knowledge in available data as they design feminist social policies?

Implications for the Politics of Social Policies with Gender Equality Concerns

The novel analysis of the CCT along this trajectory, the outcomes of which vary in each phase, is revealing and has important theoretical but also policy implications. By uncovering the trajectory of CCT design, this study sheds a different light on the "fabulous success stories of CCTs" as recounted in most of the development and social policy literature. While CCTs can improve children's health and education and mitigate poverty, they have failed to address gender inequalities despite transferring the cash to women. These findings strongly suggest that if national translation and thus internal gender-discriminatory norms matter, the way international organizations and strategic gender equality entrepreneurs in originating countries frame institutional design is important as it creates conditions for any inclusion, or not, of gender equality goals in social policies that travel.

Therefore, the book is an invitation to form transnational feminist alliances in the realm of social policy since policies travel and social policies are fundamental to altering the unjust sharing of unpaid care work. Transnational feminist agendas, with strong national and local roots and coordination, should target not only status policies, such as gender-based violence or women's political representation, but also social policies in favor of gender equality. The recent developments of the "right to care" demands from Argentinean and other Latin American activists and academics to the Inter-American Court of Human Rights are inspiring.

The findings also point to the need to design policies that invest and support gender equality entrepreneurs at multiple levels. International organizations and states need to invest in women's political apparatuses and in the training of entrepreneurs so that they might take qualitative feminist knowledge—addressing complex, fluid, intersectional, historical, and very context-specific gender relations—into account. They need to recognize women's everyday lives, their experiences of violence, care, love, and discrimination as valuable knowledge that has as much value as quantitative data. This is particularly important for the World Bank, as a Bank of knowledge, imbued as it is by neoclassical economics, and positivism and which has had a tremendous influence on what counts as "truthful" data and knowledge in matters of development and social policies.

Otherwise, without this understanding of gender relations, on the part of international development organizations and national policymakers, interacting with recognized national state machinery on gender equality and supported by strong feminist actors inside and outside the state, social policies like CCTs may simply perpetuate gender and racial inequalities. This level of understanding is of particular importance when CCTs are introduced to highly unequal societies with exclusionary social policies legacies. This book has also demonstrated the need for policymakers, strategic gender equality entrepreneurs, politicians, and feminist activists who lead or advocate for such anti-poverty programs throughout Latin America and the developing world, to integrate the meanings and implications of intersectionality. The contextual and intersectional women's knowledge, the recipients of these policies, must be recognized and used in policy design. This implies an epistemological turn toward interpretation, "thick description" (Geertz, 1973), and feminist and decolonial knowledge that takes a step back from positivism in multi-level social policies and developments agencies.

References

Adato, M., & Roopnaraine, T. (2010). Women's status, gender relations, and conditional cash transfers. In M. Adato & J. Hoddinott (Eds.), *Conditional cash transfers in Latin America* (pp. 284–314). The Johns Hopkins University Press International Food Policy Institute.

Adato, M., De la Brière, B., Mindek, D., & Quisumbing, A. (2000). *The impact of PROGRESA on women's status and intrahousehold relations*. International Food Policy Research Institute.

Altglas, V. (2018). Bricolage. In G. Ritzer (Ed.), *The Blackwell encyclopedia of sociology* (pp. 1–2). Wiley.

Altamirano, M., & Zárate-Tenorio, B. (2022). Trade unions, labor market dualization, and investment in early childhood education and care in Latin America. In J. L. Garritzmann, S. Häusermann, & B. Palier (Eds.), *The world politics of social investment: Volume I: Welfare states in the knowledge economy* (pp. 330–350). Oxford University Press.

Alvarez, S. E. (1990). *Engendering democracy in Brazil: Women's movements in transition politics*. Princeton University Press.

Ancelovici, M., & Jenson, J. (2012). La standardisation et les mécanismes du transfert transnational. *Gouvernement et Action Publique, 1*(1), 37–58.

Ancelovici, M., & Jenson, J. (2013). Standardization for transnational diffusion: The case of truth commissions and conditional cash transfers. *International Political Sociology, 7*(3), 294–312.

Anctil Avoine, P. (2022). Insurgent peace research: Affects, friendship and feminism as methods. Conflict, *Security & Development, 22*(5), 435–455.

Annesley, C. (2010). Gender, politics and policy change: The case of welfare reform under new labour. *Government and Opposition, 45*(1), 50–72.

N. Nagels, *Gender Equality in Conditional Cash Transfer Designs*, Studies of the Americas, https://doi.org/10.1007/978-3-031-60871-1

Anria, S. (2019). *When movements become parties: The Bolivian Mas in comparative perspective*. Cambridge University Press.

Anria, S. (2016). More inclusion, less liberalism in Bolivia. *Journal of Democracy, 27*(3), 99–108.

Anria, S., & Niedzwiecki, S. (2019). Participatory social policies: Diverging patterns in Brazil and Bolivia. *Latin American Politics and Society, 61*(2), 115–137.

Arroyo, J. (2010). *Estudio cualitativo de los efectos del Programa Juntos en los cambios de comportamiento de los hogares beneficiarios en el distrito de Chuschi: Avances y evidencias*. Ministerio de la Mujer y Poblaciones Vulnerables.

Arza, C., Castiglioni, R., Franzoni, J. M., Niedzwiecki, S., Pribble, J., & Sánchez-Ancochea, D. (2022). *The political economy of segmented expansion: Latin American social policy in the 2000s*. Cambridge University Press.

Bacchi, C. (2017). Policies as gendering practices: Re-viewing categorical distinctions. *Journal of Women, Politics & Policy, 38*(1), 20–41.

Barrientos, A. (2004). Latin America: Towards a liberal-informal welfare regime. In I. Gough & G. Wood (Eds.), *Insecurity and welfare regimes in Asia, Africa and Latin America. Social policy in development contexts* (pp. 121–168). Cambridge University Press.

Barrientos, A. (2009). Labour markets and the (hyphenated) welfare regime in Latin America. *Economy and Society, 38*(1), 81–108.

Barrientos, A. (2012). Dilemas de las políticas sociales latinoamericanas ¿Hacia una protección social fragmentada? *Nueva Sociedad, 239*, 65–78.

Barrientos, A. (2013). *Social assistance in developing countries*. Cambridge University Press.

Barrientos, A., & Dejong, J. (2006). Reducing child poverty with cash transfers: A sure thing? *Development Policy Review, 24*(5), 537–552.

Barrientos, A., Gideon, J., & Molyneux, M. (2008). New developments in Latin America's social policy. *Development and Change, 39*(5), 759–774.

Barrientos, A., & Villa, J. M. (2016). Economic and political inclusion in human development conditional income transfer programmes in Latin America. *Social Policy & Society, 15*(3), 421–433.

Bastagli, F. (2009). *From social safety net to social policy? The role of conditional cash transfers in welfare state development in Latin America*. International Policy Center for Inclusive Growth. UNDP.

Bastagli, F., Hagen-Zanker, J., Harman, L., Barca, V., Sturge, G., Schmidt, T., & Pellerano, L. (2016). *Cash transfers: What does the evidence say. A rigorous review of programme impact and the role of design and implementation features*. Overseas Development Institute.

Bate, P. (2004). *The story behind Oportunidades*. Banco Interamericano de Desarrollo.

Batthyány, K., Scavino, S., & Perrotta, V. (2020). Cuidados Infantiles y Trabajo Remunerado en Tres Generaciones de Mujeres Madres de Montevideo: Los Recorridos de las Desigualdades de Género. *Dados, 63*(4), 1–37.

Beach, D., & Pedersen, R. B. (2019). *Process-tracing methods: Foundations and guidelines*. University of Michigan Press.

Beaudet, P., Haslam, P. A., Caouette, D., & Benhmade, A. (Eds.). (2019). *Enjeux et défis du développement international : Acteurs et champs d'action* (Édition nouvelle et actualisée). Les Presses de l'Université d'Ottawa.

Bedford, K. (2007). The imperative of male inclusion: How institutional context influences World Bank gender policy. *International Feminist Journal of Politics, 9*(3), 289–311.

Bedford, K. (2009). *Developing partnerships: Gender, sexuality, and the reformed World Bank*. University of Minnesota Press.

Behrman, J., Parker, S., & Todd, P. (2004). Impacto de Mediano Plazo del Programa Oportunidades sobre la Educación y el Trabajo de Jóvenes del Medio Rural que tenían de 9 a 15 años de edad en 1997, In B. Hernández Prado & M. Hernández Ávila (Eds.), *Evaluación externa de impacto del Programa Oportunidades 2004* (Vol. 1). Instituto Nacional de Salud Pública.

Behrman, J. R. (2007). *Policy-Oriented Research Impact Assessment (PORIA). Case study on the International Food Policy Research Institute (IFPRI) and the Mexican Progresa anti-poverty and human resource investment conditional cash transfer program*. International Food Policy Research Institute.

Behrman, J. R. (2010). The International Food Policy Research Institute (IFPRI) and the Mexican PROGRESA anti-Poverty and human resource investment conditional cash. *World Development, 38*(10), 1473–1485.

Bejar, H. (2001). *Justicia social, política social*. CEDEP.

Béland, D. (2009). Gender, ideational analysis, and social policy. *Social Politics, 4*(1), 558–581.

Béland, D. (2019). *How ideas and institutions shape the politics of public policy*. Cambridge University Press.

Béland, D., & Cox, R. H. (2011). *Ideas and politics in social science research*. Oxford University Press.

Béland, D., Howlett, M., & Mukherjee, I. (2018). Instrument constituencies and public policy-making: An introduction. *Policy and Society, 37*(1), 1–13.

Benería, L. (2003). *Gender, development and globalization: Economics as if all people mattered*. Routledge.

Benería, L., & Sen, G. (2021). Feminist challenges to development economics. In G. Berik & E. Kongar (Éds.), The routledge handbook of feminist economics (1re éd., pp. 25–33). Routledge.

Bennett, A., & Checkel, J. T. (2015). *Process tracing: From philosophical roots to best practices*. Cambridge University Press.

Bereni, L., Chauvin, S., Jaunait, A., & Revillard, A. (2012). *Introduction aux études sur le genre*. De Boeck.

Bergeron, S. (2003). The post-Washington consensus and economic representations of women in development at the World Bank. *International Feminist Journal of Politics, 5*(3), 397–419.

Berik, G. (2017). Beyond the rhetoric of gender equality at the World Bank and the IMF. *Canadian Journal of Development Studies/Revue Canadienne d'études Du Développement, 38*(4), 564–569.

Beyeler, M., & Annesley, C. (2011). Gendering the institutional reform of the welfare State: Germany, the United Kingdom, and Switzerland. In M. L. Krook & F. Mackay (Eds.), *Gender, politics and institutions: Toward a feminist institutionalism* (pp. 79–94). Palgrave.

Bilge, S. (2009). Théorisations féministes de l'intersectionnalité. *Diogène, 225*(1), 70–88.

Blackden, C. M., & Bhanu, C. (1999). *Gender, growth, and poverty reduction: Special program of assistance for Africa, 1998 status report on poverty in Sub-Saharan Africa*. World Bank.

Blofield, M., Pribble, J., & Giambruno, C. (2023). *The politics of social protection during times of crisis*. Cambridge University Press.

Blofield, M., & Martínez Franzoni, J. (2015). Maternalism, co-responsibility, and social equity: A typology of work–family policies. *Social Politics, 22*(1), 38–59.

Boesten, J. (2009). *Intersecting inequalities. Women and social policy in Peru, 1990–2000*. The Pennsylvania State University Press.

Boesten, J. (2014). *Sexual violence during war and peace: Gender, power and post-conflict justice in Peru*. Palgrave.

Bohn, S., & Levy, C. (2019). The Brazilian women's movement and the state under the PT national governments. *European Review of Latin American and Caribbean Studies, 108*, 245–266.

Borges, F. A. (2022). *Human capital versus basic income: Ideology and models for anti-poverty programs in Latin America*. University of Michigan Press.

Boserup, E. (1970). *Women's role in economic development*. George Allen & Unwin Ltd.

Boutron, C. (2019). *Femmes en armes. Itinéraires de combattantes au Pérou (1980–2010)*. Presses universitaires de Rennes.

Bradshaw, S. (2008). From structural adjustment to social adjustment: A gendered analysis of conditional cash transfer programmes in Mexico and Nicaragua. *Global Social Policy, 8*(2), 188–207.

Brooks, S. M. (2015). Social protection for the poorest: The adoption of antipoverty cash transfer programs in the global South. *Politics & Society, 43*(4), 551–582.

Buss, D. (2015). Measurement imperatives and gender politics: An introduction. *Social Politics, 22*(3), 381–389.

Butler, J. (1990). *Gender trouble. Feminism and the subversion of identity*. Routledge.

Butler, J. (1994). *Undoing gender*. Routledge.

Calkin, S. (2015). Feminism, interrupted? Gender and development in the era of 'smart economics.' *Progress in Development Studies, 15*(4), 295–307.

Calvès, A. (2009). "Empowerment": généalogie d'un concept clé du discours contemporain sur le développement. *Revue Tiers Monde, 200*(4), 735–749.

Campbell, J. (2004). *Institutional change and globalization*. Princeton University Press.

Campbell, J. L., & Pederson, O. K. (2010). Knowledge regimes and comparative political economy. In D. Béland & R. H. Cox (Eds.), *Ideas and politics in social science research* (pp. 167–190). Oxford University Press.

Carnes, M., & Mares, I. (2015). Explaining the "return of the State" in middle-income countries: Employment vulnerability, income, and preferences for social protection in Latin America. *Politics & Society, 43*(4), 525–550.

Carstensen, M. B. (2011). Paradigm man vs. the bricoleur: Bricolage as an alternative vision of agency in ideational change. *European Political Science Review, 3*(1), 147–167.

Caulier, M. (2011). La conquête du « genre » et l'anthropologie au Mexique. *Journal Des Anthropologues, 2*(124–125), 117 à 136.

Cecchini, S., & Madariaga, A. (2011). *Programas de transferencias condicionadas. Balance de la experiencia reciente en América latina y el Caribe*. CEPAL, ASDI.

CEDLA. (2006). *Legitimando el orden neoliberal. 100 días de gobierno de Evo Morales*. Centro de Estudios para el Desarrollo Laboral y Agrario, Documento de Coyuntura 12.

CEPAL. (2006). *Estadísticas sociales*. CEPAL.

CEPAL. (2018) *Non-contributory social database protection programmes in Latin America and the Caribbean: Conditional cash transfers, social policy division*, DATE, https://dds.cepal.org/bpsnc/cct, accessed 31 January 2024.

Cerva, D. (2006). *Análisis sociopolítico de los procesos de institucionalización de la perspectiva de género en el estado: avances y retrocesos en el contexto de transformación del sistema político mexicano* (PhD Thesis), UNAM, CDMX, México.

Cerva, D. (2006). Trayectorias de los mecanismos institucionales a favor de la equidad de género en México. In *Avances de la perspectiva de género en las acciones legislativas* (pp. 253–271). Santillana/Comisión de Equidad y Género, Cámara de Diputados, LIX Legislatura.

Cerva, D. F. C. (2010). Cultura organizacional e institucionalización de las políticas de género en México: Notas para el debate. *GénEroos. Revista de investigación y divulgación sobre los estudios de género, 16*(6), 55–70.

Chanfreau, J. (2022). The persistence in gendering: work-family policy in Britain since Beveridge. *Journal of Social Policy*, 1–18.

Chant, S. (2016). Women, girls and world poverty: Empowerment, equality or essentialism? *International Development Planning Review, 38*(1), 1–24.

Chappell, L. (2000). Interacting with the state: Feminist strategies and political opportunities. *International Feminist Journal of Politics, 2*(2), 244–275.

Chappell, L. (2006). Comparing political institutions: Revealing the gendered "logic of appropriateness." *Politics & Gender, 2*(02), 223–235.

Chappell, L., Grey, R., & McLoughlin, K. (2021). Gender and judging at the International Criminal Court: Lessons from 'feminist judgment projects'. *Leiden Journal of International Law, 34*(1), 247–264.

Charlesworth, H. (2005). Not waving but drowning: Gender mainstreaming and human rights in the United Nations. *Harvard Human Rights Journal, 18*, 1–18.

Childs, S., & Krook, M. L. (2009). Analysing women's substantive representation: From critical mass to critical actors. *Government and Opposition, 44*(2), 125–145.

Coenga-Oliveira, D. (2019). Challenges Announced to Gender Equality in Current Brazil: A "Democratic State" as a danger to Women's Rights. In M. Machado & D. Andrade (Eds). *Women's Rights: International Studies on Gender Roles and its influence on contemporary Democracy*. (pp. 11–44). Erechim: Deviant.

Collier, R. B. (2021). Reflections on two episodes of popular inclusion: structuring and restructuring arenas of participation. In D. J. Yashar, D. Kapiszewski, & S. Levitsky (Eds.), *The inclusionary turn in Latin American Democracies* (pp. xxv–xviii). Cambridge University Press.

Collier, R. B., & Collier, D. (1991). *Shaping the political arena: Critical junctures, the labor movement, and regime dynamics in Latin America*. Princeton University Press.

Collier, R. B., & Collier, D. (2002). *Shaping the political arena: Critical junctures, the labor movement, and regime dynamics in Latin America*. Notre Dame University Press.

Cohen, E., & Franco, R. (2006). *Transferencias con coresponsabilidad. Una mirada latinoamericana*. FLASCO.

Cookson, T. P. (2016). Working for inclusion? Conditional cash ytransfers, rural Women, and the reproduction of inequality. *Antipode, 48*(5), 1187–1205.

Cookson, T. P. (2018). *Unjust conditions. Women's work and the hidden cost of cash transfer programs*. University of California Press.

Cornia, G. A., Jolly, R., & Stewart, F. (Eds.). (1987). *Adjustment with a human face*. Clarendon Press.

Cornwall, A., Harrison, E., & Whitehead, A. (2008). Gender myths and feminist fables: The struggle for interpretative power in gender and development. In

A. Cornwal, E. Harrison, & A. Whitehead (Eds.), *Gender myths and feminist fables: The struggle for interpretative power in gender and development* (pp. 1–19). Blackwell Publishing.

Correa Aste, N., & Roopnaraine, T. (2013). *Pueblos Indígenas y programas de transferencias condicionadas. Estudio etnográfico sobre le implementación y los efectos socioculturales del Programma Juntos en seis comunidades andinas y amzónicas de Perú.* IFPRI, PUCP, BID.

Craske, N. (2003). Gender, poverty and social movements. In S. Chant & N. Craske (Eds.), *Gender in Latin America* (pp. 46–71). Rutgers University Press.

D'Aoust, A.-M., & Châteauvert-Gagnon, B. (2022). Feminist perspectives on foreign policy. In R. Marlin-Bennett (Eds.), *Oxford Research Encyclopedia (ORE) of International Studies.*

Daly, M. (2018). Care policies for children and adults in high-income countries. In S. Shaver (Ed.), *Handbook on gender and social policy* (pp. 215–231). Edward Elgar Publishing.

Daly, M. (2022). The resilience of maternalism in European welfare states. *Contemporary Social Science, 17*(4), 313–325.

Deacon, B. (2007). *Global social policy & governance.* Sage Publications.

De Brauw, A., Gilligan, D. O., Hoddinott, J., & Roy, S. (2014). The impact of Bolsa Família on women's decision-making power. *World Development, 59*, 487–504.

Debusscher, P., & Van der Vleuten, A. (2017). Equality policies in the EU through a feminist Historical Institutionalist Lens. In H. Macrae & E. Weiner (Eds.), *Towards gendering institutionalism. Equality in Europe* (pp. 3–23). Rowman & Littlefield Publisher.

Degregori, C. I. (2000). *La década de la antipolítica: auge y huida de Alberto Fujimori y Vladimiro Montesinos.* IEP.

De La Cadena, M. (2010). Indigenous cosmopolitics in the Andes: Conceptual reflections beyond 'politics.' *Cultural Anthropology, 25*(2), 334–270.

De la O, A. (2015). *Crafting policies to end poverty in Latin America.* Cambridge University Press.

Delpeuch, T. (2008). L'analyse des transferts internationaux de politiques publiques: un état de l'art. *Questions de Recherche, 27*, 1–69.

Dezalay, Y., & Garth, B. G. (2002). *The internationalization of palace wars: Lawyers, economists, and the contest to transform Latin American states.* University of Chicago Press.

Diaz Carrasco, M. (2010). Desarrollo y chacha-warmi: Lógicas de género en el mundo aymara. *Revista Casa de La Américas, 258*, 10–24.

Díez, J. (2015). *The politics of gay marriage in Latin America: Argentina, Chile, and Mexico.* Cambridge University Press.

Dion, M. (2006). Women's welfare and social security privatization in Mexico. *Social Politics: International Studies in Gender, State & Society, 13*(3), 400–426.

Dip, A. (2018). *Em nome de quem? A bancada evangélica e seu projeto de poder*. Civilização brasileira.

Do Alto, H. (2007). Le MAS-IPSP d'Evo Morales, à la croisée des politiques institutionnelles et contestataires. In D. Rolland & J. Chassin (Eds.), *Pour comprendre la Bolivie d'Evo Morales* (pp. 94–104). L'Harmattan.

Diario Oficial de la Federación (DOF). (1999). Lineamientos Generales para la Operación del Programa de Educación, Salud y Alimentación (PROGRESA), Estados Unidos Mexicanos.- Secretaría de Desarrollo Social, 26 February, https://www.dof.gob.mx/nota_detalle.php?codigo=4944430&fecha=26/02/1999#gsc.tab=0, accessed 17 February 2024.

Dore, E., & Molyneux, M. (Eds.). (2000). *Hidden histories of gender and the state in Latin America*. Duke University Press.

Dorlin, E. (2008). *Sexe, genre et sexualité. Introduction à la théorie féministe*. Presses Universitaires de France.

Eisenstein, H. (1996). *Inside agitators: Australian femocrats and the state*. Temple University Press.

Emmerij, L. (1998). Bolivia: Permanent revolution and permanent failure? In P. Van Dijck (Ed.), *The bolivian experiment: Structural adjustment and poverty alleviation* (pp. 1–17). CEDLA.

Enloe, C. (2004). *The curious feminist: Searching for women in a new age of empire*. University of California Press.

Escobar Latapí, A., & González de la Rocha, M. (2004). *Evaluación cualitativa del programa Oppurtunidades*. Centro de Investigación y Estudios Superiores en Antropología Social.

Esquivel, V. (2018). What is a transformative approach to care, and why do we need it? *Gender & Development, 22*(3), 423–439.

Ewig, C. (2010). *Second-wave neoliberalism. Gender, race, and health sector reform in Peru*. The Pennsylvania State University.

Ewig, C. (2018). Forging women's substantive representation: Intersectional interests, political parity, and pensions in Bolivia. *Politics & Gender, 14*(3), 433–459.

Falleti, T. G. (2010). *Decentralization and subnational politics in Latin America*. Cambridge University Press.

Falleti, T. G., & Lynch, J. F. (2009). Context and causal mechanisms in political analysis. *Comparative Political Studies, 42*(9), 1143–1166.

Falleti, T. G., & Mahoney, J. (2015). The comparative sequential method. In J. Mahoney & K. Thelen (Eds.), *Advances in comparative-historical analysis* (pp. 211–240). Cambridge University Press.

Fenwick, T. B. (2009). Avoiding governors: The success of Bolsa Familia. *Latin American Research Review, 44*(1), 102–131.

Fenwick, T. B. (2017). From CCTs to a social investment welfare state? Brazil's 'new' pro-poor strategy. *Development Policy Review, 35*(5), 659–674.

Ferguson, L. (2015). "This is our gender person": The messy business of working as a gender expert in international development. *International Feminist Journal of Politics, 17*(3), 380–397.

Filgueira, F. (1998). El nuevo modelo de prestaciones sociales en América Latina: residualismo y ciudadanía estratificada. In B. Robert (Ed.), *Ciudadanía y política social* (pp. 71–116). FLACSO.

Filgueira, C. H., & Filgueira, F. (2002). Models of welfare and models of capitalism: The limits of transferability. In E. Huber (Ed.), *Models of capitalism. Lessons for Latin America* (pp. 127–157). The Pennsylvania State University Press.

Fioretos, O., Falleti, T. G., & Sheingate, A. (2016). *The Oxford handbook of historical institutionalism*. Oxford University Press.

Fiszbein, A., & Schady, N. (2009). *Conditional cash transfers. Reducing present and future poverty*. World Bank.

Foli, R., Béland, D., & Beck Fenwick, T. (2018). How instrument constituencies shape policy transfer: A case study from Ghana. *Policy and Society, 37*(1), 108–124.

Franceschet, S. (2011). Gendered institution and women's substantive representation: Females legislators in Argentina and Chile. In M. L. Krook & F. Mackay (Eds.), *Gender, politics and institutions: Toward a feminist institutionalism* (pp. 58–78). Palgrave.

Francke, P., & Mendoza, A. (2006). Perú: programa JUNTOS. In E. Cohen & R. Franco (Eds.), *Transferencias con corresponsabilidad. Una mirada latinoamericana* (pp. 391–432). FLACSO.

Fuentes, L., & Cookson, T. P. (2020). Counting gender (in)equality? A feminist geographical critique of the 'gender data revolution.' *Gender, Place & Culture, 27*(6), 881–902.

Gains, F., & Lowndes, V. (2014). How is institutional formation gendered, and does it make a difference? A new conceptual framework and a case study of police and crime commissioners in England and Wales. *Politics & Gender, 10*, 524–548.

Garay, C. (2016). *Social policy expansion in Latin America*. Cambridge University Press.

Gautier, A. (2000). Les droits reproductifs, une nouvelle génération de droits? *Autrepart, 15*, 167–180.

Gideon, J. (1998). The politics of social service provision through NGOs: A study of Latin America. *Bulletin of Latin American Research, 17*(3), 303–321.

Gideon, J. (2014). *Gender, globalization, and health in a Latin American context*. Palgrave Macmillan.

Gil-García, Ó. F. (2015). Gender equality, community divisions, and autonomy: The Prospera conditional cash transfer program in Chiapas, Mexico. *Current Sociology, 63*(4), 447–469.

González de la Rocha, M. (2000). Lo vigente y lo emergente: Tendencias recientes en la política social en México. In Agustín Escobar Latapí & M. González de la Rocha (Eds.), *Logros y retos: Una evaluación cualitativa de Progresa en México* (pp. 31–38). Secretaría del Desarrollo social.

González de la Rocha, M. (2006). Vanishing assets: Cumulative disadvantage among the urban poor. *The annals of the american academy of political and social science, 606*(1), 68–94.

Gray Molina, G. (2007). El reto post-neoliberal de Bolivia. *Nueva Sociedad, 209* (mayo-junio), 118–129.

Griffin, P. (2009). *Gendering the World Bank: Neoliberalism and the gendered foundations of global governance*. Palgrave Macmillan.

Guerrina, R., Chappell, L., & Wright, K. A. M. (2018). Transforming CSDP? Feminist triangles and gender regimes. *JCMS: Journal of Common Market Studies, 56*(5), 1036–1052.

Mackay, F., Kenny, M., & Chappell, L. (2010). New institutionalism through a gender lens: Towards a feminist institutionalism? *International Political Science Review, 31*(5), 573–588.

Haas, P. M. (1992). Introduction: Epistemic communities and international policy coordination. *International Organization, 46*(1), 1–35.

Haas, L. (2010). *Feminist policymaking in Chile*. Penn State University Press.

Haddad, L. (2007). Comment on "the role of social risk management in development: A world bank view." *IDS Bulletin: Debating Social Protection, 38*(3), 14–16.

Haggard, S., & Kaufman, R. R. (2008). *Development, democracy, and welfare states: Latin America, East Asia, and Eastern Europe*. Princeton University Press.

Hall, P. A. (1993). Policy paradigm, social learning, and the state: The case of economic policymaking in Britain. *Comparative Politics, 25*(3), 275–296.

Hall, P. A. (2003). Aligning ontology and methodology in comparative research. In J. Mahoney, D. Rüschemeyer, & D. Rueschemeyer (Eds.), *Comparative historical analysis in the social sciences* (pp. 374–404). Cambridge University Press.

Hall, A. (2008). Brazil's *Bolsa Família*: A double-edged sword? *Development and Change, 39*(5), 799–822.

Hall, I. (2020). Le « bien-vivre » (sumaq kawsay) et les pommes de terre paysannes: Du délicat exercice de la diplomatie ontologique. *Anthropologie et Sociétés, 43*(3), 217–244.

Hammer, P. J. (2013). *Change and continuity at the world bank*. Edward Elgar Publishing.

Hassenteufel, P. (2005). De la comparaison internationale à la comparaison transnationale. Les déplacements de la construction d'objets comparatifs en matière de politiques publiques. *Revue française de science politique, 55*(1), 113–132.

Hassenteufel, P., & Maillard, J. (2013). Convergence, transferts et traduction, Les apports de la comparaison transnationale. *Presses de Sciences Po, 3*(3), 377–393.

Hassim, S., & Razavi, S. (2006). Gender and social policy in a global context: Uncovering the gendered structure of 'the social.' In S. Razavi & S. Hassim (Eds.), *Chapter one: Gender and social policy in a global context: Uncovering the gendered structure of "the Social"* (pp. 1–39). Palgrave.

Hernández, S. (2018). Women in Mexican politics since 1953. In S. Hernández (Ed.), *Oxford research encyclopedia of Latin American History*. Oxford University Press.

Heintz, J., Staab, S., & Turquet, L. (2021). Don't let another crisis go to waste: The COVID-19 pandemic and the imperative for a paradigm shift. *Feminist Economics, 27*(1–2), 470–485.

Hevia de la Jarra, F. J. (2007). *El programa Oportunidades y la construcción de la ciudadana. Ejercicio y protección de derechos en un programa de transferencias condicionadas en México*. Centro de investigaciones y estudios superiores en antropología social.

Holmes, R., Jones, N., Vargas, R., & Veras, F. (2010). *Cash transfers and gendered risks and vulnerabilities: Lessons from Latin America*. Overseas Development Institute.

Holmes, R., & Jones, N. (2013). *Gender and social protection in the developing world. Beyond mothers and safety nets*. Zed Books.

Howlett, M., Ramesh, M., & Saguin, K. (2018). Diffusion of CCTs from Latin America to Asia: The Philippine 4Ps case. *Revista De Administração Pública, 52*, 264–284.

Htun, M., & Ossa, J. P. (2013). Political inclusion of marginalized groups: Indigenous reservations and gender parity in Bolivia. *Politics, Groups and Identities, 1*(1), 4–25.

Htun, M., & Weldon, L. (2017). States and gender justice. In K. J. Morgan & A. Orloff (Eds.), *The many hands of the state. Theorizing political authority and social control* (pp. 158–177). Cambridge University Press.

Htun, M., & Weldon, L. (2018). *The logics of gender justice: State action on women's rights around the world*. Cambridge: Cambridge University Press.

Huber, E., & Stephens, J. (2005). *Successful social policy regimes? Political economy, politics, and the structure of social policy in Argentina, Chile,*

Uruguay, and Costa Rica. Presented at the Conference on Democratic Governability, Kellogg Institute, University of Notre Dame, October 7–8.

Huber, E., & Stephens, J. D. (2012). *Democracy and the left. Social policy and inequality in Latin America*. The University of Chicago Press.

Huber, L., Zárate, P., Durand, A., Madalengoitia, Ó., & Morel, J. (2009). *Programa JUNTOS. Certezas y malentidos en torno a las transferencias condicionadas. Estudio de caso de seis distritos rurales del Perú*. IEP, UNICEF, UNFPA.

Hunter, W. H., & Sugiyama, N. (2014). Transforming subjects into citizens: Insights from Brazil's Bolsa Familia. *American Political Science Association, 12*(4), 829–845.

Hunter, W., Patel, L., & Sugiyama, N. B. (2021). How family and child cash transfers can empower women: Comparative lessons from Brazil and South Africa. *Global Social Policy, 21*(2), 258–277.

ILO. (2011). *Social protection floor for fair and inclusive globalization. Report of the advisory group chaired by Michelle Bachelet convened by the ILO with the collaboration of the WHO*. Organisation internationale du travail, Bachelet Report.

Jacquette, J. S., & Staudt, K. (2006). Women, gender, and development. In J. S. Jacquette & K. Staudt (Eds.), *Women and gender equity in development theory and practice. Institutions, ressources, and mobilization* (pp. 17–52). Duke University Press.

Jacquot, S., & Mazur, A. (2019). Genre et politiques publiques. In L. Boussaguet et al. (Ed.), *Dictionnaire des politiques publiques* (pp. 289–297). Presses de Sciences Po.

Jackson, C. (2008). Resolving risk? Marriage and creative conjugality. In A. Cornwall, E. Harrison, & A. Whitehead (Eds.), *Gender MYTHS & FEMINIST FABLE. The struggle for interpretative power in gender and development* (pp. 105–126). Blackwell Publishing.

Jaquette, J. S., & Summerfield, G. (2006). *Women and gender equity in development theory and practice. Institutions, resources, and mobilization*. Duke University Press.

Jenson, J. (1986). Gender and reproduction: Or, babies and the state. *Studies in Political Economy, 20*, 9–46.

Jenson, J. (1989). Paradigms and political discourse: Protective legislation in France and United States before 1914. *Canadian Journal of Latin American and Caribbean Studies, XXII, 2*, 235–258.

Jenson, J. (1997). Who cares? Gender and welfare regimes. *Social Politics: International Studies in Gender, State & Society, 4*(2), 182–187.

Jenson, J. (2009). Lost in translation: The social investement perspective and gender equality. *Social Politics: International Studies in Gender, State and Society, 16*(4), 446–483.

Jenson, J. (2011). Politiques publiques et investissement social : quelles conséquences pour la citoyenneté sociale des femmes? *Cahiers Du Genre, hors-série*, 21–43.

Jenson, J. (2015). The fading goal of gender equality: Three policy directions that underpin the resilience of gendered socio-economic inequalities. *Social Politics, 22*(4), 539–560.

Jenson, J. (2017). The new maternalism: Children first; women second. In Y. Ergas, J. Jenson, & S. Michel (Eds.), *Reassembling motherhood: Procreation and care in a globalized world* (pp. 269–286). Columbia University Press.

Jenson, J. (2020). Beyond the National: How the EU, OECD, and the World Bank Do Family Policy. In R. Nieuwenhuis & W. Van Lancker (Eds.), *The Palgrave handbook of family policies* (pp. 45–68). Palgrave Macmillan.

Jenson, J., & Mahon, R. (2022). Multiple sources of the social investment perspective: The OECD and the World Bank. In J. L. Garritzmann, S. Häusermann, & B. Palier (Eds.), *The world politics of social investment: Volume I* (pp. 109–131). Oxford University Press.

Jenson, J., Marques Pereira, B., & Nagels, N. (2017). Peut-on professionnaliser et institutionnaliser le féminisme sans les féministes? Les cas du Chili et du Pérou. In P. Meier & D. Paternotte (Eds.), *La professionalisation des luttes pour l'égalité: enjeux théoriques et politiques* (pp. 87–108). Academia L'Harmattan.

Jenson, J., & Mérand, F. (2010). Sociology, institutionalism and the European Union. *Comparative European Politics, 8*(1), 74–92.

Jenson, J., & Nagels, N. (2018). Social policy instruments in motion. Conditional cash transfers from Mexico to Peru. *Social Policy & Administration, 52*(1), 323–342.

Jenson, J., & Nagels, N. (2014). Social policy for institutional change. In J. L. Garritzmann, S. Häusermann, & B. Palier (Eds.), *The world politics of social investment: Volume II* (pp. 358–378). Oxford University Press.

Jenson, J., & Sineau, M. (2001). *Who cares? Women's work, childcare and welfare state redesign*. University of Toronto Press.

Jhonson, B. (2010). Decolonization and its paradoxes: The (re)envisioning of health Policy in Bolivia. *Latin American Perspectives, 37*(172), 139–159.

Jones, N., Vargas, R., & Villar, E. (2007). El programa Juntos y el bienestar de la infancia. In M. E. Mannarelli (Eds.), *Relaciones con condiciones: el Estado peruano frente a su infancia* (pp. 53–90). DFID, Niños del Milenio.

Jones, N., Vargas, R., & Villar, E. (2008). Cash transfers to tackle childhood poverty and vulnerability: An analysis of Peru's Juntos programme. *Environment & Urbanization, 20*(1), 255–273.

Kabeer, N. (1994). Gender-aware policy and planing: A social-relations perspective. In M. Macdonald (Ed.), *Gender planning in development agencies* (pp. 80–98). Oxfam.

Kapiszewski, D., Levitsky, S., & Yashar, D. J. (Eds.). (2021). *The inclusionary turn in Latin American Democracies*. Cambridge University Press.

Kaufmann, D., Mastruzzi, M., & Zavaleta, D. (2003). Sustained macroeconomic reforms, tepid Growth: A governance puzzle in Bolivia? In D. Rodrik (Ed.), *In search of prosperity: Analytic narratives on economic growth* (pp. 1–51). Princeton.

Kenny, M. (2007). Gender, institutions and power: A critical review. *Politics, 27*(2), 91–100.

Kergoat, D. (2009). Dynamique de consubstantialité des rapports sociaux. In E. Dorlin (Éd.), *Sexe, race, classe. Pour une épistémologie de la domination* (pp. 111–125). PUF.

Mackay, F., & Krook, M. L. (Éds.). (2011). *Gender, politics and institutions: Towards a feminist institutionalism*. Palgrave Macmillan.

La Paz López, M., & Salles, V. (2006). *El Programa Oportunidades examinado desde el género*. Opportunidades, Unifem, el Colegio de Mexico.

Laplante, L., & Theidon, K. (2007). Truth with consequences: Justice and reparations in post-truth commission Peru. *Human Rights Quarterly, 29*(1), 228–250.

Lavinas, L. (2015). 21st century welfare. *New Left Review, 84*(6), 5–40.

Lavrard-Meyer, C. (2010). *Pauvreté et démocratie au Pérou. Le vote des pauvres depuis la transition démocratique*. L'Harmattan.

Leisering, L. (2019). *The global rise of social cash transfers. How states and international organizations constructed a new instrument for comabating poverty*. Oxford University Press.

Leite, I. C., Pomeroy, M., & Suyama, B. (2015). Brazilian South-South development cooperation: The case of the Ministry of Social Development in Africa. *Journal of International Development, 27*, 1446–1461.

Lévi-Strauss, C. (1966). *The savage mind*. Weidenfeld & Nicolson.

Levitsky, S., & Way, L. (2002). The rise of competitive authoritarianism. *Journal of Democracy, 13*(2), 51–65.

Levy, S. (1991). La pobreza extrema en México: una propuesta de política. *Estudios Económicos, 6*(1), 47–89.

Levy, S. (2006). *Progress against poverty: Sustaining Mexico's Progresa-Oportunidades program*. Brookings Institution Press.

Levy, S. (2008). *Good intentions, bad outcomes. social policy, informality, and economic growth in Mexico*. Brookings Institution Press.

Levitt, P., & Merry, S. (2009). Vernacularization on the ground: Local uses of global women's rights in Peru, China, India and the United States. *Global Networks, 9*(4), 441–461.

Lewis, J. (1992). Gender and the development of welfare regimes. *Journal of European Social Policy, 2*(3), 159–173.

Liebowitz, D. J., & Zwingel, S. (2014). Gender equality oversimplified: Using CEDAW to counter the measurement obsession. *International Studies Review, 16*, 362–389.

Lindert, K., Linder, A., Hobbs, J., & De la Brière, B. (2007). *The nuts and bolts of Brazil's Bolsa Família program: Implementing conditional cash transfers in a decentralized context*. World Bank. WB social protection discussion paper 709.

Lister, R. (1994). She has other duties—Women, citizenship and social security. In S. Baldwin & J. Falkingham (Eds.), *Social security and social change: New challenges to the Beveridge mode* (pp. 31–44). Harvester Wheatsheaf.

Llanos, D., & Rosas, N. (2010). *Cry over spilled milk: Improving targeting outcomes in social programs in Peru*. JF Kennedy School of Government.

Lomeli, E. (2008). Conditional cash transfers as social policy in Latin America: An assessment of their contributions. *Annual Review of Sociology, 34*, 475–499.

Lopez-Estrada, S. (2017). Políticas de cuidado infantil en América Latina. Análisis comparado de Chile Costa Rica, Uruguay y México. *Frontera Norte, 29*(58), 25–46.

Lopreite, D., & Macdonald, L. (2014). Gender and Latin American welfare regimes: Early childhood education and care policies in Argentina and Mexico. *Social Politics, 21*(1), 80–102.

Lovenduski, J. (Foreword). In M. L. Krook & F. Mackay (Eds.), *Gender, politics and institutions: Toward a feminist institutionalism*. Palgrave Macmillan.

Macdonald, L., & Ruckert, A. (2009). Post-neoliberalism in the Americas: An introduction. In L. Macdonald & A. Ruckert (Eds.), *Post-neoliberalism in the Americas* (pp. 1–18). Palgrave MacMillan.

Mackay, F. (2011). Conclusion: Towards a feminist institutionalism? In M. L. Krook & F. Mackay (Eds.), *Gender, politics and institutions: Towards a feminist institutionalism* (pp. 181–196). Palgrave Macmillan UK.

Mahon, R. (2021). IOs' role in global social governance: Family policy. In K. Martens, D. Niemann, & A. Kaasch (Eds.), *International organizations in global social governance* (pp. 187–206). Springer International Publishing.

Mahon, R. (2024). The Care Economy al América Latina: A Multi-scalar Feminist Project, *Social Politics,* 1-24

Mahoney, J., & Thelen, K. (2010). *Explaining institutional change: Ambiguity, agency, and power*. Cambridge University Press.

Marco Navarro, F. (2012). *El Bono Juancito Pinto del Estado Plurinacional de Bolivia. Programas de transferencias monetarias e infancia*. CEPAL.

Marino, K. M. (2019). *Feminism for the Americas: The making of an international human rights movement*. The University of North Carolina Press.

Marques-Pereira, B. (2000). Gouvernance, citoyenneté et genre. In C. Gobin & B. Rihoux (Eds.), *La démocratie dans tous ses états : systèmes politiques entre crise et renouveau* (pp. 41–49). Bruyland Academia.

Marques-Pereira, B. (2017). Resignification du maternalisme dans le cadre des programmes de transferts monétaires conditionnels. In B. Destremau & I. George (Eds.), *Le « care », face morale du capitalisme : assistance et police des familles en Amérique latine* (pp. 125–138). Peter Lang.

Martens, K., Niemann, D., & Kaasch, A. (2021). *International organizations in global social governance*. Palgrave Macmillan.

Martinez, A. (2008). Genre et développement: Enjeux et luttes des femmes du Tiers-Monde. In P. Beaudet, J. Schefer, & P. Haslam (Eds.), *Introduction au développement international: Approches, acteurs et enjeux* (pp. 70–85). Les Presses Universitaires d'Ottawa.

Martinez, A. (2022). The feminist movement and its evolution in modern Mexico, 1970s–2000s. *The Chico Historian, 31*, 128–141.

Martínez Franzoni, J. (2008). Welfare regimes in Latin America: Capturing constellations of markets, families and policies. *Latin American Politics and Society, 50*(2), 67–100.

Martínez Franzoni, J., & Voorend, K. (2011). Actors and ideas behind CCTs in Chile, Costa Rica and El Salvador. *Global Social Policy, 11*(2–3), 279–298.

Martínez Franzoni, J. M., & Sánchez-Ancochea, D. (2014). Filling in the missing link between universalism and democracy: The case of Costa Rica. *Latin American Politics and Society, 56*(4), 98–118.

Martínez Franzoni, J., & Voorend, K. (2011). Actors and ideas behind CCTs in Chile, Costa Rica and El Salvador. *Global Social Policy, 11*(2–3), 279–298.

Martínez Franzoni, J., & Voorend, K. (2012). Blacks, whites, or grays? Conditional transfers and gender equality in Latin America. *Social Politics, 19*(3), 383–407.

Martin De Almagro, M. (2018). Producing participants: Gender, race, class, and women, peace and security. *Global Society, 32*(4), 395–414.

Mathez-Stiefel, S.-L., Boillat, S., & Rist, S. (2007). Promoting the diversity of worldviews: An ontological approach to biocultural diversity. In B. Havekort & S. Rist (Eds.), *Endogenous development and biocultural diversity: The interplay of worldviews, globalization and locality* (pp. 67–81). COMPAS, CDE.

Mathieu, S. (2016). From the defamilialization to the "demotherization" of care work. *Social Politics, 23*(4), 576–591.

Mazur, A. (2002). *Theorizing feminist policy*. Oxford University Press.

Mazur, A. (2009). Les mouvements féministes et l'élaboration des politiques dans une perspective comparative. *Revue Française De Science Politique, 59*(2), 325–351.

Mazur, A. G., & McBride, D. E. (2008). State feminism. In G. Goertz & A. G. Mazur (Eds.), *Politics, gender, and concepts: Theory and methodology* (pp. 244–269). Cambridge University Press.

McAdam, D., Tarrow, S. G., & Tilly, C. (2001). *Dynamics of contention*. Cambridge University Press.

McGuire, J. (2013). *Conditional cash transfers in Bolivia: Origins, impact*. University of Pennsylvania.

McIlwaine, C., & Datta, K. (2003). From feminising to engendering development. *Gender, Place & Culture, 10*(4), 369–382.

MacRae, H., & Weiner, E. (2017). *Towards gendering institutionalism: Equality in Europe*. Rowman & Littlefield.

Meltzer, J. (2013). Good citizenship' and the promotion of personal savings accounts in Peru. *Citizenship Studies, 17*(5), 641–652.

Merry, S. E. (2011). Measuring the world: Indicators, human rights, and global governance. *Current Anthropology, 52*(S3), 83–95.

Mesa-Lago, C. (1978). *Social security in Latin America: Pressure groups, stratification, and inequality*. University of Pittsburgh Press.

Mesa-Lago, C. (2002). *Models of Development, Social Policy and Reform in Latin America*. UNRISD.

Mesa-Lago, C. (2008). Social insurance (pensions and health), labour markets and coverage in Latin America. *UNISD. Social Policy and Development. Programme Paper*, *36*(August), 1–40.

Milner, A. (2007). Bricolage. In G. Ritzer (Ed.), *The Blackwell encyclopedia of sociology*. Wiley.

Ministerio de Planificación del Desarrollo. (2006). *Plan Nacional de Desarrollo. Bolivia digna, soberana, productiva y democrática para Vivir Bien*. Bolivia.

Ministerio de Salud. (2005). *Norma técnica para la atención del parto vertical con adecuación intercultural*. Ministerio de Salud.

Mohanty, C. T. (1984). Under western eyes: Feminist scholarship and colonial discourses. *Boundary 2, 12*(13), 333–358.

Molina, R. (2005). *Los pueblos indígenas en Bolivia: diagnostico sociodemográfico a partir del censo de 2001*. CEPAL.

Molyneux, M. (2001). Gender and citizenship in Latin America: Historical and contemporary issues. In M. Molyneux (Ed.), *Women's movement in international perspective, Latin America and beyond* (pp. 163–202). Palgrave. Institute of Latin American Studies.

Molyneux, M. (2002). Gender and the silences of social capital: Lessons from Latin America. *Development and Change, 33*(2), 167–188.

Molyneux, M. (2006). Mothers at the service of the new poverty agenda: Progresa/Oportunidades, Mexico's conditional transfer programme. *Social Policy and Administration, 40*(4), 425–449.

Molyneux, M. (2007). *Change and continuity in social protection in Latin America. Mothers at the service of the state?* United Nation Research Institute for Social Development.
Molyneux, M. (2008). The "Neoliberal Turn" and the new social policy in Latin America: How neoliberal, how new? *Development and Change, 39*(5), 775–797.
Molyneux, M., & Thomson, M. (2011). Cash transfers, gender equity and women's empowerment in Peru, Ecuador and Bolivia. *Gender and Development, 19*(2), 195–212.
Monasterios, K. (2007). Bolivian women's organizations in the MAS era. *NACLA Report on the Americas, 40*(2), 33–37.
Monge, A., Vásquez, E., & Winkelried, D. (2009). *¿Es el gasto social público en programmas sociales regresivo en el Perú?* CIES. Universidad del Pacifico.
Monteiro, I. R. (2011). Integração de políticas sociais: um estudo de caso sobre o Bolsa Família. Dissertação (Mestrado Profissional em Bens Culturais e Projetos Sociais)—FGV—Fundação Getúlio Vargas, Rio de Janeiro.
Morais de Sá e Silva, M. (2017). *Poverty reduction, education and the global diffusion of conditional cash transfers.* Palgrave Macmillan.
Morales Escoffier, N. (2009). Boom or a Boomerang: Social Policy in Bolivia. *Focal Point, 8*(5), 22–23.
Moreira, N., et al. (2012). Empoderamento das mulheres beneficiárias do Programa Bolsa Família na percepção dos agentes dos Centros de Referência de Assistência Social. *Revista de Administração Pública, 46*(2), 403–423.
Moser, C. (1993). *Gender planning and development.* Routledge.
Muller, P. (2006). Référentiel. In L. Boussaguet, S. Jacquot, & P. Ravinet (Eds.), *Dictionnaire des politiques publiques* (pp. 272–278). Presses de la fondation nationale des sciences politiques.
Nagels, N. (2011). Les représentations des rapports sociaux de sexe au sein des politiques de lutte contre la pauvreté au Pérou. *Recherches Féministes, 24*(2), 115–134.
Nagels, N. (2013). *Genre et politiques de lutte contre la pauvreté au Pérou et en Bolivie: quels enjeux de citoyenneté ?* (PhD thesis). Geneva Graduate Institute, Geneva.
Nagels, N. (2014a). Programmes de transferts conditionnés et santé maternelle au Pérou et en Bolivie. *Les cahiers de santé publique et de protection sociale, 15*, 61–69.
Nagels, N. (2014b). Programmes de transferts conditionnés au Pérou et en Bolivie: entre ciblage et universalisation de l'assistance sociale. *Revue Internationale De Politique Comparée, 21*(1), 111–132.
Nagels, N. (2016). The social Investment perspective, Conditional cash transfer programmes and the welfare mix: Peru and Bolivia. *Social Policy and Society, 15*(3), 479–493.

Nagels, N. (2018). Incomplete universalization? Peruvian social policy reform, universalism, and gendered outcomes. *Social Politics, 25*(3), 410–431.

Nagels, N. (2019). Gender and conditional cash transfers: Shifting the citizenship regime in Bolivia? In M. Balán & F. Montambeault (Eds.), *What's Left?* (pp. 91–100). University of Notre Dame Press.

Nagels, N. (2021). Gender, the world bank, and conditional cash transfers in Latin America. *International Feminist Journal of Politics, 23*(5), 676–697.

Nagels, N., & Pozos Barcelata, A. (2022). Igualdad de género en el diseño del programa de transferencias condicionadad Progresa. *Clepsydra. Revista De Estudios De Género y Teoría Feminista, 23*, 271–291.

Nay, O. (2020). Knowledge battles at the World Bank: How institutional activists introduced the norm of participation into international development policy. In D. Dolowitz, M. Hadjiisky, & R. Normand (Eds.), *Shaping policy agendas* (pp. 137–161). Edward Elgar Publishing.

Nay, O. (2021). L'ouverture des organisations internationales: Trois interprétations sociologiques. In D. Lagrange, M. Louis, & O. Nay (Eds.), *Le tournant social de l'international: Les organisations internationales face aux sociétés civiles* (pp. 37–54). Presses Universitaires de Rennes.

Norris, P. (2004). *Electoral engineering: Voting rules and political behavior*. Cambridge University Press.

Noy, C. (2008). Sampling knowledge: The hermeneutics of snowball sampling in qualitative research. *International Journal of Social Research Methodology, 11*(4), 327–344.

Noy, S. (2017). *Banking on health: The World Bank and health sector reform in Latin America*. Palgrave Macmillan.

O'Connor, J. S. (1996). Understanding women in welfare states. *Current Sociology, 44*(2), 1–12.

O'Laughlin, B. (2008). A bigger piece of a very small pie: Intrahousehold resource allocation and poverty reduction in Africa. In A. Cornwal, E. Harrison, & A. Whitehead (Eds.), *Gender myths and feminist fables: The struggle for interpretative power in gender and development* (pp. 21–44). Blackwell Publishing.

Olivier de Sardan, J.-P., & Piccoli, E. (2018). *Cash transfers in context. An anthropological perspective*. Berghahn Books.

Orenstein, M. A. (2008). *Privatizing pensions: The transnational campaign for social security reform*. Princeton University Press.

Orloff, A. (1993). Gender and the social rights of citizenship: The comparative analysis of gender relations and welfare states. *American Sociological Association, 58*(3), 303–328.

Orloff, A. (1996). Gender in the welfare state. *Annual Review of Sociology, 22*, 51–78.

Orloff, A. (2009). Gendering the comparative analysis of welfare states: An unfinished agenda. *Sociological Theory, 27*(3), 317–343.

Orloff, A. (2017). Gendered states made and remade. Gendered labor policies in the United States and Sweden, 1960–210. In K. J. Morgan & A. Orloff (Eds.), *The many hands of the state theorizing political authority and social control* (pp. 158–177). Cambridge University Press.

Ortiz, I. (2007). *Social policy National development strategies: Policy notes.* United Nations Department of Economic and Social Affairs

Osorio Gonnet, C. (2017). ¿Cómo viajan las ideas? El rol de las comunidades epistémicas en el diseño de políticas sociales en América Latina. *Revista Del CLAD Reforma y Democracia, 68*, 75–112.

Osorio Gonnet, C. (2018). A comparative analysis of the adoption of conditional cash transfers programs in Latin America. *Journal of Comparative Policy Analysis: Research and Practice, 21*(4), 1–17.

Paquet, M. (2015). Bureaucrats as immigration policy-makers: The case of subnational immigration activism in Canada, 1990–2010. *Journal of Ethnic and Migration Studies, 41*(11), 1815–1835.

Parashar, S. (2014). *Women and militant wars: The politics of injury.* Routledge.

Parkhurst, J. O. (2017). *The politics of evidence: From evidence-based policy to the good governance of evidence.* Routledge, Taylor & Francis Group.

Paternotte, D. (2011). *Revendiquer le "mariage gay": Belgique.* Editions de l'Université de Bruxelles.

Platt, T. (2006). El feto agresivo. Parto, formación de la persona y mito-historia en los Andes. In G. fFrnandez Juárez (Eds.), *Salud e interculturidad en América latina. Antropología de la salud y critica intercultural* (pp. 145–172). Universitad de Castilla de la Mancha.

Peck, J., & Theodore, N. (2015). *Fast policy. Experimental statecraft at the thresholds of neoliberalism.* University of Minnesota Press.

Perea Ozerin, I. (2020). Transnational feminist movements in Latin America and the Caribbean. Contributions for the study of European activism. *Papel Político, 25*, 1–12.

Perova, E., & Vakis, R. (2009). *Welfare impacts of the "Juntos" program in Peru: Evidence from a non experimental evaluation.* World Bank.

Piccoli, E. (2014). « Dicen que los cien soles son del Diablo »: L'interprétation apocalyptique et mythique du Programa Juntos dans les communautés andines de Cajamarca (Pérou) et la critique populaire des programmes sociaux. *Social Compass, 61*(3), 328–347.

Pierson, P. (2004). *Politics in time. History, institutions and social analysis.* Princeton University Press.

Porto De Oliveira, O. (2020). Comparing international policy transfers. In B. G. Peters & G. Fontaine (Eds.), *Handbook of research methods and applications in comparative policy analysis.* Edward Elgar Publishing

PND. Ministerio de Planificación del Desarrollo. (2006). *Plan Nacional de Desarrollo. Bolivia digna, soberana, productiva y democrática para Vivir Bien.*

Pribble, J. (2006). Women and welfare: The politics of coping with new social risks in Chile and Uruguay. *Latin American Research Review, 41*(2), 84–111.

Pribble, J. (2011). Worlds apart: Social policy regimes in Latin America. *Studies in Comparative International Development, 46*, 191–216.

Prügl, E. (2017). Neoliberalism with a feminist face: Crafting a new hegemony at the World Bank. *Feminist Economics, 23*(1), 30–53.

Prügl, E. (2021). Smart economics. In G. Berik & E. Kongar (Eds.), *The Routledge handbook of feminist economics* (pp. 468–476). Taylor & Francis Group.

Quisumbing, A. (2003). *Household decisions, gender and development: A synthesis of recent research.* IFPRI/Johns Hopkins University Press.

Quisumbing, A., & McClafferty, B. (2006). *Food security in practice: Using gender research in development.* IFPRI.

Radcliffe, S. A. (2002). Indigenous women, rights and the nation-state in the Andes. In M. Molyneux & N. Craske (Eds.), *Gender and the politics of rights and democracy in Latin America* (pp. 149–172). Palgrave.

Ramm, A. (2020). Latin America: A fertile ground for maternalism. In A. Ramm & J. Gideon (Eds.), *Motherhood, social policies and women's activism in Latin America* (pp. 13–37). Springer International Publishing.

Rawlings, L. (2004). *A new approach to social assistance: Latin America's experience with conditional cash transfer programmes.* The World Bank.

Razavi, S., & Miller, C. (1995). *From WID to GAD: Conceptual shifts in the women and development discourse.* UNRISD.

Razavi, S., & Staab, S. (2018). Rethinking social policy: A gender perspective from the developing world. In S. Shaver (Ed.), *Handbook on gender and social policy* (pp. 74–89). Edward Elgar Publishing.

Razavi, S. (2020). What does the UN have to say about family policy? Reflections on the ILO, UNICEF, and UN women. In R. Nieuwenhuis & W. Van Lancker (Eds.), *The Palgrave handbook of family policy* (pp. 87–119). Palgrave Macmillan.

Riggirrozzi, P. (2010). Social policy in post-neo-liberal Latin America: The cases of Argentina, Venezuela and Bolivia. *Development, 53*(1), 70–76.

Riquer Fernández, F. (2000). Las pobres de Progresa: reflexiones. In E. Valencia Lomelí, M. Gendreau & A. M. Tepichín Valle (Eds.), *Los dilemas de la política social. ¿Cómo combatir la pobreza?* (pp. 283–310). Universidad de Guadalajara/Universidad Iberoamericana/ITESO.

Rossel, C., Antía, F., & Manzi, P. (2022). The politics of conditionality in Latin America's cash transfer reforms. In J. L. Garritzmann, S. Häusermann, & B. Palier (Eds.), *The world politics of social investment* (Vol. II, pp. 379–401). Oxford University Press.

Rostow, W. W. (2013). *The stages of economic growth*. Cambridge University Press.
Rousseau, S. (2007). Las políticas de salud reproductiva en el Perú: reformas sociales y derechos ciudadanos. *Estudos Feministas, 15*(2), 309–331.
Rousseau, S. (2009). *Women's citizenship in Peru*. Palgrave.
Rousseau, S. (2011). Indigenous and feminist movements at the constituent assembly in Bolivia: Locating the representation of indigenous women. *Latin American Research Review, 46*(2), 5–28.
Rozée, V. (2007). Les patrons culturels du comportement reproductif et sexuel dans les Andes Boliviennes. *Cuestiones Del Tiempo Presente, 7*, 1–13.
Sabatier, P. (1998). The advocacy coalition framework: Revisions and relevance for Europe. *Journal of European Public Policy, 5*(1), 98–130.
Sainsbury, D. (1996). *Gender, equality and welfare states*. Cambridge University Press.
Sainsbury, D. (2008). Gendering the welfare state. In G. Goertz & A. G. Mazur (Eds.), *Politics, gender, and concepts theory and methodology* (pp. 94–113). Cambridge University Press.
Skoufias, E., & McClafferty, B. (2001). *Is Progresa working? Summary of the results of an evaluation*. IFPRI. International Food Policy Research Institute.
Dobrowolsky, A., & Saint-Martin, D. (2005). Agency, actors and change in a child-focused future: 'Path dependency' problematised. *Commonwealth & Comparative Politics, 43*(1), 1–33.
Saxonberg, S. (2013). From defamilialization to degenderization: Toward a new welfare typology. *Social Policy & Administration, 47*(1), 26–49.
Scott, J. W. (1986). Gender: A useful category of historical analysis. *The American Historical Review, 91*(5), 1053–1075.
Secretaría de Desarrollo Social (SDS). (1999). Más oportunidades para las familias pobres. *Evaluación de Resultados del Programa de Educación, Salud y Alimentación. Primeros Avances*. Secretaría de Desarrollo Social, Progresa.
Segura-Ubiergo, A. (2012). *The political economy of the welfare state in Latin America: Globalization, democracy, and development*. Cambridge University Press.
Sen, A. (1999). Democracy as universal value. *Journal of Democracy, 10*(3), 3–17.
Schady, N. (2000). The political economy of expenditures by the Peruvian Social Fund (FONCODES), 1991–95. *American Political Science Review, 94*(2), 289–304.
Shaver, S. (2018). Introduction to the handbook on gender and social policy. In S. Shaver (Ed.), *Handbook on gender and social policy* (pp. 1–18). Edward Elgar Publishing.
Siim, B. (1994). The gendered Scandinavian welfare states: The interplay between women's roles as mothers, workers and citizens in Denmark. In J. Lewis (Ed.),

Women and social policies in Europe. Work, family and the state (pp. 27–48). Edward Elgar Publishing Company.
Skocpol, T. (1992). State formation and social policy in the United States. *American Behavioral Scientist, 35*(4–5), 559–584.
Skoufias, E. (2005). *PROGRESA and its impacts on the welfare of rural households in Mexico.* IFPRI.
Skoufias, E. (2007). Poverty alleviation and consumption insurance: Evidence from PROGRESA in Mexico. *The Journal of Socio-Economics, 36*(4), 630–649.
Staab, S. (2012). Maternalism, male-breadwinner bias, and market reform: Historical legacies and current reforms in Chilean social policy. *Social Politics, 19*(3), 299–332.
Staab, S. (2017). *Gender and the politics of gradual change: Social policy reform and innovation in Chile.* Palgrave Macmillan.
Streeck, W., & Thelen, K. A. (Eds.). (2005). *Beyond continuity: Institutional change in advanced political economies.* Oxford University Press.
Stone, D. (2012). Transfer and translation of policy. *Policy Studies, 33*(6), 483–499.
Sugiyama, N. (2011). The diffusion of conditional cash transfer programs in the Americas. *Global Social Policy, 11*(2–3), 250–278.
Sugiyama, N. B., & Hunter, W. (2020). Do conditional cash transfers empower women? Insights from Brazil's Bolsa Família. *Latin American Politics and Society, 62*(2), 53–74.
Tabbush, C. (2010). Latin American women's protection after adjustment: A feminist critique of conditional cash transfers in Chile and Argentina. *Oxford Development Studies, 38*(4), 437–459.
Taylor, M. (2009). The contradictions and transformations of neoliberalism in Latin America: From structural adjustement to "empowering the poor." In L. Macdonald & A. Ruckert (Eds.), *Post-neoliberalism in the Americas* (pp. 21–36). Palgrave Macmillan.
Teichman, J. (2007). Multilateral lending institutions and transnational policy networks in Mexico and Chile. *Global Governance, 13*(4), 557–574.
Teichman, J. (2008). Redistributive conflict and social policy in Latin America. *World Development, 36*(3), 446–460.
Thelen, K. (1999). Historical institutionalism in comparative politics. *Annual Review of Political Science, 2*(1), 369–404.
Tickner, J. A. (1992). *Gender in international relations: Feminist perspectives on achieving global security.* Columbia University Press.
Tomasso, L. (2022). *Rien de personnel. Politisation des violences sexuelles et reproductives et actions collectives des femmes au Pérou et au Guatémala* (Thèse de doctorat) UQAM.

Tomazini, C. (2016). *L'État et ses pauvres : La naissance et la montée en puissance des politiques de transferts conditionnels au Brésil et au Mexique*. 2016 (PhD Thesis). Université Paris II Universidade Estadual de Campinas, Paris.

Tomazini, C. (2022). Pioneering anti-poverty policies in Brazil and Mexico: Ambiguities and disagreements on conditional cash transfer programs. *International Journal of Sociology and Social Policy, 42*(1/2), 7–22.

Tripp, A. M. (2010). Toward a comparative politics of gender research in which women matter. *Perspectives on Politics, 8*(1), 191–197.

Tronto, J. (2008). Du Care. *Revue Du MAUSS, 32*, 243–265.

Unidad ejecutora del Bono Juancito Pinto. (2008). *Informe de cierre preliminar del Bono Juancito Pinto al 31 de diciembre 2008*. Ministerio de Educación y de Cultura.

Ulloa Pizarro, C. (2013). La institucionalización de la perspectiva de género en México: una política pública en transición. *Revista Análisis Público, 2*(2), 15–35.

Valderrama, J. (2009). *Propuesta Metodologica Para Identificación a los Potenciales Beneficiarios de los Programas Sociales en el Peru*. Ministerio de Economía y Finanzas. Dirección General de Asuntos Económicos y Sociales. Sistema de Focalización de Hogares. SISFOH.

Vargas, V. (2002). The struggle by Latin american feminism for rights and autonomy. In N. Craske & M. Molyneux (Eds.), *Gender and the politics of rights and democracy in Latin America* (pp. 199–221). Palgrave Publishers; Women Studiers at York Series.

Vargas, R. (2010). *Gendered risks, poverty and vulnerability in Peru: A case study of the Juntos Programme*. Overseas Development Institute.

Vargas, R., & Salazar, X. (2009). Concepciones, expectativas y comportamiento en población pobre beneficiaria del Programa JUNTOS en Apurímac, Huancavelica y Huánuco. In R. Díaz, L. Huber, Ó. Madalengoita, R. Saldaña, & C. Trivelli (Eds.), *Análisis de implementación del Programa JUNTOS en las regiones de Apurímac, Huancavelica y Huánuco* (pp. 97–130). CIES, Care.

Vásquez Huamán, E. (2005). *¿Los niños ... primeros? Niveles de vida y gasto público social orientado a la infancia: 2004–2005*. Universidad del Pacífico. Centro de Investigación. Save the Children Suecia.

Vasquez del Aguila, E. (2006). Invisible women: Forced sterilization, reproductive rights, and structural inequalities in Peru of Fujimori and Toledo. *Estudos e Pesquisas em Psicologia, 6*(1), 109–124.

Vergara, A., & Encinas, D. (2016). Continuity by surprise. Explaining institutional stability in contemporary Peru. *Latin American Research Review, 51*(1), 159–180.

Verschuur, C. (2015). Une histoire du développement au prisme du genre. Perspectives féministes et décoloniales. In C. Verschuur, I. Guérin, & H.

Guétat-Bernard (Eds.), *Sous le développement, le genre* (pp. 43–71). IRD Éditions.

Vetterlein, A. (2007). Economic growth, poverty reduction, and the role of social policies: The evolution of the World Bank's social development approach. *Global Governance, 13*, 513–533.

Vidal Fuertes, C., Martínez, S., Celhay, P., & Claros Gómez, S. (2015). *Evaluación de Impacto del Programa de Salud Materno Infantil "Bono Juana Azurduy."* Unidad de Análisis de Políticas Sociales y Económicas BID Banco Mundial.

Villatoro, S. P. (2004). *Programas de reducción de la pobreza en América latina. Un análisis de cinco experiencias*. CEPAL.

Vite Pérez, M. À., & Rico Martínez, R. (2001). *Neoliberalismo y urbanización popular en la zona metropolitana de la ciudad de México*. Plaza y Valdés.

Von Gliszcsynski, M., & Leisering, L. (2016). Constructing new global models of social security: How international organizations defined the field of social cash transfers in the 2000s. *Journal of Social Policy, 45*(2), 325–343.

Voß, J.-P., & Simons, A. (2014). Instrument constituencies and the supply side of policy innovation: The social life of emissions trading. *Environmental Politics, 23*(5), 735–754.

Walby, S. (2005). Gender mainstreaming: Productive tensions in theory and practice. *Social Politics: International Studies in Gender, State & Society, 12*(3), 321–343.

Waylen, G. (2011). Gendered institutionalist analysis: Understanding democratic transitions. In M. L. Krook & F. Mackay (Eds.), *Gender, politics and institutions: Towards a feminist institutionalism* (pp. 147–162). Palgrave.

Waylen, G. (2014). Informal institutions, institutional change, and gender equality. *Political Research Quarterly, 67*(1), 212–223.

Welti Chanes, C. (2014). El Consejo Nacional de Población a 40 años de la institucionalización de una política explícita de población en México. *Papeles De Población, 20*(81), 25–58.

Whitehead, C. (1995). Emergency social funds: The experience of Bolivia and Peru. *Development in Practice, 5*(1), 53–57.

Wiebe, N. (2021). Case study F: The challenges of moving towards universal social protection in Bolivia. In S. Esther & L. Markus (Eds.), *Handbook on social protection systems* (pp. 210–216). Edward Elgar Publishing.

Woodward, A. (2003). Building velvet triangles: Gender and informal governance. In *Informal governance in the European Union* (T. Christiansen & S. Piattoni, pp. 76–93). Edward Elgar.

Yashar, D. (2005). *Contesting citizenship in Latin America: The rise of indigenous movement and the postneoliberal challenge*. Cambridge University Press.

Yaschine, I., & Orozco, M. (2010). The evolving antipoverty agenda in Mexico: The political economy of PROGRESA and Oportunidades. In M. Adato & J.

Hoddinott (Eds.), *Conditional cash transfers in Latin America* (pp. 55–77). Intl Food Policy Research Institute.
Ybarnegaray Ortiz, J. (2011). Feminismo y descolonización. *Nueva Sociedad, 234*, 159–171.
Young, I. M. (2000). *Inclusion and democracy*. Oxford University Press.
Young, I. M. (2002). Lived body vs gender: reflections on social structure and subjectivity. *Ratio, 15*(4), 410–428.
Zwingel, S. (2012). How do norms travel? Theorizing international women's rights in transnational perspective. *International Studies Quarterly, 56*(1), 115–129.

Index

A
Alianza Popular RevolucionariaAmericana (APRA), 137
Andean ontology, 168
Auxílio Gás, 78

B
Bacchi, C., 28
Bank of knowledge, 3
Bartolina Sisa, 138
Biomedical, 164
Blofield, M., 43
Bolivia, 2
Bolsa Alimentação, 78
Bolsa Escola, 77
Bolsa Escola Federal (BEF), 77
Bolsa Família, 2
Bolsonaro, Jair, 179
Bono Juana Azurduy, 2
Bono Juancito Pinto, 2
Borges, F.A., 6
Boserup, E., 102
Brazil, 2
Brazilian South–South cooperation, 116
Bricolage, 38
Buarque, C., 77

C
Cardoso, F.H., 77
Care
  caregivers, 10
  unpaid female labor, 103, 126
CEPAL, 6
Certification, 40, 97
Childbirth, 8, 162
Clausen, A.W., 101
Clientelism, 55, 141
Clinton, Bill, 103
Colonialism, 135, 140
Comedores Populares, 139
Conditional Cash Transfers (CCTs), 1, 57, 61, 76, 80, 125
  non-contributory cash transfer, 77
  standard model, 111
  subnational, 76
Conflicts, 91

N. Nagels, *Gender Equality in Conditional Cash Transfer Designs*, Studies of the Americas, https://doi.org/10.1007/978-3-031-60871-1

Consejo Nacional de Población (CONAPO), 61
Cooking, 14
Cooks, 46, 111
Cookson, T.P., 8
Co-responsibilities, 64
 extra-official conditions, 8, 161
Coverage, 4
Crisis, 61
 internal conflict, 146
 Tequila crisis, 59

D
Decolonization, 150
Decontextualization, 40, 97
De la O, A., 7
de León, José Gómez, 61
Demography, 69
Depatriacalización Unit, 150
Designers, 15
Development, 1, 102
Disappearing, 3
 weaken, 128

E
Economic sciences, 69
Economist, 98
Education, 4
Entrepreneurs, 42
Eugenics, 165
Ewig, C., 32
Expansionary era, 177
Experts, 80, 113

F
Feminism
 feminist, 66, 69
 feminist movements, 57, 75
 feminist policies, 88
 gender/feminism institutionalization, 65, 66, 69
 global feminism, 57, 105
 women's rights, 149
 World Conference of Women, 67
Fieldwork, 4
Fome Zero, 80
Fondo de Cooperación para el Desarrollo Social (FONCODES), 139
Food subsidies, 59
Fourth International Conference in Beijing, 57
Fragmentation, 93
Framing, 40, 97
Fujimori, 139

G
Garay, C., 56
Gender
 conditions/conditionalities, 1, 7
 empowerment, 1
  financial autonomy, 2
 gendered configuration, 52
 gendered division of labor, 11, 29, 57, 99
 gender equality, 1
  gender equality goals, 1
  explicit gender equality objectives, 95
  implicit gender equality objectives, 86
 gender inequalities, 3
 gendering, 26
 girls, 58, 117
 intra-household relationships, 5
 mainstreaming, 105
 men, 27, 158
 traditional gender roles, 2, 5
 women, 19
 women, 158

Gender and Development (GAD), 105
Gender machinery/women's political agency (WPA), 2, 87
Gideon, J., 32

H
Health, 4
Historical institutionalism, 17, 173
Human development, 104
Hygienic vision, 163

I
Indigenous, 6, 109
Informal workers, 137
Innovation, 77, 144
Institutional births, 164
Institutional designs, 15
Institutional feminism, 94
Institutional legacies, 14, 43, 103, 121
Institutional venues, 44
 bureaucracy, 44
Instrumentalist, 49
Instrumentalist rationale, 76
Instrument communities, 26
Inter-American Development Bank (IADB), 10, 72
International Food Policy Research Institute, 19
International organizations, 11
Interpretative turn, 179
Intra-household bargaining power, 85

J
Jenson, J., 1
Juntos, 1

K
Knowledge, 3
 bank, 104
 contextual, 22
 data, 71, 75, 182
 economic, 22
 evaluations, 40, 131, 145
 evidence, 51, 75, 98
 evidence-based policies, 14
 expertise, 50, 99
 feminist knowledge, 149
 feminist studies, 68
 gender knowledge, 100
 gender studies, 91
 ideas, 36
 indicators, 70
 knowledge on gender, 13, 126
 qualitative, 22, 124
 quantitative, 22, 124
 research, 108
 scientific proof, 70

L
Latin America, 33
Law of Popular Participation, 138
Left
 center-left, 76, 95, 135
Levy, Santiago, 59, 115
López, Dr. Paz, 65
Lula da Silva, Luiz Inácio, 76, 78

M
Martínez Franzoni, 11, 111
Marques-Pereira, B., 43
Mason, Karen, 107
Massachusetts Institute of Technology (MIT), 123
Maternalism, 11, 43, 157
 families, 159
 maternal roles, 165
 mothering, 167
 mothers, 2, 100
McNamara, 100

Mechanism, 13
Mechanistic approach, 15
Mexico, 1
Ministry of finance, 46
Ministry of Food Security and Struggle against Hunger (MESA), 80
Ministry of Social Assistance and Promotion (MAPS), 81
Ministry of Social Development and Fight against Hunger (MDS), 84
Modernization, 101
Molyneux, M., 9, 43
Morales, Evo, 135
Motherhood, 5
Movimiento al Socialismo (MAS), 138
Movimiento Nacionalista Revolutionario (MNR), 137

N
Nationalization, 147
National Program for Food Assistance (PRONAA), 139
National revolution of 1952, 137
Neoclassical economics, 104, 130
Neoliberalism, 23
Neo-Malthusian, 100
1988 Constitution, 57, 76
Non-governmental organizations (NGOs), 147

O
Obrador, López, 180
Orloff, A., 28

P
Paniagua, 142
Partido dos Trabalhadores (PT), 54
Partido Revolucionario Institucional (PRI), 54
Party of Democratic Revolution (PRD), 56, 60
Peasants, 137
Personal links, 64
Peru, 2
Plurinational Constitution, 148
Policy communities, 152
  friends, 94
  intimate/informal instrument communities, 46, 60
  intimate relations/links, 65, 94
  personal relations/links, 63, 82
Policy designs, 1
Political configuration, 3, 13
Political parties, 142
Poverty, 10
  poor, 43
  poverty reduction, 58, 104
Process tracing, 17
Programa Alimentación, Salud y Educación (PASE), 61
Programa do Cartão Alimentação, 80
Programa Nacional de la Mujer (PRONAM), 68
Programa Nacional de Solidaridad (PRONASOL), 56
Progresa, 1
Prügl, E., 105

R
Racial inequalities, 3
Recipe, 14
Renda Minima, 77
Reproductive labor, 29
Right
  center-right, 23, 95

S
Schady, N., 121
Secretariat de Desarrollo Social (SEDESOL), 59

Secretariat of Public Policies for Women, 81
Sen, A., 104
Sendero Luminoso, 141
Sequence, 16, 174
 time, 89
Sistema de Focalización por Hogar (SISFOH), 142
Smart Economics, 110
Social investment, 2
 capabilities, 104
 children, 3, 111
 human capital, 145
Social policy(ies), 1
 methodological, 179
Social policy legacies/institutional social policy legacies, 1, 3, 136, 160, 161
Social protection unit (PREM), 98
Sociology, 69
Staab, S., 42
Standardization, 14
Standard model, 17
Strategic (gender equality) entrepreneurs, 3, 53
 international entrepreneurs, 118
 policy entrepreneurs, 40, 94
 policymakers, 16
 strategic entrepreneurs, 98, 144
 technocratic entrepreneurs, 62
 transnational entrepreneurs, 48
Structural adjustment policies (SAP), 101
Success stories, 125
Suplicy, E., 76

T
Targeting, 10, 142
 means-testing, 142
Toledo, Alejandro, 135
Traditional childbirth, 163
Trajectory, 21
Translation, 14
Translators, 136
Travel, 3, 4, 36
 diffusion, 4
 policy transfer, 12, 173
Truman, Harry S., 100
Truth and Reconciliation Commission (TRC), 143

U
Unidad de Análisis de Políticas Sociales y Económicas (UDAPE), 164
United Nation Development Program (UNDP), 103
United Nations, 100
Universalism, 6, 148, 154
Universalization, 155

W
Washington Consensus, 101
Welfare states/regimes, 16, 30, 136
 basic income, 97
 social rights, 57, 161
 social security system, 55
Wolfensohn, James, 80, 103
Wolfowitz, Paul, 109
Women in Development (WID), 102
Workers, 56
World Bank, 3
World Conference, 66

Z
Zedillo, Ernesto, 59, 116
Zero Hunger program, 80

The manufacturer's authorised representative in the EU is Springer Nature Customer Service Centre GmbH, Europaplatz 3, 69115 Heidelberg, Germany. If you have any concerns regarding our products, please contact ProductSafety@springernature.com

Printed and bound by CPI Group (UK) Ltd, Croydon, CR0 4YY
01/10/2026
02225854-0002